CHURCH MATTERS

If, as human beings, we are 'hardwired' for belonging, then the shape of our *ecclesial* belonging must be both mirror and lamp to this universal vocation. Such is Catholicism's unique and abiding charisma — a mark of the church which matters deeply, and one expounded here with a rare combination of rigour and reverence. Cowdell writes with the authority of 'a critical friend', who for more than twenty-five years as a scholar-priest has wrestled with the church as experienced by many postmodern Australians, provoking it to become more visibly what it actually is: an instrument of God's just and inclusive reign.

The Rt Revd Dr Richard Treloar,
Bishop of Gippsland

Scott Cowdell's aim is 'to keep the Church and the Eucharist at the heart of Christian life and imagination'. He does this as a thoroughly well educated, urbane Anglican, open to the good influence of other faith traditions and ever attentive to the many fine fruits of secularisation in contemporary Australia. He exudes hope and joy from the Gospels, despite the clunkiness of so many church structures – what he felicitously calls 'institutional cluelessness and dysfunction in the Church'. He insists that 'it is not acceptable for churches to assume that their beliefs and structures are preserved infallibly from distortion so that sin adheres only to individual Christians'. He's real and he is good company on the page. He deftly draws on theologians of many traditions, bringing us back to the bread and the word so that the Eucharistic community can be Christ's Body in the world, 'as a desperately needed alternative to consumerism and to a worsening global culture of dog eat dog'.

Fr Frank Brennan SJ AO,
Rector, Newman College
The University of Melbourne

In this fine collection, Scott Cowdell offers a vision of the church which avoids the extremes of theological liberalism and fundamentalist conservatism: both sides of the same coin. Instead, he calls for a comprehensive reclaiming of the church grounded in the biblical story and the historical tradition. This vision is centred not on individualism but on the living presence of the Spirit in the eucharistic community, leading it more deeply and authentically into worship and mission.

The Revd Canon Professor Dorothy A. Lee,
Stewart Research Professor of New Testament
Trinity College Theological School
University of Divinity, Melbourne

CHURCH MATTERS

ESSAYS AND ADDRESSES ON ECCLESIAL BELONGING

SCOTT COWDELL

Foreword by Hugh Mackay AO

COVENTRY
PRESS

Published in Australia by
Coventry Press
33 Scoresby Road
Bayswater VIC 3153

ISBN 9781922589255

Copyright © Scott Cowdell 2022

All rights reserved. Other than for the purposes and subject to the conditions prescribed under the *Copyright Act*, no part of this publication may be reproduced, stored in a retrieval system, or transmitted in any form or by any means, electronic, mechanical, photocopying, recording or otherwise, without the prior permission of the publisher.

Scripture quotations are from the *New Revised Standard Version Bible*, copyright 1989, Division of Christian Education of the National Council of the Churches of Christ in the United States of America. Used by permission. All rights reserved.

Catalogue-in-Publication entry is available from the National Library of Australia
http://catalogue.nla.gov.au

Cover design by Ian James – www.jgd.com.au
Cover photograph: Mass at Corpus Christi parish, Oklahoma City, USA
Author: Jzsj
Wikimedia Commons: Creative Commons Attribution-Share Alike 4.0
Text design by Coventry Press
Set in EB Garamond

Printed in Australia

In memoriam

James Warner, priest

1937–1993

Also by Scott Cowdell ...

Mimetic Theory and its Shadow: Girard, Milbank, and Ontological Violence
(Studies in Violence, Mimesis, and Culture. East Lansing, MI.: Michigan State University Press, forthcoming 2023)

René Girard and the Nonviolent God
(Notre Dame, IN.: The University of Notre Dame Press, 2018)

René Girard and Secular Modernity: Christ, Culture, and Crisis
(Notre Dame, IN.: The University of Notre Dame Press, 2013)

Abiding Faith: Christianity Beyond Certainty, Anxiety, and Violence
(Eugene, OR.: Cascade, 2009; Lutterworth, UK.: James Clark, 2010)

The Ten Commandments and Ethics Today
(Melbourne: Acorn Press, 2008)

God's Next Big Thing: Discovering the Future Church
(Melbourne: John Garratt Publishing, 2004)

A God for This World
(London and New York: Continuum, 2000)

Is Jesus Unique? A Study of Recent Christology
(Theological Inquiries. Mahwah, NJ.: Paulist Press, 1996)

Atheist Priest? Don Cupitt and Christianity
(London: SCM Press, 1988)

Contents

Foreword by Hugh Mackay AO	7
Acknowledgments	11
Preface	13
1. The Postmodern Church (1996)	17
2. Lay Vocation and Worship (1998)	35
3. On Loving the Church (2006)	50
4. Holy Spirit and Mission: Concerns about *Mission-Shaped Church* (2006)	75
5. Baptismal Ecclesiology and its Enemies (2006)	95
6. An Abusive Church Culture: Sexual Abuse and Systemic Dysfunction (2008)	104
7. Baptism in Australia: 'Civil Baptism' and the Social Miracle (2009)	126
8. Church and Faith as if Easter Makes a Difference (2012)	141
9. The Eucharist Makes the Church (2013)	149
10. The Church of the Apostles, Seattle (2013)	174
11. Two Cheers for the Parish (2015)	178
12. Mimesis and Ministry (2016)	191
13. Catholic Anglicanism for Evangelicals (2016)	206
14. How Can We Sing the Lord's Song in a Strange Land? (2017)	216
15. Theology in the School of Humility (2021)	227

Foreword by Hugh Mackay AO

Does Church matter?

It certainly matters to the people most likely to read this book: theologians and theology students, ordained ministers and other church leaders, ardent Anglicans—especially those who embrace the Anglo-Catholic tradition—and Christians from other traditions who are concerned by the decline in church attendance and might be looking for ways to make their own church more appealing or more relevant to the wider community.

As a social psychologist who falls into none of those categories, I have been struck not only by the obvious depth of scholarship in this collection of Scott Cowdell's writing but also by his powerful insights into a contemporary culture which, at first glance, seems to have relegated 'church' to the margins of society.

It's true Australians attend services of Christian worship less often now than at any previous time in our post-colonial history: fewer than ten percent attend church weekly, rising to about 25 percent at Christmas and Easter. It's also true that, according to the 2021 Census, the number of Australians who identify as Christian has dropped below 50 percent for the first time in Census history.

Such figures tell us nothing about the prevalence of religious faith since, as Cowdell has noted, much of the practice (if that's the right word) of religion (if that's the right word) has moved from the public to the private realm, often in the guise of 'therapeutic spirituality'. He sees this as part of a major culture-shift towards a rampant individualism at the expense of community, whether in local neighbourhoods, faith communities or elsewhere. Yet, because we humans are a social species hardwired for co-operation and togetherness, the sense of belonging is fundamental to our mental and emotional health. The inevitable consequences of increasing social fragmentation can be seen in our present epidemics of loneliness, anxiety and depression.

Many observers of the human condition have pointed to the despair that grips societies that move from faith in 'something greater than ourselves' to mere faith in the self. Cowdell's analysis of this phenomenon helps to explain the appetite for terminal bleakness in contemporary literature and dystopian narratives more generally, as well as the mad rush into consumerist materialism.

The place of the church—and religion more generally—in all this has become more complex. If you were only to look at attendance figures, you might be at risk of missing a bigger and more nuanced picture. While only 44 percent of Australians now identify as Christian, the steady rise of other religions (Hinduism the fastest-growing of them) means that almost two-thirds of Australians still identify with some religion. And over 90 percent of *non-churchgoers* say they like having a church in their local neighbourhood.

There's an intriguing paradox in Australians' current attitudes to church: while church attendance is going through the floor, attendance at church schools is going through the roof. Almost 50 percent of secondary-school pupils now attend non-government schools, and the vast majority of those are run by churches. Clearly, many parents who eschew church for themselves nevertheless want their children to be educated in a church-based ethos.

We rely heavily on faith-based organisations when it comes to charitable work, too. And, as Cowdell reminds us, it's often to religious language that we turn for solace in a crisis.

But the very word 'church' has taken on a dark connotation since the extent of sexual abuse by clergy and other church leaders has come to light. And, on this point, Cowdell offers one of his most illuminating essays. In Chapter 6, he shows how the institutional culture of the church, the training of its ministers and the arrangements for discipline of wrongdoers all fall far short of the standards expected by our society—churchgoers and non-churchgoers alike. That essay is one of several in this collection where Cowdell boldly imagines a church that would be more faithful to its essence and more responsive to the needs of the wounded society it is meant to serve.

Cowdell's insider account of the Anglican church, and the harsh realities of its shift towards managerialism on the one hand and fundamentalism on the other, makes compelling and dispiriting reading, as does his description of parish life too often based on the exploitation of Anglicanism as a badge of middle-class respectability.

Lord Acton's famous dictum about power—*all power corrupts, and absolute power corrupts absolutely*—surely applies as much to institutions as to individuals. There is, therefore, a good argument to be made—and Cowdell makes it very effectively in Chapters 12 and 14—that a decline in the power of the church, including its declining membership, may be just the thing that is needed to bring it to a fresh understanding of its reason for being, and its proper role and function in a secular society. He writes of 'the gift of secularisation'.

My own rather simple understanding of God as the loving spirit within and among us—not *out there* but *in here*—leads me to think of the church as being, ideally, a body of people living in harmony with the spirit of love (the spirit that makes us whole; aka the holy spirit). In turn, that suggests the primary role of the church is to encourage and nurture the work of that loving spirit.

Cowdell is wary of some recent initiatives for stimulating church attendance, fearing that the pursuit of 'relevance' might compromise the Church's very nature. But he writes appreciatively of old things done in creative new ways, for instance in his chapter on The Church of the Apostles in Seattle. Cowdell's message—and perhaps it is the core message of this collection—is that the challenge is not to 'do church' in new ways, but to 'be church' in more committed, more *essential* ways and to accept that the concept of the church as 'the body of Christ' implies a cessation of hostilities between its constituent parts, among many other things.

One of the loveliest things about this creative and courageous collection is the opportunity it gives us to see a formidable intellect and a human personality evolving over a 25-year period. When Cowdell notes in the Preface that he has become 'more generous and I hope more mature', the claim rings true in the discernible growth of tolerance, humility and sensitivity in his writing.

Hugh Mackay

Acknowledgments

I am grateful to Hugh McGinlay at Coventry Press for taking on this publication so readily and getting it out so expeditiously. For permission to reproduce previously published material I thank the following: Fr Michael Goonan, SSP (St Pauls Publications, for Chapter 7), Hilary Regan (ATF Press, for Chapters 3 and 5), and Dr Michael Gladwin (*St Mark's Review*, for Chapters 1, 2, 4, 6, 12, 13, 14 and 15). Permission was not required for me to reproduce Chapter 8. Thanks, too, to Robert Lentz, OFM (and his agents: Trinity Religious Artwork & Icons, of Lone Tree, Colorado) for permission to reproduce his icon of St Ignatius Loyola, appearing in Chapter 15.

I thank my old friend and now fellow Canberran, Hugh Mackay, for his Foreword. We have been talking about faith and Church matters off and on for the whole period covered by this collection, and now meet regularly over coffee to discuss this and much more besides. We have very different views of the Church's nature and significance, though our being able to have an open and mutually respectful dialogue about this actually shows the Church in a good light.

Hugh and I were on the short-lived Strategic Issues Advisory Panel of the Anglican Church. In proposing such a panel, Bishop Bruce Wilson memorably informed our General Synod that the Anglican Church of Australia is 'a Royal Family Church in a Princess Diana world'. We were shut down after three years for not achieving enough, though a group that represented the full range of Australian Anglicanism and managed to develop fruitful conversations and trusting friendships represented an achievement in itself.

This book is dedicated to the memory of Canon James Warner, who, from 1982 to 1988, was Principal of St Francis Theological College, Brisbane. During his time there, I had five wonderful and formative years as a theological student. Jim was the model of a faithful, godly, learned and cultured priest.

Preface

This volume is an edited selection of my talks and writings on the Church over the last quarter century, set out here in date order. Though I hope that some improvement might be evident across the years, the reader will soon realise that some preoccupations have remained unchanged. My central concern is to keep the Church and the Eucharist at the heart of Christian life and imagination.

For me, belonging to the community that gathers week by week around the two tables of word and sacrament is of the essence. It is integral to personal faith, and anything but the optional extra to which it is widely reduced. This is a view that I hold up in the face of today's accelerating decline of the Church in Australia and elsewhere in the West. I argue for it against influential current alternatives, chiefly the annexing of spirituality by individualism and commodification, offering a stubborn apologia for Catholic ecclesiology. As a High-Church Anglican, and perhaps perversely, I can do this despite not (currently!) being in communion with the Bishop of Rome.

With this central conviction about where Christianity grounds its incarnational vision comes a set of implications for Christian faith and practice. I emphasise a 'whole people of God ecclesiology', with the expectation that the Church needs to be an intentional community—'mature, mystical, and militant', as I put it in my 2004 book *God's Next Big Thing: Discovering the Future Church*, though by 'militant' I simply mean intentional and certainly not combative or triumphalist. A Vatican II Catholic should be entirely comfortable with what I am commending. This intentionality has implications for all those drawn through baptism into Christ's ongoing life and mission, touching every Christian in one way or another with the magic wand of vocation.

I combine an emphasis on lay vocation, which needs permission and encouragement, with a high view of the ordained ministry. But, please God, not a clericalist one. I once set an examination (yes, an actual sit-down examination) in an ecclesiology course, inviting discussion of the statement, 'I don't care how high your doctrine of the priesthood is as long as your doctrine of the Church is higher, and I don't care how high your doctrine of the Church is as long as your doctrine of the Kingdom of God is higher'. This statement captures my view of the priesthood within the divine economy: as a significant but not a superior state of life, integral to a larger organic reality.

Lest the reader think that I want to lock God up in 'churchiness', as High-Church Anglicans have been known to do, I affirm that God is bigger than the Church and that God is anything but absent from the secular. The sacramental Church—properly enculturated in every time, place and language—affirms God's incarnational investment in the world God loves. This respectful acknowledgment properly precedes the critiques that I offer of modern and postmodern Western life. This is the world I live in and only as a postmodern Westerner can I know God and make my own sense of the world. I do not believe in nostalgic retreat or the attempt to make heaven on earth. In fact, I argue that the gospel has played a crucial role in birthing the secular, and that retreating to a closed world of allegedly greater religious purity goes against the grain of where God in Christ is leading us.

So, I hope to be seen neither as a theological liberal nor as any sort of conservative (Evangelical or Catholic). Perhaps 'liberal Catholic' would be a fair description, as long as it remains clear which of these two words is the noun and which is the adjective. 'Progressive Orthodoxy', the descriptor favoured by a former Anglican Primate, Archbishop Peter Carnley, would be better, though I want to keep my emphasis on the Catholic. I believe it to be a generous and inclusive thing, Catholicism, and would not want to suggest any narrowing intent in my use of the term.

Preface

Apart from my ecclesial location, I should say a little more to clarify my particular perspective. I am a theologian who has served in parish and theological college leadership, with the last fifteen years devoted to research and writing. The occasional pieces in this volume have emerged as needed on the sidelines of my main work, which since 2007 has been theological engagement with the mimetic theory of René Girard (some chapters following, drawn from that period, include discussion of Girard). As I negotiated various vocational challenges in mid-life and had to deal with institutional cluelessness and dysfunction in the Church—to which I occasionally contributed through a lack of adequate self-awareness—I learned to temper idealism with patience, and frustration with compassion.

When deciding what should go into this volume (about two-thirds of what was available is included) I left certain pieces in well-deserved obscurity. Portions here and there from items that I included have been removed, mostly for the sake of enhanced clarity. Some deleted sections and statements were of no continuing relevance while a few others no longer seemed either right, fair or appropriate—very occasionally all three! I have become more generous and I hope more mature over this past quarter century.

Nevertheless, I doubt that writing about the Church today can avoid the tension between God's gracious acceptance of us just as we are and God's urgent call for us to actually be the Church more intentionally and confidently. The people of God in both Testaments of the Bible faced this tension—what else is the Bible about? And so must we.

Scott Cowdell

Canberra

Mary, Mother of Our Lord / Feast of the Assumption,
15 August 2022

1

The Postmodern Church (1996)

> *This chapter explores options for the Church in an emerging postmodern paradigm, beyond former apostolic and Christendom paradigms. Following Stanley Hauerwas, I argue for an intentional, liturgically-formed Church with a confident narrative identity rooted in the gospel. I develop this in dialogue with Richard Adams' much-loved novel* Watership Down. *The fruit of my reflections while in my first parish—All Saints', Chermside, in Brisbane (1992-1997)—is evident in this agenda-setting piece. It was the annual Fellowship of St John Lecture, given at St John's College within the University of Queensland on 22 May 1996, and subsequently published as 'The Postmodern Church', St Mark's Review 168 (Summer 1997): 14-20. It is reproduced here with kind permission.*

In a secular society like ours, the Church does not feature prominently—not in the public life of our nation nor in the private thoughts and actions of most individuals. Spirituality maybe, the Church—No! But after the 1995 Port Arthur atrocity, things were different. Eyes turned to the Church, where a robust vision long nurtured in word, sacrament and lives of faith was brought to public attention.

I remember particularly the televised liturgy from St. David's Anglican Cathedral in Hobart, and the witness of Bishop Philip Newell. His sermon offered no glib answers, no quick fix—in that sense the Church shared fully in the nation's ambient mood of shock and sadness. But while fully involved in the silent pain of the world at large, nevertheless the Church was not reduced to mute incomprehension and stunned silence. The Church was somehow able to speak. The Church responded to wounded humanity by rehearsing that great story of suffering met and overcome, with evil named and disempowered: the story of Jesus Christ. But that story was introduced gently and with respect for the diversity of opinion, of belief and unbelief, in the world to which the Church spoke.

Rounding out the Church's words on that occasion, giving them resonance, was the rich tradition of Western liturgy, religious architecture and church music. The power of that tradition is still real for people in such grave moments when support and reassurance are sorely needed. Evident in the Church's response was a confident assurance that God has called it to be an agent of Christ's transforming work in the world. The Church not only speaks, of course. It also listens and supports. In addition, it unashamedly stands on its historical dignity, its still lingering gravitas, in the face of such an atrocity, demanding appropriate political action such as tightened gun control.

Here then is something of what I see the Church becoming in a postmodern Western world. I would first like to put these thoughts into historical context by saying something about the Church's existence in previous ages. Then I am going to tell you a story about rabbits, about how to be good rabbits, which will tell us something about how to be good Christians in a difficult environment. So, with the help of theologian Stanley Hauerwas, we will revisit Richard Adams' wonderful story *Watership Down*, which in addition to being a delight for older children is a powerfully allegorical story for adults about community. Then I want to say more about how the postmodern Church might look in the West. And in that context, I will conclude with a word about how well placed the Anglican Church is to take a leadership role in postmodern Christianity—if it has the nerve.

The Postmodern Church (1996)

I

It is now recognised that human understanding comes in historical wholes, called paradigms or epistemes. At one time, we all tended to see things in a certain way, taking all sorts of things for granted about aspects of the world and our lives in it. Then things happened that strained this overarching consensus, to the point that it ceased working. A period of uncertainty, even of crisis, follows, until a new and more successful paradigm settles into place.

This is an idea from the history and philosophy of science. In physics, there have been paradigm shifts in the twentieth century, with quantum mechanics and Einstein's special and general theories of relativity ushering in completely new ways of imagining and understanding the workings of nature. The older theories still work up to a point, but a lot of new problems arose that the old worldview could not explain. The evolutionary paradigm in the biological sciences is another example. Evolution is more than just one more theory, as the creation scientists claim; it is a whole way of viewing things, and a framework for theories. We can see the same thing at work in human life. A classical Greek lived in a very different mental world from a medieval European, not to mention an American colonist in revolutionary mood when modernity, science and Enlightenment were banishing the tyranny of heteronomous authority and uncritical traditionalism.

Now a postmodern paradigm has come to birth, with people in the West feeling differently about who they are, about what right and wrong mean, about what might constitute the good life and about where to find their bearings. Since the Second World War, and increasingly since the 1960s and 1970s, confident expansionist dreams have crumpled somewhat in the modern West, except perhaps in the blind march of its technological innovation. The confident individualism of modernity, and its rationalist, empirical turn of mind, has lost its edge—nineteenth-century cultural anthropology, along with early twentieth-century linguistics and linguistic philosophy, have shown us just how much in our individual lives is the product of culture and language. These public, collective realities create us as much as we create them.

In reviewing the history of Christian thought and life, the paradigm approach is helpful. In *The Once and Future Church*,[1] Loren Mead sees the Church today in the midst of a paradigm shift. And not for the first time either.

First, there was what he calls the apostolic paradigm, represented in New Testament Christianity and in that of the early centuries, before Christianity became 'established'. This apostolic Christianity was intense, committed, highly self-conscious, and lived in a world understood to be a foreign, even a hostile environment. We saw a glimpse of this understanding in a recent Sunday Gospel, where the writer has Jesus say in his high priestly prayer that 'I am not asking on behalf of the world, but on behalf of those whom you gave me, because they are yours' (John 17:9).

The apostolic paradigm gave rise to confessors and martyrs and required an intensive catechumenate before people were deemed ready to make a thoroughgoing lifetime commitment to Christ in the symbolic death and resurrection of baptism. This was the Christian world in which every believer was responsible for the mission going forward, for bearing personal witness to Christ in word and in manner of life, and in contributing to the kind of church life that would impress and win over 'the world' by its radical goodness and mutual love. Again, the Gospels and epistles through the Sundays of the Easter season have given ample illustration of this vision. Mead points out that the missionary frontier stood at the edge of every congregation according to this mindset—that frontier was at the front door of the church, if you like.

---

[1] Loren B. Mead, *The Once and Future Church: Reinventing the Congregation for a New Missionary Frontier* (New York: The Alban Institute, 1991).

The Postmodern Church (1996)

But this was not true in the next and longest period of Christian history, which Mead calls the Christendom paradigm. There, the Church and the world were made one, the civic and social life of the Empire was baptised, Christian civilisation was born, and the good Christian became the good citizen. And there, by and large, the Church has remained, from the fourth century when Christianity became 'official' until well into the twentieth century. In the Christendom paradigm, the mission frontier ceases to be the edge of the congregation, because the congregation blurs invisibly into the society around it. The mission frontier becomes the edge of the Empire itself, as we saw at the nadir of Christendom in the extraordinary worldwide missionary expansion of the nineteenth century, dovetailing as it did with the unprecedented European colonialism of that period.

The Christendom paradigm bred the sort of Christians still well represented in our congregations in their old age. Their Christian faith is not usually understood as distinctive and different from other worldviews and lifestyle options, or not at least from 'respectable' ones. Nor is it primarily or even partly a doctrinal issue because doctrine tends to be really important only in times of controversy. Faith for such Christians is diffused throughout their general sensibilities; it is an unreflective, morality-centred ambience rather than a belief vis-à-vis other beliefs. Its essence is more likely to be the ten commandments than the creed. Its almost invariable concomitant is good citizenship and a sense of civic duty. It is politically, socially and liturgically conservative.

Richard Hooker, the great Anglican apologist of the Elizabethan Settlement in sixteenth-century England, eagerly merged citizenship and religion in his famous understanding of the Church of England and the nation as two sides of the one coin. The Church of England is still wedded to this fiction, despite today's very different secular and multifaith conditions.

Throughout the world, the Church clings to establishment fantasies where it can, with Roman Catholicism much criticised for its establishment attitudes by the Liberation Theologians of South America, with the WASP establishment of the United States receiving feminist and other left-wing Christian criticism, and with the Anglican Church of Australia desperate to recover an identity now that the Christendom paradigm has begun to collapse and our whole institution is reeling. For collapsing it is. The entire Christendom paradigm is falling over worldwide.

II

So many things have happened, at so many levels. At the level of culture, the Western vision has become increasingly suspect and marginalised, the West having been unable to prevent the monstrous evils of two world wars plus Cold War xenophobia. The Enlightenment dream of progress to a better future is everywhere problematic, and an increasingly uniform, media-driven mass culture now competes with extensive religious and moral pluralism to create a radically destabilising shock of the new. The existentialist void identified in mid-twentieth century philosophy and cultural studies remains, but reliably filling that void has proved increasingly difficult. And instead of one authentic identity there are now many selves on offer that we might adopt. Where, nowadays, are the colossal individuals of the modern period—where are they among the middle aged and elderly, let alone among the dazed and readily manipulable young?

For churches, the primary factor in the decline of Christendom has been secularisation, by which is meant the marginalising and relativising of the religious institution and its claims. Even the morality and respectability nexus, which extended the Christendom paradigm through taking on board the moralistic reductionism of Enlightenment religious philosophy, has been robbed of its former power. In Australia, as a notable case, the various churches from the beginning saw themselves as exercising a civilising influence in a society that grew from largely amoral convict beginnings,[2] and still Church leaders seek to be the conscience of our society on a range of issues. But is anyone listening? The modern Church's claims to be a moral guide are held in increasing disrepute as more and more instances of sexual impropriety and other abuses of power are brought to light by a gleeful media and fed upon by an eager populace.

The Church was once synonymous with meaning in the West. Now its last efforts to maintain this Christendom paradigm, through commissions, public statements and such, are either unnoticed, or if noticed disregarded, or if occasionally taken notice of, then treated as but one more among a range of possible opinions.

The inability to pass on the faith to the next generation is at the heart of the Church's crisis, yet so-called youth ministry is often uninspiring. Poor quality entertainment in an atmosphere of pious individualism is frequently the best we can offer our young people in the mainstream churches, as an alternative to the disorienting, value-soft but nevertheless potent bombardment of imagery and stimulus that constitutes today's highly commercialistic, frequently destabilising youth culture.

Already we see faulty adaptions to new ecclesial conditions. With the aim of keeping Christendom alive, of maintaining the link between Christ and culture, the Church reduces its vision to morality, to psychotherapy, or to the championing of whatever current politically correct obsession of the left. What was often a right wing conservatism in Christendom's heyday very often gives way to declining Anglicanism's mildly left-wing Christian activism, in an attempt to preserve a public role for the Church. But in all these cases, Christianity is essentially little more than

---

[2] See e.g., Ian Breward, *Australia: 'The Most Godless Place Under Heaven'?* (Melbourne: Beacon Hill Books, 1988).

software for personal or social transformation, and like all software it is readily discarded when a better package comes along.

On the other hand, we see flawed attempts to revive the apostolic paradigm in the resurgence of various so-called conservative Christianities. These have the sectarian-style elements of the apostolic, and a cognitive distance from the mindset of the prevailing culture up to a point. But they are really about self-preservation, and they are innately fearful. Where do we see in them the genuine fearlessness and zeal of the apostles to win the world to Jesus Christ, to engage and adapt, to converse and confute with the world, and to invest the talent God has given? On the contrary, too much conservative Christianity is like the third servant in that shocking Gospel parable, whose careful self-preservation in burying the talent given him by his master earned him a definitive rebuke—his strategy was the one deemed most inimical to the cause of the gospel.[3]

In these two approaches we see something like the main options that Peter Berger identified in Christian responses to the modern world. In his book *The Heretical Imperative*, Berger makes the point that we must all now be heretics, which means that we have to *choose* what to believe.[4]

One popular choice is the reductive option, as he calls it. The Church gives up its distinctive claims, devalues its traditional practices and assimilates with modern society thinking that this will preserve its influence. Alternatively, there is what Berger calls the deductive option, whereby traditional beliefs and practices are reasserted in the teeth of modernity, so that a strongly ideological, confrontational Christianity emerges. This we see today in Protestant biblical fundamentalism, in the tyranny of born-again romanticism, which is never far away in the Charismatic Movement, and in the renewed authoritarianism of

---

[3] See Mark 13:33-7, Matthew 25:14-30, Luke 21:34-46.
[4] Peter Berger, *The Heretical Imperative* (New York: Doubleday, 1979).

Pope John Paul II's post-Vatican II Roman Catholicism. The third option, and the one favoured by Berger, he calls the inductive approach. The tradition is unpacked to lay bare its core experiences, whereupon a new expression can be found that is more faithful to the original vision. Like him, I would support this difficult third way beyond religious indifferentism, on the one hand, and cognitively isolated sectarianism on the other. To draw some implications of this third way, in comparison to the other two, I am now going to talk about rabbits.

III

Richard Adams' rabbit epic *Watership Down* is about a community on a long and difficult journey. They seek a place of their own where they can be fully themselves—fully alive as rabbits.[5] It begins with a piece of unlikely prescience. A rabbit given to strange feelings is overcome with dread, and with the few others who trust him he leaves the warren. Soon it is revealed that the old warren was in the way of a pending land development—the rabbits not gassed in their burrows were shot and the land torn up. A journey ensues in which rabbits find themselves in all sorts of alien situations, involving extended travel in the open, crossing rivers and finding shelter in unfamiliar country. Along the way, other rabbits join them, some of whom seem most unprepossessing, like the young dreamer who started them on their quest.

In the midst of their frequent perplexity, fear and indecision, however, there is one rallying point, and that is the telling of sacred rabbit stories. These were the stories of El-ahrairah, mythical prince of rabbits, whose courage, cunning tricks and quick-wittedness delivered his warren again and again from its enemies. The telling of these stories kept the rabbits inventive and protected them from any false sense of security. It also fostered the mutual dependence

---

[5] Richard Adams, *Watership Down* (London: Penguin, 1974).

that is essential for rabbits, so that by journey's end even the most unlikely of rabbits had made a crucial contribution to the eventual happy outcome.

Along the way, two other warrens are discovered. These are highly allegorical episodes. Encountering the first warren, our travellers are surprised at how sleek and well fed the rabbits are, how fine their coats. They have a communal space underground, rather than simply individual burrows, though it is little used. And here Stanley Hauerwas discerns a link to modern liberal societies in decline, with the communal dimension no longer working. The rabbits in this newly discovered warren no longer tell the stories of El-ahrairah. They cannot make much sense out of them. Instead, they tell tragic stories, and the does compose grim, existentialist-sounding poetry. There is not much closeness and interdependence in the warren.

The good condition of the rabbits is explained by the fact that the local farmer leaves out vegetables for them every day—normally a great and rare treat for rabbits. All of this surprises the travellers as being most un-rabbit like. Unease develops, and with good reason. The bitter truth is that the farmer feeds the rabbits in order to save himself the trouble of keeping his own. And when he wants a rabbit to eat, he simply snares one. This is the dark secret of this modern, liberal-minded warren. A pact has been made which ensures comfort and prosperity without any of the old skills and dreams and stories being necessary.

But there is a terrible cost. These rabbits have capitulated to the prevailing culture and forgotten who they are. They may be sleek and fat, but there are casualties, and the group as a whole has lost its way. Endemic divorce, endemic child and spousal abuse, endemic addiction, endemic youth disillusionment and suicide—these are some features of life in the West today that echo the dark secret of this outwardly healthy and progressive-looking warren.

The next warren the travellers encounter is militaristic and totalitarian. All else is sacrificed for security and certainty, which is the abiding personal need of its fearsome chief rabbit, General Woundwort. Life is totally regimented, and the unhappy rabbits are driven to unnatural practices like fixed supervised feeding times come rain or shine, and long confinements underground. Dissent is harshly suppressed. The biggest rabbits are sent out on patrols to capture travellers who might attract predators. It is a thing of pride that these rabbits stand and fight with cats and stoats, rather than running away like the cunning spiritual descendants of El-ahrairah. It is a bleak warren, and the does are frequently infertile. Needless to say, the old stories are not valued there either.

If the first warren was meant to represent the declining liberal democracies and late capitalism, perhaps the second represents the Soviet alternative where control was everything and life was often miserable. For Stanley Hauerwas, however, both these warrens also stand for types of the Church.[6]

Hauerwas represents the newly emerging postliberal trend in theology, which advocates a more sectarian style of Christianity in the face of the collapsing Christendom paradigm. These postliberals, chiefly Protestant but with Roman Catholic sympathisers, are not biblical fundamentalists or Papal conservatives, though they are attracted to strong ideals of Christian community as represented in Roman Catholic religious life and in the alternative communities of radical Protestantism.

According to Hauerwas and other postliberals, Christianity has little to gain and everything to lose by giving in to the dubious charms of what amounts to Berger's reductive option, abandoning the story in favour of rapprochement with 'the world'. Instead, he opts for the postliberal solution of seeking identity within a

---

[6] Stanley Hauerwas, *A Community of Character: Toward a Constructive Christian Social Ethic* (Notre Dame, IN.: The University of Notre Dame Press, 1981), Chapter 1.

narrative world opened up by the Bible. Others of this school point to the tradition and the liturgy as disclosing an alternative cognitive world to that of wider culture.

For Hauerwas, *Watership Down* shows how a story can form a community—how in the telling and retelling a community can be reconstituted in accordance with its foundational vision. The stories of El-ahrairah shaped this rabbit community, preserving it from the distortions fallen into by others encountered along the way.

IV

What the Church can learn from this allegorical tale of rabbits is that many features of the apostolic paradigm would re-emerge should it rediscover itself as a story-formed community. We would see a revival of biblical theology and a rediscovery of the power of liturgy. We would see a recovery of Christian distinctiveness. This would be manifest in Christianity recovering a characteristic vocation within secular culture, rather than continuing as merely an optional perspective on how to live a civic-minded moral life within that culture.

Apart from this apostolic vision, there is now little or nothing to draw the young to the mainstream churches. While the Charismatic churches can offer an intense though often short-lived transitional experience in young adulthood, it is only a great adventure that will decisively lure young people away from the dubious priorities and impoverished ways of being to which late capitalist society regularly consigns them. There is evidence that mainstream churches are at last beginning to realise this. But it would help if the worshipping parents and grandparents of these wavering young Christians saw their own faith as the adventure of a lifetime—if they saw it in apostolic terms. Only the summons of an adventurous calling will galvanise the young and win their lives for the Church.

The Postmodern Church (1996)

Another aspect of this sense of Christian distinctiveness is the growing recognition that Christianity is different from other religions and world views—that Christianity and Buddhism, for instance, are two quite different ways of understanding human life and ultimate reality. This flies in the face of much *avant garde* theology born in the 1960s and 1970s which saw all the different religions as simply different reifications of the one basic divine or else human experiential reality. For some with this view, it was enough to say that all the religions represented a universal ethic, as if the true adherent of whatever religion would be satisfied to be summarily grouped with others of quite different traditions—or, worse, to be told that what is for them a rich spiritual and intellectual vision could be reduced to the mundanity of a mere code of behaviour. In the 1990s, however, there is a growing theological awareness that different religions, different traditions, different stories, really are *different*, and that salvation, for instance, is a Christian concept only really explicable through inhabiting Christianity's story of God. The Buddhist tells quite a different story, without the transcendent God of history, without the incarnation, without the covenant and without any perseverance of the human self with God in eternity.[7]

So, a story-formed community will live distinctively in the world. It will be a city set on a hill—to use the Gospel image—with an expectation that being a Christian will occasionally, perhaps frequently, mean something different from what it meant for our forebears of the Christendom paradigm. It will mean more than being a good person, which in my experience is often no more than a euphemism for morally undeveloped bourgeois conformism. It will mean more than being a good citizen—it may mean just the opposite, as it did for Jesus of Nazareth. It will certainly mean

---

[7] See e.g., Gavin D'Costa, ed., *Christian Uniqueness Reconsidered: The Myth of a Pluralistic Theology of Religions* (Maryknoll, NY.: Orbis, 1990); S. Mark Heim, *Is Christ the Only Way? Christian Faith in a Pluralistic Perspective* (Valley Forge, PA.: Judson Press, 1985).

the sort of commitment to worship, involvement in Christian education and eagerness to share the story in evangelisation that was once the sole preserve of sectarian Christians.

We see the stirrings of this transformation throughout mainstream churches today, with an emphasis on lay ministry challenging the clergy-dominated ministry style of Christendom, and with a revived catechumenate aiding the rediscovery of more intentional discipleship. The story-telling rabbits of *Watership Down* can point the way.

V

I want to say, however, that a sole emphasis on story cannot be the whole answer. It is part of the answer only, though a part that has often been neglected. The main problem I have with thoroughgoing postliberals is that the question of truth gets sidelined. I want to know whether the story of Jesus Christ is true. Or is it just a personal favourite at best, and a piece of unrealistic wish-fulfilment at worst? To be sure, the Christian story cannot be proven, if proof means establishing a direct correspondence with reality, using a correspondence theory of truth. But it can be believed on the basis of its coherence, both internally and with experience of life and the world, using a coherence model of truth.

I am most sympathetic to theologies that acknowledge the age of proof and objective certainty to be over, concluding that religious conviction will only take hold once we open ourselves to the story of Jesus Christ and put it to work in our lives. But at the same time these are theologies that are not content to retreat into a cognitive vacuum—a narrative enclave of meaning. Instead, they develop the method of correlation pioneered in Paul Tillich's theology in the 1950s. Nowadays, it is done in more sophisticated ways that acknowledge a newly sprung environment of relativism, pluralism and scepticism about Christianity's exclusive claims. The

Chicago Roman Catholic theologian David Tracy is today's chief exponent of a theology that takes seriously the postliberal call to be rooted in our own story as Christians, allowing our sensibilities to be formed by it, while maintaining a respect for the wider reach of God's truth, God's love and God's action outside the Christian story.[8]

My concern, then, is to avoid a world-denying sectarianism while preserving the heightened intensity that a story-formed community can discover. And it must be said that this is the abiding tone of Christianity's story properly understood. It is not a story that condemns or fears the world. Rather, it tells of a God who continually creates and redeems the world. Interestingly, this is also the case with *Watership Down*. When the travellers finally establish their own warren, they include in it the large communal space they found at the first warren, and aspects of the tight organisation they found at the militaristic second warren. And why not? It was part of their sacred story to be adaptive, inventive and open minded, as is true of the Christian story as well.

Christianity so conceived will *engage* with the world, rather than beating a retreat from the world into sectarianism. This engagement will not just mean a mind and heart open to God's truth in the world, but also a commitment to the betterment of that world because it is the world God loves. Such genuine zeal for the life of the world is far from the politically correct do-goodism that Christendom in decline often lapses into. It will not forget the God-centred nature of the Christian story for any human-centred activism or, worse, messianism—the Christian story is a story that will not be finished by our best efforts within the limits of world history alone. Having said that, it should be noted that even the most eschatological of theologians today, the most oriented toward hope for God's inbreaking future, maintains

---

[8] See especially David Tracy, *Plurality and Ambiguity: Hermeneutics, Religion, Hope* (London: SCM Press, 1988).

a firm commitment to Christian struggle in the present toward a better world. The theologian referred to here, Jürgen Moltmann, expects that Christians will be made restless by God's promises, seeking signs of them coming to fulfilment within the events of history.[9]

As for the Christian's role in changing the world, it will, of course, be political, and it will occasionally be partisan. The Christendom-style Christian was intensely political, in the sense that Christianity and the social *status quo* were wedded, though it was not characteristically partisan in politics. Hence the phenomenon of staunch monarchist Anglicans demanding prayers for the Queen one week while the next week condemning as too political a sermon advocating native title or nuclear disarmament.

The sort of political stance typical of the postmodern Christianity I envisage is not the 'Christ of Culture' sort that H. Richard Niebuhr names,[10] characteristic of the Christendom paradigm, nor the 'Christ against Culture' option beloved of the sectarian mindset in its misguided attempts to recapture the apostolic 'good old days'. Rather, it will be the option that Niebuhr calls 'Christ the Transformer of Culture', emphasising ongoing creative engagement with the culture in which the Church abides, though as a story-formed community that stands at some distance from that prevailing culture.

The Church so conceived will seek to recapture the zeal and the focus of the apostolic paradigm without any sectarian fearfulness, which at best only mimics the truly apostolic. And it can do this because today's Church is an inheritor of all that was good in the Christendom paradigm, with its affinity between the Church and the world. There is nothing to be gained by joining the sectarian push to separate Church from world. Why not, for

---

[9] Jürgen Moltmann, *Theology of Hope: On the Ground and Implications of a Christian Eschatology*, trans. James W. Leitch (London: SCM Press, 1967).
[10] H. Richard Niebuhr, *Christ and Culture* (New York: Harper & Row, 1951).

present purposes, use the hard-won resources, the structures and the spiritual capital of the Christendom centuries and trade on the residual goodwill still accruing to the Church?

My own Anglican tradition can offer leadership for the postmodern Church, should it dare. It can offer today's pluralistic postmodern world a long experience in the reconciling of pluralism within its own fold. It can offer a commitment both to the story and to the world at large in its unique dual identity as a natural law tradition that nevertheless locates its essence most definitively in its liturgical life. And it can offer its innate publicness, forged in the bosom of the English nation and somehow preserved throughout the Anglican Communion in its aspiration to engage with public life and open debate wherever it incarnates itself.

This recognition is the burden of Bruce Kaye's book about Australian Anglicanism called *A Church Without Walls*.[11] Bruce Kaye's vision is grounded in the Christian story, but it is precisely this story that drives him to envision a gracious Church open to the world and its people. This is the sort of religion that I discerned in our Church's response to Port Arthur, with that memorial liturgy from St David's Cathedral, Hobart.

In closing, I offer a word of warning. It is tempting to seek a way forward by concentrating on technique. We ask what program or policy we must institute to get the desired results. To be like the Church portrayed in the Acts of the Apostles, for instance, we tend to think that it is a matter of setting about sharing our goods in common, or trying to pray more, or some such. This forgets two things. One is the fact that God is Lord of the Church, as of history, and committed to the Church's reform. So, we do not have to stage-manage the next phase of Church history. The message of the Acts of the Apostles, particularly in its imaginative version of the first Pentecost, is that God's Spirit is at work to the extent that

---

[11] Bruce Kaye, *A Church Without Walls: Being Anglican In Australia* (Melbourne: Dove, 1995).

even Christian fearfulness and lack of imagination will not thwart God's emerging future.

Dare we trust that love and devotion for God and God's cause is sufficient for us at this as at any perplexing time? In the Acts of the Apostles, the Christians simply loved Jesus and were open to God's Spirit. All the details of their life and witness seemed to fall more or less into place subsequently. So it will be with the Church today. The way forward is not that of finding the right technique. It is, as ever, simply a matter of opening our hearts to the story of God's love in Jesus Christ and to God's voice in the wise voices of the world in which we live. Whenever the Church does this, it has got it right.

2

Lay Vocation and Worship (1998)

> *Living the Christian life constitutes the primary vocation for all Christians, who are called to be the Church in the world. In this endeavour, worship constitutes the Church's defining vocation, also helping to inspire and empower individual Christians in their further vocational callings. This essay was prepared at a time when Lay Presidency of the Eucharist (which its proponents in the Diocese of Sydney call lay administration of the Lord's Supper) was being debated by the Doctrine Commission of the Anglican Church of Australia, of which I was a member (1995-2009). I offer a counter-position on lay vocation that is fundamentally ecclesial and Eucharistic though not locked up in 'churchiness', which finds its proper outworking in the wider world where lay people actually live. Published as 'Lay Vocation and Worship', St Mark's Review 172 (1998): 14-20, it appears here by kind permission.*

The individual Christian, whether or not pursuing a vocation as normally understood, is nevertheless invited to adopt a vocational self-understanding in living as a disciple of Jesus Christ, and worship is central to this. Appropriate vocational activity will subsequently emerge for every Christian, both in terms of contributing to the witness of the Church as a whole, understood as a community at a critical distance from the social mainstream, and in the way that each individual Christian approaches the constitutive realities of their life in society: work, relationships, money and status, community activity and civic responsibility.

It will help first to reflect on the meaning of 'vocation' and how we might understand the Christian life vocationally. Next, the nature of worship and its role in fostering this sense will be considered. The vocation of each lay person and the laity as a whole will then be discussed, introducing Anglican perspectives that locate lay vocation as part of being the Church 'in the world' rather than confined within the Church's own institutional life. Some practical suggestions about aspects of lay vocation will be offered in conclusion, with some thoughts about how we might better develop lay vocation in relation to worship. The present push in Evangelical Anglican circles for Lay Presidency is mentioned in this context as a misunderstanding of lay vocation in the Church.

The meaning of vocation

'Vocation' arises in significant, responsible contexts where ability and inclination are matched by opportunity and wherewithal. It is a concept not to be trivialised, as well-meaning persons do when they indiscriminately refer to any job as a 'vocation' regardless of the significance of the job, the peculiar abilities it calls for, its difficulty, the way it is approached or the motive for doing it. Vocation is about a level of purpose and significance, a level of ability and commitment beyond the ordinary, so that certain doctors, teachers, scientists, thinkers, artists and priests, for instance, can be said to be pursuing a vocation, or parents, or married couples, or celibates consecrated in the religious life. In each case, the loftiness of the enterprise, the special abilities required and the disciplined lifetime commitment that is called for all contribute to our appreciating its vocational quality.

Vocation emerges independently of specific employment for many, who may be leaders or carers or prophets, either through or apart from their job as needs be, exercising their vocation in a variety of contexts throughout life. Further, in the sense that any worker consciously pursues a significant goal, as when police officers commit themselves to serving the public, or machinists take active responsibility for workplace safety, there is a sense in which any occupation or undertaking can be elevated to the vocational level because of the meaning and purpose brought to the work by a vocationally-minded individual performing it.

In the same way, vocation can be ascribed to communities, devolving upon their individual members consequently, as when a nation must pull together in time of war, or a town in the face of natural disaster or local economic downturn. It would not be unreasonable, for instance, to talk about a vocation emerging for today's industrialised West in leading the world toward environmental sustainability, with each individual's consequent vocation expressed in habitual recycling, the purchase of green products etc., with the loftiness of the overall cause elevating the individual's modest domestic efforts to the realm of the vocational.

Ministries in the Church are traditionally called vocational, such as ordination and missionary work, along with certain states of life, chiefly either celibacy or else marriage and parenthood. We recognise some lay ministries in the Church as vocational, like youth work and church music. Most importantly, however, we have recovered a sense that all Christians share a vocation by virtue of their baptism (an insight due both to the liturgical revival and the Biblical Theology Movement). The Church is thus rediscovering itself as a community with a mission, with every baptised member of the community bearing responsibility for that mission.

Some achieve this end through specific identifiable vocational callings within the institutional Church. Most Christians, however, pursue secular occupations and states of life, albeit with the possibility of doing so in a vocational manner. Their job, their social location, the circumstances of their life and its opportunities can all be understood as the arena of Christian mission and service, as a place to serve God and advance the Kingdom through dealing with both good and bad elements in whichever situation. Here a significant cause is discerned in what may outwardly seem the insignificant comings and goings, work and relationships of an ordinary life. Indeed, extra skills and commitment are sometimes required to do a job or negotiate a situation *as a Christian* than are required to do so without that overarching commitment.

Theological reflection being one thing, however, the lived truth of the Church and its people is often another. The frequent failure of this vocational reality to establish itself is multi-stranded, with its cure relying on the constant work of the Holy Spirit to rekindle the Christian vision in the hearts of Christians and in the Church as a whole. Religious education has a part to play, but it cannot always provide the impetus and the sustained energy to drive the deep individual and collective change called for. Here, worship can take the Church further, where the vision is rehearsed, preached, explored, sung and sacramentally enacted week by week.

Worship: a conversational event

Worship honours God and ascribes ultimate 'worth-ship' to God. There is a functional sense in which all human beings worship something, whatever represents ultimate concern for them. For the Christian, however, in the words of Hopkins' hymn, 'Jesus calls us from the worship of the vain world's golden store'. So, worship rightly understood becomes a critical action. Indeed, it becomes a socio-political act, in that it tacitly relativises every other priority in the name of life's greatest priority, which has consequences for worshippers relating to money, people and society. In the modern West, where identity is regularly found in work and personal achievement, worship recaptures the sense of 'liberating feast' that has not fared well since the Reformation.[12] Instead of the holiday as today's favoured Western site of renewal and transcendence,

---

[12] Jürgen Moltmann, 'The Liberating Feast', *Concilium* 92 (1974): 74-84.

worship offers renewal from a genuinely transcendent source. This discovery of God with us in the midst of life and work, in what for many could otherwise be an alienating place of exile, can be liberating indeed.

Worship is not just our honouring of God, then. At the same time, it is also God honouring us—God offering to us the true selves-in-relation-to-other-selves that we have failed to lay hold of. In this sense, we can see worship as a dynamic, conversational reality—not just an offering to God, as the Anglo-Catholic tradition rightly sees it, but also as God's offering to us, and not just in the very real sense of receiving Christ sacramentally. God offers to the Church in worship the transformation of its life, the forgiveness of sin, the reorientation of priorities, and hence a vocational imperative: 'Go in peace to love and serve the Lord'.

Worship is an alternative reality into which the assembled congregation enters, constituted by narrative, symbol and sacrament. The church building, the vesture of ministers, the music and singing, the sights and smells of the liturgy can all contribute to this sense of 'liminality', of being in an alternative world-between-the-worlds. In that environment, the story of Jesus Christ is told and reflected upon, and ideally it engages with people's lives in the world. That way, their liminal state in church is not one of escape from the world outside but rather a platform set at a distance from that world to allow a reorientation of perspective upon life in that world. It is as much a mistake to make church entirely remote from life (in terms of archaic language, etc.), which is often done in the supposed interests of enhanced spirituality, as it is to downplay a sense of otherness and specialness, which is often done in the supposed interests of enhanced relevance. Worship needs to be a piece of the world's life where God's presence in that life is laid bare, rather than missing God's involvement in that life by sundering transcendence from immanence.

The Eucharist is the great sacramental focus of God's new creation coming to birth, and of our incorporation into it—not as an infallible Church or a purely heavenly society but as a pilgrim community with a vision and a mission for our own salvation and that of the world around us. At the end of worship, as is especially evident in the deacon's dismissal that concludes the Eucharist, there is a symbolic departure from the sacred time and space of the liturgy, an end to the liminality, and thence a return to the space of life in 'the real world'. There the outworking of lay vocation takes place.

The gap between theory and practice is as wide here, however, as it is everywhere else in the Church's life. Sunday worship can take on aspects of a leisure activity, offering 'infotainment', diversion and even escapism rather than a transforming perspective. Hence the liberating feast dimension is lost. It is also lost when worship ceases to be an inspiring and equipping event. How many parish Eucharists have we attended where we have felt insulted, cheated and let down by poor or even non-existent presentation of the vision in liturgy and preaching, or felt excluded by virtue of our gender, our age, our social location, our presence with a family, or without one? Surely this state of affairs must be addressed without delay, and our parishes, theological schools and bishops must all take responsibility. In his work on pastoral liturgy, Robin Green points out that, like good art, good worship is born out of discipline, and 'the task of enabling a community to carry the whole of human life into God is a costly business'.[13]

The intentional community

Worship can create a grand vision of God's cosmic purpose and of humanity within it, renewing the Church in its vocation to be a community of grace and prophetic witness, with each individual Christian energised to take his or her part. And it is

---

[13] Robin Green, *Only Connect: Worship and Liturgy from the Perspective of Pastoral Care* (London: Darton, Longman & Todd, 1987), 130.

this very grandeur of perspective that makes vocational language appropriate for Christian endeavour, be it the vocational work of the priest in celebrating and proclaiming the vision and striving for its actualisation in Church life, or of the lay person whose 'secular' life and labours can also be understood in the light of worship as a site of God's new creation coming to birth.

But before discussing forms that individual Christian lay vocation might take in the world, it is necessary to put such vocational talk in its larger context. The Church is not a collection of individuals each fulfilling separate missions, but rather a collective reality with a single purpose. Paul's strikingly organic image of Christians as members of Christ's body is nowhere more forcefully rendered than in Bishop John A.T. Robinson's preferred translation of 1 Corinthians 12:27, 'Ye are the body of Christ and severally *membranes* thereof'.[14] For Paul, the vocation of the Christian is in terms of the body first and foremost, with various parts contributing to the success of the whole.

Hence, the Christian does not stand aloof in mission and vocation, as if the eye or the ear were to say that it has no need of the hand or the foot (1 Corinthians 12:21). Taking one's part in the life and identity of the body is paramount. In this sense, the primary vocation of the Christian is 'being the Church', attending worship, receiving the sacraments and under-standing (standing-under) the story of Jesus Christ. This becomes clearer when the Church's role as an alternative community is appreciated. The Church can be a focused community of discipline where social alternatives are lived out. For a society choked with material consumption, coarsened by the depersonalising of sexuality and disoriented by the loss of shared meaning, the Church can be what the Jesus of Matthew's Gospel imagined: a city set on a hill; an exemplary community challenging and encouraging the world by modelling a different

---

[14] John A.T. Robinson, *The Body: A Study in Pauline Theology* (Philadelphia: Westminster Press, 1952), 51 (italics mine).

way. Without any holier than thou sectarianism, nevertheless the Church as intentional community is an idea emerging from the collapse of a flabby Christendom, beyond lacklustre personal moralism and bourgeois conformism.

William Diehl points out that churches that are growing give responsibility for the mission to all their members—to the laity—while those churches that are dwindling tend to lock up the mission institutionally, with nothing vocational for the laity to do. This malaise is reflected in widespread boredom with and disconnection from worship in mainstream churches.[15]

Stanley Hauerwas comments on this decline, criticising the thin soup that lay people are offered throughout liberal churches, with little to get their teeth into in an agenda of well-intentioned sentiment, mild social concern and friendly worship. 'Churches characterised by compassion and care', Hauerwas writes, 'no longer are able to sustain membership, particularly of our own children'.[16] Elsewhere, Hauerwas states that only a sense of participating in an adventure will galvanise young people and render involvement in worship and Christian life attractive. In the matter of commending Christian sexual morality to the young, for instance, Hauerwas recognises the sheer impossibility of this patently counter-cultural task apart from the inculcation of a grand vision: 'Our children have to see that marriage and having children, and the correlative sexual ethic, are central to a community's political task', he argues, 'For only then can they be offered a vision and an enterprise that might make the disciplining of sex as interesting as its gratification'.[17] It is this empowering perspective that is properly

---

[15] William Diehl, *The Monday Connection: A Spirituality of Competence, Affirmation, and Support in the Workplace* (San Francisco: HarperCollins, 1991), 16-17.

[16] Stanley Hauerwas, *After Christendom: How the Church is to Behave if Freedom, Justice and a Christian Nation are Bad Ideas* (Sydney: Lancer, 1991), 99.

[17] Stanley Hauerwas, *A Community of Character: Toward a Constructive Christian Social Ethic* (Notre Dame, IN.: University of Notre Dame Press, 1981), 183.

the content and the purpose of worship, fit to render the ordinary lives of Christian laity vocational.

Agents of grace

The Christian vocation to worship God and be the Church will lead to lifestyle choices, affect the way that relationships are approached and employment is undertaken, suggest causes to adopt and occasionally call for brave and sacrificial action. It is well to remember the great cloud of witnesses whose vocation proved ultimately to be martyrdom, which is the act of being the Church most radically.

It is well to remember, too, that some of these martyrs, and certainly countless other Christians whose travail did not cost them their lives, have suffered at the Church's own hand. Here the issue of prophecy arises, and the possibility that one can oppose the Church on behalf of the Church. Who would deny that protest by visionary Christians is God's regular leaven in the ecclesial lump? This occurs when criticism of injustice or immoral collaboration on the Church's part in a particular place or time is made on behalf of the Church's overall identity and mission, with the Protestant Reformation and the Catholic Counter-Reformation providing classic examples. One also thinks of protests that led to the various renewals of religious life, to the acceptance of modern science as theologically valid, to freedom for slaves, to labour reform and to women's ordination.

However, it cannot be denied that the Church has not always been able to reform itself from within, having to rely on prophetic insights from outside its fold such as Marxist and feminist social analysis. Yet it has been Christians who have taken up these insights and, as it were, brought them aboard. For the lay Christian, then, fidelity to the vision will sometimes mean opposition to aspects of the Church's present polity, which is the longstanding witness of faithful Christian radicalism.

Yet there is Dietrich Bonhoeffer's challenge to remember here, that to love your idea of the Church rather than the actual Church is to be an enemy of the Church. Here is a warning that helps distinguish wholesome radicalism from angry fanaticism and loyal opposition from adolescent rebellion. It is only a fitting lay vocation to challenge and castigate the Church if it arises from a love for the Church as well as from a vision of God's Kingdom, and if it is done in sackcloth and ashes—that is, if the lay prophet is also the lay penitent, and if the critic is willing to stand with the criticised; if it is '*our* problem in the Church' rather than '*your* problem in the Church'.

The vision of worship that calls the Church into being and critiques its life calls for lay Christians to live out its post-tribal, non-sexist vision, loving the world of God's creation and respecting living things. Christians will recognise the fact of human evil and not despise just opposition to it—even, I suggest, to the point of sanctioning 'just war', though some Christians of great courage and deep conviction differ on this last assessment. Christians cannot be gnostic in their approach to material reality, but neither can they be imprisoned in the frequently empty materialism of modern Western life. Christians cannot be suspicious of human sexuality, either, but must recognise its profoundly symbolic character, psychological power and political resonances, conducting themselves with care and responsibility.

Christians must be change-agents for God's new future. It may seem that an ordinary life provides few opportunities. But apart from the great works that God requires of some lay Christians, there is much ultimate significance in the way that quite normal things are done. Here one thinks for instance of the great service that lay Christians can perform in the covenant of marriage, being the sacramental agents of God's love and grace for one another, liberating each other from lonely self-possession or else from predatory shallowness. One thinks also of the service to humanity that good parents perform, and here lay Christians have perhaps their greatest chance to affect the world's future by passing on a vision, a taste for grace, and an ethic beyond prudent pragmatism.

In the workplace, lay Christians can be agents of grace and sanity, of perspective and compassion. They can redeem a bitter environment by their perseverance, care and humour, supported as this stance must be by habits of intercessory prayer. They can be the leaven in the lump of organisations by demonstrating a diligence beyond that of timeserving colleagues. They can model a way of redeeming work from the abyss of alienation that many modern Westerners find it to be by 'going the extra mile'. William Diehl advocates what he calls 'a spirituality of competence, affirmation and support in the workplace'. He challenges and seeks to equip lay Christians to catch a vision in Church on Sunday that they can carry into the working week.[18]

Of course, many workplace situations call for more than Christian leaven in the lump. Creative protest of all sorts is often required. Sometimes this is simply the initiative that all good organisations welcome from their members. But sometimes lay vocation demands even more. Christians in a workplace may choose to sacrifice pay so the need for downsizing will be removed and workmates will keep their jobs. Management may need to be confronted over some moral wrong and a Christian may be the one prepared to risk the consequences of doing it, having been made restless in worship for the values of God's Kingdom.

Conscientious objection, of the sort that led to the founding of the Friends' Ambulance Brigade in First World War England, is a special instance of the sort of stance lay Christians may feel compelled to take. Another Christian who would not sign up even when offered non-combatant status was the young Austrian Catholic farmer Franz Jaggerstatter, guillotined in 1943

---

[18] Diehl, *The Monday Connection*, 52ff.

for refusing to join Hitler's army.[19] In this particular case, we see how the discernment of lay vocation can be complicated, with conscience set against what many would regard as plain duty. Yet Jaggerstatter chose to leave his three young daughters the memory of a father who sought to follow Christ's way of the cross, refusing to follow the prudent, self-preserving course recommended by his parish priest and diocesan bishop.

Dimensions of lay vocation as the Anglican tradition sees it are summarised by Fredrica Harris Thompsett. 'The theology of vocations in the English Reformation was not so much a simple imitation of the Lutheran doctrine of a "priesthood of all believers"', she writes, 'but rather an English assertion of encompassing vocations bound together in charity'.[20] This she identifies as the joint witness of the early English prayer books. There is also the dimension of faith education for the laity present from the earliest days of Anglican reform, with the expectation that they will read the newly printed books and the English Bible and be instructed by set homilies.

The *Book of Common Prayer* collect for the second Sunday of Advent, about reading marking, learning and inwardly digesting Scripture, is echoed in the bishop's charge to the congregation at the end of Confirmation according to *An Australian Prayer Book*. There the people are reminded that all the baptised and confirmed are called to study and seek to understand the Bible and the Christian faith more fully, to share in the faith and worship of the Church and be committed to evangelisation. That this charge has been watered down slightly in *A Prayer Book for Australia*

---

[19] See e.g., Joan Chittister and Robert Lentz, *A Passion for Life: Fragments of the Face of God* (Maryknoll, NY.: Orbis, 1996), 64-67.
[20] Fredrica Harris Thompsett, 'The Laity', in *The Study of Anglicanism*, eds. Stephen Sykes and John Booty (London: SPCK; Philadelphia: Fortress Press, 1988), 245-60, at 248.

may indicate a recognition that many lay Anglicans feel no such responsibility.

Worship and life

Worship can support lay vocation if lay people are able to make connections between worship and life. This comes easily to some but requires 'conscientisation' before others will achieve it. Interestingly, too, such influence can go in the opposite direction. Jim Forest, a companion of the Berrigan brothers in Catholic Worker protests against the Vietnam war in America, rediscovered a heart and a will for worship through his Christian activism. The public burning of draft cards struck him as a ritual act in fidelity to the gospel and reopened his eyes to the gospel character of the Mass.[21]

Emphasising lay vocation taking place in the world of work and life is crucial. But it is not necessary, or even helpful, for lay Christians to be aggressively evangelistic in the workplace. Christians are called to 'Always be ready to make your defence to anyone who demands from you an accounting for the hope that is in you; yet do it with gentleness and reverence' (1 Peter 3:15-16), which both establishes the expectation of evangelistic outreach and sets limits to it. Christian witness in the highways and byways of life need not be intensively evangelistic to be fruitful.

Nor is it appropriate that lay people whose proper ministries are in 'the world' are wholly caught up in ministries serving the institutional Church. Rostered duties in worship that serve to build up the body of Christ are one thing, such as the ministries of welcome at the door, reader/lector and liturgical assistant, but to overdo this commitment and effectively to clericalise particular

---

[21] Jim Forest, 'Communities of Resistance', in *A Reader in Political Theology*, ed. Alistair Kee (London: SCM Press, 1974), 161-67, at 163.

laity is to dishonour their true vocation in the world, where nowadays it is they and no longer the clergy who constitute the Church's front line. It is a sorry Church that has numerous licensed priests who have dropped out of active ministry and now work at purely secular occupations with little if any disciplined ecclesial function while countless lay people are propping-up the Church's worship and its committee structures with no encouragement to discover what their Christian calling in life outside the institutional Church might be.

And here it is necessary to name today's Evangelical push for Lay Presidency at the Eucharist as poor ecclesiology and misdirected pastoral concern. This is because Christian worship and the question of who leads it should be seen more holistically, with 'intensive liturgy' in Church and 'extensive liturgy' out in the world.[22] It is the vocation of lay people to preside at 'extensive liturgy'—following Christ in living out their Christian calling in the world—while the priests' building up of the Church entails presiding at its 'intensive liturgy'. Both groups need 'liturgical assistants' in their respective spheres: in the intensive liturgy of the Church, the priest presides and the laity properly assist; in the extensive liturgy of lay vocation in the world, the laity preside and the priest properly assists. The priest is the liturgical assistant of the laity in the extensive liturgy of life.[23] Lay Presidency, by further locking-up the laity in the Church's institutional life, risks becoming a closet clericalism denying the genuineness and dignity of lay vocation in the world.

I have argued that the primary lay vocation is to be the Church, rather than focus first and foremost upon specific ethical or political projects (as well-meaning souls, often with a yen for

---

[22] Charles Price and Louis Weil, *Liturgy for Living* (New York: Seabury, 1979), 23.
[23] See my paper, 'Priestly Leadership, Eucharistic Presidency and Lay Vocation', in *Who May Celebrate? Boundaries of Anglican Order*, ed. Ivan Head (Sydney: Doctrine Commission of General Synod, 1996), 59-65.

Christian activism, often present the case). In the collective vision and collective responsibility that properly emerges from worship, lay vocation finds its true bearings.

3

On Loving the Church (2006)

> *This piece is from a volume of essays marking the retirement of Revd Dr Bruce Kaye as General Secretary of the Anglican Church of Australia. After considering some identity challenges facing Australian Anglicanism, I explore two possible responses to failings and decline in the Church. I call these the pneumatology of despair and the pneumatology of hope. The former covers both a range of wrongheaded and dysfunctional options as well as a more reflective mood of tragic pathos. The latter expresses a stubborn confidence that God is still at work in the Church and that despair is unrealistic. These reflections drew on my experience in two challenging appointments: as Principal of St Barnabas' Theological College, Adelaide (1998-2002), and as Rector of St Paul's, Manuka, in Canberra (2002-2007). This piece appeared in* Agendas for Australian Anglicanism: Essays in Honour of Bruce Kaye, *eds. Tom Frame and Geoffrey Treloar (Adelaide: ATF Press, 2006), 249-270, and is reproduced here with the kind permission of ATF Press.*

He who loves his dream of a community more than the Christian community itself becomes a destroyer of the latter, even though his personal intentions may be ever so honest and earnest and sacrificial.

Dietrich Bonhoeffer[24]

---

[24] Dietrich Bonhoeffer, *Life Together* 5th edn. (1949), trans. John W. Doberstein (London: SCM Press, 1954), 17.

Anglicanism, in its origins as a distinctive take on Catholic Christianity and in its ongoing witness to unity in diversity, demonstrates a love for the actual Christian community beyond anyone's particular dream for that community. The Church exists; it is a part of God's activity in Christ, as Scripture and creed testify; and its facticity, its historical givenness and innate spiritual dignity as the body of Christ, precedes anything anyone might try to make of it. Dietrich Bonhoeffer ought to be able to rest easy, then, that at least one major Christian tradition stands as a witness to the Church being more than its parties.

Reformation Anglicanism was Catholicism reforming itself without dismissing the legacy of English Christianity, including the traditional essentials of faith and order. Just so, subsequent Anglicanism has contained the zeal of Evangelicals and Anglo-Catholics, allowed Christ and culture to negotiate their ongoing relationship without recourse to dogma and authoritarianism, and generally demonstrated a respect for the actual Church able to welcome parties and enthusiasms while not being annexed by them.

Dietrich Bonhoeffer was concerned for a Church that could be hijacked by culture, as the so-called German Christians demonstrated with their Nazification of the gospel, or by pietism, which sought a better Church, a 'real' Church, holier than the actual Church that God loves. Sixteenth-century Anglican reform honoured the actual Christian community and the forms of its historical manifestation. It represented continuity in change, demonstrating God's continuing faithfulness to a Church that is intuitively grasped as a divine gift before it is set about as a human project. Anglicanism's emerging vocation as a partner in twentieth-century denominational mergers, and more recently in concordats with Lutherans, demonstrates a further dimension of this respect for the actual Church—to the extent that some have seen the Anglican vocation in terms of relinquishing its prerogatives in the cause of a respectful Christian *oikumene*.[25]

But all is not well in Anglicanism, and the splendid experiment is widely thought to be in crisis. In earlier times, Anglicans faced crises when the unassimilable, radical end of the Puritan movement gained political power during the English Commonwealth, dismissing both the bishops and the prayer book, and when some Anglicans felt conscience-bound to retain their allegiance to James II after the Glorious Revolution (giving rise to the first of several breakaway Anglican Churches in the Non-Juring schism). Later, the importation of Romish ritual practices, or else distaste for religious enthusiasm, threatened Anglican unity (indeed, we lost the Methodists). Nowadays, the main internal conflict is broadly that of culture-embracing liberals versus tradition-affirming conservatives, with the situation in American Episcopalianism amounting to mutual excommunication.[26] This has blown up into a North-South divide in global Anglicanism with homosexuality as the trigger, so that local self-definition is outpacing Anglican solidarity. Hence, we see American impatience[27] on the same-sex issue up against third-world resistance to Western cultural dominance, employing the authority of Scripture as a cultural equaliser.[28] In both cases, despite the purest of motives, the actual Church is at risk as different ideas of the Church compete.

This is sometimes perceived to be a matter of truth versus unity—better to salvage a true Church from the break-up than

---

[25] Stephen Neill, *Anglicanism* (1958) (London: Mowbray, 1977), 406.

[26] Daniel Hardy, 'The Situation Today: March 2001', in *Finding the Church: The Dynamic Truth of Anglicanism* (London: SCM Press, 2001), 199-206, at 202-03.

[27] Richard F. Tombaugh, 'Ecclesial Impatience: The Windsor Report: A Response to The Lambeth Report', *Conversations in Religion and Theology* 3, no. 1 (May 2005), 105-08.

[28] Paula D. Nesbitt, 'The Future of Religious Pluralism and Social Policy: Reflections from Lambeth and Beyond', in *Religion and Social Policy*, ed. Paula D. Nesbitt (Walnut Creek, CA.: Altamira Press, 2001), 244-61.

maintain a united one that has lost its way. Yet a united Church that struggles with the fact of its brokenness can also be a powerful sign of Christ's truth, beyond what pristine ideological purity, be it liberal or conservative, can demonstrate. I will have more to say about this aspect of loving the actual Church later in this chapter when I engage with the work of Rusty Reno and Ephraim Radner.

Yet the Church faces a more general and more insidious malaise in contemporary culture. I refer to the volatilising of ecclesiology characteristic of postmodern, consumer-driven Western life. And here Anglicanism is not alone. We must all face growing pressures to make the Church relevant to today's perceived priorities, particularly those concerning personal needs. This is not just about a liberal, culture-friendly agenda versus a conservative one, because the personal annexing of religion goes on apace in both versions of Church life. A case can be made that the more structural, large-scale threats to Church unity to which I have been referring all run on the fuel of privatised religious meaning, revealing the schismatic impulse to be characteristic of modern Western sensibility.

In what follows, I will explore the contemporary attitudes that are making it hard for many Anglicans, and modern Western Christians more generally, to love the actual Christian community, preferring their dream for that community. How does this play out in the widespread dysfunction and loss of nerve manifest throughout Western Church life, and not least in Australian Anglicanism?

What are the options for us if we have come fundamentally to mistrust the Spirit of God in guiding the Church today? These I will discuss under the heading 'Pneumatology[29] of despair', and beyond its widespread 'fleeing, fawning or fighting' options I will focus on the more sophisticated but no less discouraging proposal of the conservative Episcopalian thinker Ephraim Radner, advocating dogged perseverance despite God's

---

[29] Pneumatology is that branch of systematic theology dealing with the person and work of the Holy Spirit (*pneuma* is a biblical word for Spirit).

apparent abandonment of the Church. Alternatively, what are our options if we pursue what I am calling 'Pneumatology of hope', believing that God's Spirit is still making the Church? This is what Bishop John Zizioulas argues, against what he identifies as the characteristically bogged-down institutionalism of Western Christianity. Following God's perennial reforming impulse in fidelity to the actual Church, of which this reforming impulse is always an integral part, I want to follow the Catholic theologian James Alison in learning how to let go of anger, with a love for the actual Christian community that does not mean leaving everything in the Church just as it is.

Alternative ideas of Church

Throughout the Western world, paradigmatically in America but also plainly in Australia, the Church risks being annexed to the needs and priorities of the sovereign autonomous individual. In an increasingly therapeutic and managerial society, where everything is voluntary and associational, this utilitarian and expressive individualism has supplanted more traditional versions of human abiding. The social contract view of national life, from Thomas Hobbes to Margaret Thatcher, nowadays leaves a vacuum of personal meaning beyond the individual, and beyond the narrowly altruistic horizon of (currently) significant others within the household. It is within these confining limits that the churches are expected to perform.

Sociologist Robert Bellah charts the impact of this thinking in America, but his conclusions have a wider resonance. Human beings still access the depths of God yet increasingly they lack a language to express these depths, with church involvement firmly annexed to an agenda of personal fulfilment for individuals craving identity, meeting the fellowship needs of urbanised isolates for human contact and solidarity. While claiming a traditional pedigree for their version of religion, nevertheless conservative believers are engaged in the same culturally captive quest as a reaction against the affectively challenged, take-it-or-leave-it pluralism that characterises postmodern Western life.

An overwhelming trend in American religion—Catholic and Protestant, regardless of doctrine and worship style—is for congregations to define themselves as 'communities of personal support'. And there is a familiar cost, as Bellah recognises. This is why congregational life, as with other voluntary organisations and the contemporary family, can be so fragile—why it requires so much energy to keep it going and why it has so faint a hold on commitment when such needs are not met.[30] Every pastorally energetic parish priest in Australia will immediately recognise this as a true assessment of the situation we face, too, in terms of the tenuousness of attachment to the Church, the high expectations of lay people, the enormous scope for disappointment they demonstrate, and the amount of effort necessary to fulfil the diverse expectations of a congregation—let alone to lead it.

This state of affairs recalls the eudaemonistic[31] and pietistic focus against which Dietrich Bonhoeffer issued his prophetic warning.[32] Here is the universal religious impulse according to Bonhoeffer, from his prison poem 'Christians and Unbelievers':

> All go to God when they are sorely placed:
> They plead to him for help, for peace, for bread,
> For mercy, for them sinning, sick or dead.
> We all do so in faith or unbelief.[33]

---

[30] Robert N. Bellah, et al, *Habits of the Heart: Individualism and Commitment in American Life* (1985) (Berkeley and Los Angeles: The University of California Press, 1996), 232.

[31] Eudaemonism is the perspective (in ethical theory) that happiness is the highest good.

[32] This insight jelled for me listening to Thorwald Lorenzen lecturing on Church renewal and faith as discipleship in Bonhoeffer; see his 'Dietrich Bonhoeffer's Legacy: 60 Years On', *St Mark's Review* 199 no. 2 (2005): 12-19.

[33] See Dietrich Bonhoeffer, *Letters and Papers from Prison*, trans. Reginald H. Fuller (New York: Macmillan, 1953), 224; this more contemporary (and singable!) translation is by W. H. Farqharson, appearing at #240 in *Together in Song: Australian Hymn Book II* (Melbourne: HarperCollinsReligious, 1999).

The natural human version of religion is thus exposed as equivalent to magic, seeking to enlist sacred power to our own ends—our wellbeing, our happiness, and our sense of purpose in life. Bonhoeffer, however, and before him Karl Barth, saw the gospel of Jesus Christ as the critique of this typical human religiosity. God goes to human beings, embracing their cause in Jesus Christ, doing for us what we cannot do for ourselves by religious let alone secular means. God places God's cause in our hands, calling on us to take up and further that cause. This is the road less travelled along which Bonhoeffer's poem leads us, to a God who shares the threatened condition of human existence and supports us in it, not to give us a quiet and untroubled life but empowering us to live by faith. And this faith is about discipleship, not standing-off from God in attitudes of private satisfaction but caught up in God's purposes as disciples of Christ.

This is the religionless Christianity for which Bonhoeffer is justly famous, though regularly misunderstood. It prefigures later Protestant 'death of God' theology, though it does not emphasise the dissolution of God into secular life without remainder as is sometimes thought. Rather, it is a call to spiritual maturity in which God's life and agenda in the world becomes the centre of the disciple's life, rather than God and religion being annexed for that individual's ends. It represents a truly Copernican revolution, and if it is about secularity then that is because the modern, secular world is where God now chooses to take God's age-old stand in solidarity with human beings.

But who wants it? Who in the Church today would call such 'religionless Christianity' relevant to their needs? As Jesus was crucified for not fitting-in with the religious culture of his day, so Pastor Bonhoeffer went to the scaffold for his ill-fitting version of Christianity. And so, too, today: if God offers modern Westerners the meaning, comfort and fellowship they seek from the Church, it is only in the context of greater challenge and potential difficulty—of a greater missional intensity and burden of discipleship than many in today's Church will not recognise let alone welcome.

In Australian Anglicanism, the preferred options for the Christian community appear to be an ideology strong enough to stabilise and galvanise the individual, on the one hand, versus a retreat from difficult engagement into nostalgic comfort and safe bourgeois predictability on the other hand. The latter option, widespread in Middle-to-High expressions of Anglicanism, is plainly not the religionless Christianity—of faithful discipleship at home in the world God loves—to which Bonhoeffer points. But neither is the more sectarian, zealous, Evangelical alternative, with its culture critique of secular values mixed with a highly culture-affirming commitment to meeting the meaning and fellowship needs of individuals, with the multiplication of warm, personal and 'relevant' fellowships tailored to the needs and preferences of every age group, locality and subculture. Two recent Australian books set out and critique these options.

Most insightful on the situation in Middle-to-High Anglicanism in Australia is Melbourne writer Caroline Miley in *The Suicidal Church*.[34] The gist of her argument is this: that Middle-to-High Anglicanism in Australia, the ongoing decline of which is widely acknowledged, is not dying so much as committing suicide. Miley claims, with statistics from the National Church Life Survey to back her, that many Anglican congregations, clergy and laity, are committed to a middle-class worldview quite incompatible with energy, change and growth in the Church. If I were paraphrasing Martin Luther, I would call what she describes the middle-class captivity of Anglicanism. She argues that we are bourgeois, timid, conventional, stiflingly hierarchical, and dismissive of competence and enthusiasm because these are thought to be showy and

---

[34] Caroline Miley, *The Suicidal Church: Can the Anglican Church be Saved?* (Sydney: Pluto Press, 2002).

even vulgar—an affront to the sturdy culture of middle-class amateurishness.

Most importantly, Miley blames middle-class values for the sheer incomprehension or else visceral distaste many Anglicans in her tradition feel for evangelism, and for the sort of unseemly religious enthusiasm that might lead to livelier worship, growing congregations and the threat to quiet, established habits that these inevitably bring. In short, Miley believes that many lay people, many congregations, many priests and bishops, resist the Spirit of God, refusing spiritual intensity, mission and growth for the sake of familiarity in what fragment of the Church is remaining, along with control of that fragment: 'holding to an outward form of Godliness, but denying its power' (2 Timothy 3:5).

Chris McGillion examines the other, more ideological option. In *The Chosen Ones*[35] he offers a thorough overview of the rise of a new conservative orthodoxy in the Anglican Diocese of Sydney, 'the Jensen Ascendency'. It was held up during the moderate Goodhew years (1993-2001) but emerged with Archbishop Peter Jensen's ambitious ten-year plan for Sydney's religious renewal. McGillion sees Jensen's aim of attracting ten percent of Sydney into 'Bible based' churches by 2011 as a religious undertaking unprecedented in our time. His book is a history of the parties and the personalities, the various leagues, Synod voting tickets and back-room politics. The robust secularity of these processes, free of any pious reserve or spiritual squeamishness, is what many find most striking about this avowedly spiritual movement.

This in-your-face Christianity, sceptical about God's presence in the world apart from the Bible—a movement close to fundamentalism in several respects—strikes me as a too-desperate expedient. This is a faith confronting the world from a position of spiritual superiority (despite what many will see as a rather

---

[35] Chris McGillion, *The Chosen Ones: The Politics of Salvation in the Anglican Church* (Sydney: Allen and Unwin, 2005).

worldly way of going about it), tuned-in to the needs of many individuals to find steadfast bearings in life. Yet the downplaying of ecclesiastical tradition and worship habits that is characteristic of this movement, favouring instead the embrace of American-style praise worship, family-friendly 'meetings' and a gospel tailored to our culture's individualistic focus, all point to a cultural captivity every bit as real, albeit different in its expression, from the more parlous situation that Miley brings to light in the Middle-to-High zone of Australian Anglicanism.

What are we to make of these options? I am reminded of some acute pastoral wisdom from Rowan Williams that I have found unerringly helpful for interpreting the behaviour of others (and my own) as it bears on situations of pastoral conflict. This principle can extend beyond the personal to the institutional. In seeking to assess a problem individual, Williams commends questions like, 'Is there a pattern of behaviour here suggesting an unwillingness to learn or be enlarged?' or 'Is there an obsessive quality to acts of self-presentation (in speech especially) that would indicate a fixed and defended image of needs that must be met for this self to sustain its position of power?'[36] This points to an unstable stance based on anxious self-definition, fiercely protective because tight control of religious meaning and practice is deemed necessary to meet personal needs. So too for the versions of Christian community that not only attract such individuals but come to manifest their pathology.

It is interesting that the versions of Christian community to which I am drawing attention are mutually antagonistic, with the ungracious and insecure in both camps highly antipathetic towards those of the other camp. By contrast, it is only the mature disciple from the Middle-to-High tradition who can discern and

---

[36] Rowan Williams, '"Know Thyself": What Sort of Injunction?', in *Philosophy, Religion and the Spiritual Life*, ed. Michael McGhee (Royal Institute of Philosophy Supplement, 32. Cambridge: Cambridge University Press, 1992), 211-27, at 225.

acknowledge gospel treasure in the field of Evangelicalism, for all its 'otherness', just as it is only a mature Evangelical disciple who can discern the pearl of great price in the spiritual reserve of 'central Anglicanism', or else in the more exuberant sacramentality of Anglo-Catholicism.

All this represents today's religion of expressive individualism in characteristic guises. It is impatient with the actual Christian community, seeking either to restrain its uncomfortable demands for discipleship, in one manifestation, or else transform it into a purer, more ideological version of itself—though correspondingly culturally attuned in its relentlessly personal focus—according to its other manifestation.

One of America's sharpest advocates for 'mere Christianity', eschewing both Evangelical stringency and liberal-cultural capitulation, is the Episcopalian lay theologian Rusty Reno, who has more recently become a Roman Catholic. Such a move is significant given Reno's sustained emphasis, following Ephraim Radner, on persevering with the flawed, actual (Episcopal) Church despite its current crises and divisions.

Reno's particular animus is what he and other conservative Episcopalians see as the all-too-ready abandonment of Christian distinctiveness in favour of contemporary relevance. The agenda of individual self-expression, sexual self-determination and personal authenticity dominates Episcopalian life today, according to Reno, who sheets this home to the influence of what he calls me-first humanism. But being true to yourself as the highest moral goal of modernity cannot deliver the true self it promises, so that the chronically destabilised affective and relational life characteristic of modern societies can only find relief if it embraces postmodern *apatheia* and irony, giving up the prospect of meaningful personal transformation. Thus, the redemptive project of modernity runs aground in a postmodern environment of irresolvable plurality, programmatic distractedness and consumerist excess.

On Loving the Church (2006)

While Reno is at odds with the liberal tendencies of Middle-to-High Anglicanism in America, the more conservative, family-oriented agenda is no less culturally packaged and consumer driven, as I have been suggesting. Hence my reservations about Reno's hard line, and his insufficiently critical distinction between Christ and culture that misses the culture-dependence of religious conservatism.

Apart from that, I find Reno broadly correct in his challenge to modernity in the name of orthodox Christianity as a more dependable path to sustained personal redemption. Christianity offers a better cure of the soul than modernity, achieving a more reliable at-one-ment of the individual with their 'true self' than modernity's breathless agenda of personal transformation normally allows. Reno concludes that 'Who we are now can be connected ('at-one') with who we hope to become because we are incorporated into the identity of Jesus, and what he does may be imputed to us, ensuring that we are continuous ('at-one') across the wrenching logic of change.'[37]

But of course, this is not what modern people want from the Church—a gospel that will change them, decentring their lives and providing them with a new focus in Christ. Hence today's widespread pragmatic rejection of the gospel in the Church, diluted to fit the demands of culture, when in fact it is the gospel that will reliably deliver the modern dream of personal transformation toward something really authentic.[38]

Pneumatology of despair

What are our options if we accept the mandate of contemporary Western culture and seek our own personal satisfaction from

---

[37] Russell R. Reno, *Redemptive Change: Atonement and the Christian Cure of the Soul* (Harrisburg, PA.: Trinity Press International, 2002), 229.

[38] Russell R. Reno, 'Pro Nobis: Words We do Not Want to Hear', in *In the Ruins of the Church: Sustaining Faith in an Age of Diminished Christianity* (Grand Rapids, MI.: Brazos Press, 2002), 47-61.

the Christian community, yet that community does not fulfil our expectations? Frequently, we witness one or another of the responses that I will call fleeing, fawning or fighting.

Fleeing, like divorcing, is a characteristic Western response to a difficult, unsatisfying, disappointing situation. If the actual Church does not meet our needs, we can leave it, either for another denomination, like those Anglican clergy who 'went to Rome' over women priests (some subsequently returning, even after being 're-ordained'), or else leave the Church altogether for want of any satisfying prospects.

Another dimension of fleeing, as it applies to clergy, is to move on from difficult pastoral appointments in a succession of career moves, seeking more congenial circumstances, in effect buying-in to our culture's obsession with options, choice and 'therapeutic disengagement'. The long-suffering, persevering virtues of staying put are hard to reconcile with the personal ideals of a fast-paced, postmodern society, where nothing is forever, and where sustained commitment that yields fruit only after a number of years scarcely computes. The often-rapid turnover of pastoral appointments in Australian Anglicanism, however, is surely a contributing factor to the malaise that Miley and others identify—a failure in the cure of souls through a succession of brief pastoral relationships that are inevitably superficial. Nor can any transformative engagement with Church culture occur when no one stays long enough to be an agent of positive change, while sustaining the necessary pastoral energy. So, as well as reflecting dissatisfaction with actual Church life, this type of fleeing actually contributes to the causes of that dissatisfaction.

The options I am calling 'fawning and fighting' are well drawn in terms of co-dependent behaviour by American New Testament scholar and Franciscan friar, Michael Crosby.[39] He

---

[39] Michael H. Crosby, *The Dysfunctional Church: Addiction and Codependency in the Family of Catholicism* (Notre Dame, IN.: Ave Maria Press, 1991), 217–36.

movingly describes his own struggles as an over-functioning supporter of religious authority—fawning—then as an equally over-functioning ecclesial critic and dissident—fighting.

The fighting option, identified by Crosby, is to imbibe anger and so become its prisoner, either by becoming bitter and failing in compassion, or, in Crosby's own case, by becoming a fixated critic of his Church's hierarchy caught up in a cycle of agonistic defiance and controlling behaviour. The fawning option is to deny the problems to which ecclesiastical obedience and a culture of clerical compliance give rise by striving to soften the Church's official line, interpreting this or that indefensible ruling as more subtle, context-dependent and secretly inclusive than appearances would indicate. This is a widespread tactic, and not only in Roman Catholicism. A more complete version of this response is to become an apparatchik in the system, finding identity and purpose by serving its version of God and Christianity.

In all three cases, the actual Christian community is sacrificed for the sake of a preferred version of it—by leaving that community (fleeing), by integrity-sacrificing collusion with its dysfunction (fawning), or by becoming embittered, sometimes to the point of assaulting that community (fighting). In all these cases, the actual Christian community is the loser.

The only healthy alternative, according to Crosby, is to break free of the addictive pattern of behaviour and its reactive control. Not as a dissident locked into a co-dependent struggle with it, however. Rather, by eschewing the 'control without care' characteristic of his dissident phase, Crosby became a more mature and well-intentioned critic of the system—more cool-headed and effective, no longer bitter and twisted but penitent and forgiving. James Alison makes a similar point in his discussion of the 'false sacred' that all religious structures generate, demanding compliance from their adherents, or else subtly remaining in control of dissidents by setting the agenda for their angry responses to the system, so that in opposing the system they remain controlled by it.[40]

This points us in a hopeful, persevering direction, and I will be pursuing it in the next section. First, however, I extend my pneumatology of despair category by introducing a further option as it emerges in Rusty Reno and Ephraim Radner (upon whom Reno draws).

Reno takes a very dim view of current Episcopalian conditions, which recall Nehemiah for him, and a city of broken-down walls. Yet from Ezra and Nehemiah also comes his faith in the eventual resurrection of Western Christianity, in God's good time, from the body of its faithful remnant. So, Reno counsels a sort of dogged perseverance with the Church as it is. He refuses both versions of dispensing with the actual Church: the liberal, more obviously culturally-accommodating one (which he regularly identifies with Bishop Spong), but also the conservative ideological version, preferring its dream of the Christian community over the actual community (to this end, he offers a sharp critique of the Radical Orthodoxy push in contemporary Anglican and Roman Catholic theology).[41]

For all his critique, however, Reno makes a virtue out of the necessity of inhabiting a broken Church, in an argument derived from Origen's defence of the regular intractability of Scripture. Origen believed that God's power is evident in the weaknesses of Scripture as a medium for conveying divine truth, with its many incompletenesses and contradictions. So too with the capacity of a

---

[40] James Alison, *On Being Liked* (London: Darton, Longman & Todd, 2003), especially the Chapters entitled 'Confessions of a Former Marginaholic' (65-77) and 'The Importance of Being Indifferent' (114-30).
[41] Russell R. Reno, 'The Radical Orthodoxy Project', in *In the Ruins of the Church*, 63-79.

necessarily imperfect Church to still mediate the reality of God—a treasure in earthen vessels.[42]

But it is the Episcopalian theologian Ephraim Radner to whom Reno regularly points, and in Radner's work we find a fuller version of Reno's case for persevering with a broken Church. Drawing on the scriptural figures of exile, brokenness and the passion of Christ, Radner calls for patience, reticence and foregoing any expectation of a too pure, too-perfect Church, pointing out that Jesus himself was willing to receive communion with Judas.[43] Significantly, Radner denies any conflict between preserving the truth and preserving the unity of the Church, because Christ's solidarity with his people, no matter what, is at the heart of gospel truth. Radner addresses directly the frustration that leads many to prefer their dream of the Christian community to the actual community, referring to his own frustrations with the Episcopal Church.

> Why stay within this church, within this denomination in particular, even within this or that diocese or session or district where the burdens often seem intolerable? Because it is the most evangelical thing one might do, witnessing not to weakness, not to compromise, not to disingenuity, but witnessing to the reality of the power of the cross of Jesus Christ in history... Why then would we be anxious that staying put, in the form of Jesus, could ever obscure the clarity of the gospel? Just the opposite will be the case.[44]

---

[42] Russell R. Reno, 'Towards a Postliberal Ecclesial Spirituality', in *In the Ruins of the Church*, 129-47.

[43] Ephraim Radner, 'The Figure of Truth and Unity', in *Hope Among the Fragments: The Broken Church and its Engagement with Scripture* (Grand Rapids, MI.: Brazos Press, 2004), 111-20, at 116.

[44] Ephraim Radner, 'Enduring the Church: How to be a Fool', in *Hope Among the Fragments*, 199-214, at 210, 211.

So far, so good, surely. Why am I calling this a 'pneumatology of despair'? Because there is more here than following Christ in a difficult calling. Behind Radner's spiritually bracing advice lurks a startlingly downbeat assessment of the present age of our 'Church of Churches',[45] with its chronic denominational divisions, its self-definitional strategies, its preference for 'fixing' over deep soul-searching and repentance. All this strikes Radner as a call to patient, repentant dying on the part of a Church that has so resisted the loving, unifying work of the Spirit that it must now see itself as bereft of the Spirit. Penitence is the only option he allows for a Church that God is abandoning to a radically cleansing and not-soon-to-be-resolved fate. And this 'penitence of the pneumatically deprived Church is maddeningly antiprogrammatic'.[46] As Jeremiah resisted the 'alluring but mendacious optimism concerning the brevity of Israel's captivity',[47] which lasted a whole lifespan of seventy years, so the best Radner can commend to today's Christian on God's behalf is 'dying where one is and asking for no more than that God bless this dislodged place of standing'.[48]

Radner did his doctorate on the Jansenists, and from the Abbé Saint-Cyran he seems to have discerned this radical call to long-term ecclesial detoxification—a call manifest as a penitential spirituality of faithful perseverance within the actual Church. One's separation, according to the Jansenists, was inner, in terms of the pursuit of patient holiness, not outer, in pursuit of a Church more to one's liking. Saint-Cyran is even supposed to have told St Vincent de Paul that trying to reform the Church was wrong-headed—that 'It would be the height of temerity to oppose the designs of God and decide to defend the Church

---

[45] Ephraim Radner, *The End of the Church: A Pneumatology of Christian Division in the West* (Grand Rapids, MI.: Eerdmans, 1998), 333.
[46] Radner, *The End of the Church*, 352.
[47] Radner, *The End of the Church*, 332.
[48] Radner, *The End of the Church*, 352.

which he has decided to let go of'.[49] This is the pneumatology of despair that I discern in Radner—not his advocacy of what my theological college Principal, James Warner, called 'stickability'; not Radner's refusal of any reform 'unrooted in the soil, deep and dark, of penitence';[50] not his sense that God is letting go of certain forms of the Church, despite calling us to persevere with them in the meantime. None of this is necessarily despairing. But what is despairing is the suggestion that God has withdrawn God's Spirit from God's people, even if only for a season.

Pneumatology of hope

The pneumatology of despair, as I have called it, has lost confidence in God inhabiting the present Church. The fleeing, fawning and fighting options are each, in their own way, signs of thwarted expectation. The apparent Godlessness of the Church is such that we leave. Or else we give up in resignation but will not leave, prepared to keep the system going, settling for empty institutional 'belonging' at the expense of spiritual life and mission. Anger and conflict with the present Church in favour of our dream for it completes this range of standard reactions to the regular disappointments of ecclesial life.

The more theologically reflective position of Reno, and even more so that of Radner, cannot be reduced to the fawning option, though in its emphasis on perseverance there is a limited similarity. It is a far more conscious, critical, high temperature version of the range of moods, from resignation to cynicism, that constitute fawning as I have described it. Yet it, too, is despairing, reading today's ecclesial situation figurally in negative terms only—of brokenness, exile and passion. There appears to be no room for confidence in God's embrace of the Church that is. Radner appears

---

[49] Radner, *The End of the Church*, 353.
[50] Radner, *The End of the Church*, 352.

to have lost faith in the Spirit's ongoing work, not just *enlivening* the Church but actually *constituting* its present Eucharistic life and ministerial order, expressing some of its anticipated eschatological perfection.

Here I am helped by the ecclesiology of a leading Greek Orthodox theologian, Bishop John Zizioulas. He strikes at the heart of our Western moroseness about the Church—our fretting over its relevance, our eagerness to fix it and make it more dynamic—with a dose of Eastern Christian confidence in the role of the Holy Spirit. We in the Western Church have too institutional, too structural and too backward-looking an ecclesiology—too Christological, also, in the sense of being too tied to origins, foundations and faith-once-delivered-to-the-saints. Instead of looking back in nostalgia, looking around in despair and looking forward in morose resignation, feeling that the divine thread has snapped and that the Church needs to be reconnected to God by our efforts—otherwise abandoned, fought over, or just grimly, resignedly inhabited—we can instead embrace with hope what Zizioulas calls 'The epicletic conditioning ... of the Church's continuity'.[51]

Here, beyond the glum Christological figures offered by Radner, we discover Christ as an always-present personal reality in the Spirit, constantly re-establishing relationship and forming *persons* in the Church out of the isolated, needy *individuals* that our culture makes us. 'Christ *in-stitutes* and the Spirit *con-stitutes*',[52] as Zizioulas memorably puts it, and we need not fear for the institutional Church, abandon it or enterprise it, if we are

---

[51] John D. Zizioulas, *Being as Communion: Studies in Personhood and the Church* (1985) (Contemporary Greek Theologians, 4. Crestwood, NY.: St Vladimir's Seminary Press, 1997), 186. Zizioulas' reference here is to 'epicletic conditioning': the root word 'Epiclesis' refers to the calling down of the Holy Spirit—on the Eucharistic elements but meant more generally here.

[52] Zizioulas, *Being as Communion*, 140.

confident that its life in Christ *institutionally* is secured by the Holy Spirit *constitutionally*.

Such a vision allows us to retain assurance, poise and engagement, confident that God is leading the Church toward God's dream for it—that fleeing, fawning and fighting are unnecessary counsels of despair, and that our best efforts involve more (though certainly not less) than dogged perseverance. We can be confident that God is continuing to strive with the Church for the expression of Christ's mind within it, and that God's faithfulness to the bride of Christ is at the heart of the Church's reality—dynamic and on-the-move, not static and paralysed.

I have written a book about signs of tomorrow's Church coming to birth in the midst of today's mixed ecclesial indicators in the West.[53] Unwittingly at the time, I was tapping into a whole new sense of something exciting happening in Western Christianity, beyond the various despairing options that I have identified, as a Google search of 'Emerging Church' will demonstrate. This future Church is emerging in tandem with the strong impetus throughout today's West toward what Anthony Giddens[54] calls life politics, which is manifest most obviously in the proliferation of New Social Movements (NSMs). I describe this mood as 'mature, mystical and militant'—the latter term referring not to ideological hardness but simply to a renewed intentionality in witness and discipleship. Most importantly, I do not see the Emerging Church as anti-liturgical, non-traditional or otherwise entirely a different sort of thing from what the Church has always been in every age through the Spirit. My faith is simply that God is continuing to make the Church, and that staying on board with the actual

---

[53] Scott Cowdell, *God's Next Big Thing: Discovering the Future Church* (Melbourne: John Garratt Publishing, 2004).

[54] See Anthony Giddens, *The Consequences of Modernity* (Cambridge: Polity, 1990), 156-63. Here he defines life politics as the politics of self-actualisation, as against the emancipatory politics that addresses inequality.

Christian community can be a joyful, hopeful position—beyond the depleted options I have set out, including Radner's sanctified gloominess.

Loving the Christian community itself

Following on from our discussion of the Church as always a Church in and of the Spirit, beyond anything that repels and disheartens us in the actual Church's life, it is now clear that the path to loving the actual Church is that of faith. Not faith in the institution, but in the Holy Spirit of God who ensures that Christ remains the living Lord of the Church in every age. The reforming work of the Spirit is perennially, universally part of the Church's integral life. This was the burden of a moving essay by Hans Küng, who remained a loyal and upbeat priest in the Roman Catholic Church despite his serious conflict with its Magisterium. The Church remains truly Catholic in every age and place because there are saints in it who demonstrate the Spirit's presence.[55] It is perhaps among those saints that Radner would have us abide, but the mark of the saints is joy, not resignation. Küng guides us more reliably with his notion of the Church's 'indefectibility'—not its infallibility, but its graced status as a bearer of God's Spirit that will not ultimately fail to manifest God's light and truth.

This same faith is the root cause of James Alison's love for the actual Church, even though many of his fellow gay Catholics are consumed with anger at their Church for its homophobic stance. Alison has moved beyond rivalry and defensiveness, thanks to the insights about human culture of the French American theorist René Girard. Universally, we humans attain peace and social order thanks to the safety valve of scapegoating, according to Girard,

---

[55] Hans Küng, 'Why I Remain a Catholic', in *The Church Maintained in Truth: A Theological Meditation*, trans. Edward Quinn (London: SCM Press, 1980), 75-87.

with the regulated violence that is the price of our stability folded into our conceptions of the sacred. For Alison, following Girard, faith is not the embrace of a sacred order, let alone a metaphysical worldview but, instead, faith means abandoning 'the temple' with Jesus, in favour of a resurrected way of life beyond the nervous boundary-setting characteristic of human institutions.[56]

Of course, we still occupy institutions, including religious ones, but their agenda is not ultimate, and we no longer need to fret over them—by fearing them or else trying to save them. Loving the actual Church becomes possible when we no longer expect too much of the Church, accepting its flawed reality because that is what Christ did, while recognising that human liberation and thriving—Zizioulas' epicletic living—is reliably found in the Church despite its many flaws.

Alison has learned not to be dominated by dysfunction in the Church, standing more lightly to the Church's failings than the 'pneumatology of despair' allows, and certainly without what we could call the sanctified moroseness of Radner. There is an altogether more impish, ironic, debonair ordinariness in Alison's ecclesial perseverance. He concentrates contemplatively on the presence of Christ and the Spirit in word and sacrament at the heart of the flawed, actual Church, finding himself able to get on with feeding the sheep as a priest because he discerns the new reality of post-resurrection forgiveness, of new creation, present in word and sacrament and Christian witness in the flawed, actual Church, and tries not to worry about the rest.[57]

---

[56] See e.g., René Girard, *I See Satan Fall Like Lightning* (1999), trans. James G. Williams (Maryknoll, NY.: Orbis, 2001).

[57] Of a number of useful essays by James Alison, I recommend his excellent piece on God helping Jonah overcome his anger, entitled 'Spluttering up the Beach to Nineveh...', and his fine treatment of Ezekiel living with a broken heart but not giving way to hating, in 'Moving On: The Exilic Transformation of Anger into Love', in James Alison, *Faith Beyond Resentment: Fragments Catholic and Gay* (London: Darton, Longman & Todd, 2001), 86-124.

The major exponent of this kind of vision right in the thick of the institutional Church is the Archbishop of Canterbury, Rowan Williams. A significant theme in his theology is the role of 'the other'—the unassimilable, the ill-fitting—and a religion of creation and incarnation fit for limited, historically bound human beings. We find the truth of God and ourselves in demanding encounter with the life of a community, with strangers who devoutly disagree with us, and with the challenges of brute existence—with the often-unsympathetic grain of reality.[58]

Jesus' temptations in the desert are of this sort, according to Williams, but Jesus refuses Satan's magical alternative in favour of sticking with the actual, imperfect world. And so it is for Williams in his advocacy of what we might call ecclesial staying put out of love for the actual Christian community. He has a more confident assessment of its prospects than those who opt for fleeing, fawning or fighting. Also, the work of God's Spirit is more plainly evident to Williams in quotidian ecclesial reality than is the case for Radner, despite strong similarities in the form of their 'spirituality of perseverance'. The actual Church establishes its spiritual credentials for Williams in

> the daily prayer of believers, the constant celebration of the Eucharist, meeting the same potentially difficult or dull people time after time, because they are the soil of growth. It insists that we go on reading the same book and reciting the same creeds ... an inexhaustible story, a pattern of words and images given by God that we shall

---

[58] Rowan Williams, *On Christian Theology* (Oxford: Blackwell, 2000). See especially the essays 'Trinity and Revelation' (131-47), and 'Trinity and Ontology' (148-66), on revelation emerging through closure-defying spiritual struggle within the Christian community; also 'Between the Cherubim: The Empty Tomb and the Empty Throne' (183-96), on the necessary limitations of institutional faith and practice; and 'Nobody Knows Who I am Till the Judgement Morning', 276-89, on finding ourselves only through struggle with demanding others and not in some easier version of life (or Church).

never come to the end of. ... In very unmagical settings indeed, inner cities and prisons, and remote hamlets and struggling mission plants, the church remains pledged; its pastors and people and buildings speaking of God who is not bored or disillusioned by what he has made—and so they speak of the personal possibilities for everyone in such a situation.[59]

This is a spirituality of disciplined abiding, contemplatively tuned to the active presence of God rather than prematurely convinced that ours is not a season of the Spirit, as Radner would have it. It is from this spirituality that Rowan Williams draws his pattern of leadership for the Anglican Communion, patiently calling for sustained engagement with difference and with disappointment in the Church.

This unwearied love of the actual Christian community, believing it to be the continuing site of God's investment in Christ as actualised in the Spirit, is fully compatible with seeking spiritual renewal in the Church. Yet, as we have seen thanks to James Alison, this will be a renewing impulse free of personal disappointment and the hatreds it can spawn. Hence, beyond the us-and-them of party rivalry in our Church, communion in the Spirit genuinely can be 'achieved through the sacrifice of purity', as English theologian Martyn Percy puts it. For Percy, good manners in the midst of conflict represents a distinctively Anglican witness to confidence in the Spirit's continuing guidance of the Church.[60]

---

[59] Rowan Williams, *Silence and Honey Cakes: The Wisdom of the Desert* (Oxford: Lion Publishing, 2003), 92-93.
[60] Martyn Percy, 'Reluctant Communion: On Sacrificing Purity', in *Theological Liberalism: Creative and Critical*, eds. J'annine Jobling and Ian Markham (London: SPCK, 2000), 114-25, at 123. (Author's Note: Percy's subsequent lengthy struggle with a hostile Council as Dean of Christ Church, Oxford, and his eventual loss to the Church in 2022, shows what a demanding expectation this can be).

Happily, I am able to conclude this discussion about loving the actual Church with an apt, home-grown example. Bruce Kaye, the leading scholar-statesman of Australia's diverse and fractious Anglican community—to whom this volume of essays by some of his many admirers stands in tribute—is a major witness to the attitude I am commending.[61] In a steady flow of books and articles, in networks of ideas and influence, and in a wide range of personal friendships, Dr Kaye has demonstrated what it means to love the actual Christian community, to relish its difference as a rich source of stimulus, and yet to pursue a clear-eyed prophetic program, confident that much is being achieved. His latest book, *Reinventing Anglicanism*,[62] is rich in scriptural, historical and theological warrants for confidence in God's continued prosecution of the Anglican story. Bruce Kaye is no benumbed apparatchik, grim-faced stoic or fuming zealot, but a churchman who richly embodies what loving the Church can and should mean. He is living proof that any hope we might have for Australian Anglicanism is justified.

---

[61] (Author's Note: I refer here to the original volume of essays in which this Chapter was first published.)

[62] Bruce Kaye, *Reinventing Anglicanism: A Vision of Confidence, Community and Engagement in Anglican Christianity* (Adelaide: Openbook Publishers, 2003). See my review of this book in *St Mark's Review* 195 no. 1 (2004): 48-49.

4

Holy Spirit and Mission: Concerns about *Mission-Shaped Church* (2006)

The Doctrine Commission of the Anglican Church of Australia responded to a major report from the Church of England that had created a lot of interest among Evangelicals, by affirming their widespread desire to move beyond present ecclesial priorities and structures with renewed missionary zeal. My brief was to consider the report, called Mission-Shaped Church, *with regard to the Holy Spirit. This whole issue remains a live one, even if the report is now dated. I argue that the promised renewal ought to be possible without wholesale abandonment of our ecclesial past, as the report itself hopes. Though it may entail changes in doctrinal emphasis that are less palatable to Evangelicals. I suggest that a suitably dynamic and collaborative ontology of ministry is conceivable in the Spirit that can satisfy the demands both of continuity and change, as I argue in conversation with insights from science and from management theory. Hence, I call for trust in the Holy Spirit's continued constituting of the Church's life and mission. This essay was published as 'Holy Spirit and Mission: Captivity and Charism in* Mission-Shaped Church', St Mark's Review *200 (2006): 43-49, alongside the other Commission members' contributions. It appears here by kind permission.*

The Church of England is increasingly disconnected from the life of the nation in which it claims a privileged spiritual location. *Mission-Shaped Church*—otherwise known as the Cray Report (named after the chair of the commission that produced it, the Evangelical leader Graham Cray, who became the Bishop of Maidstone)—goes some way to addressing this challenge.[63] It offers a valuable analysis of life and culture in postmodern Britain, with a variety of good-news stories about church plants and other 'fresh expressions' understood to represent tomorrow's Church. It also reflects on the praxis of this Emerging Church, for the benefit of practitioners seeking to get on board.

My focus is on three issues that I take to be important in our reception of *Mission-Shaped Church*. First, I affirm the Holy Spirit's constant impetus toward creative ecclesial reformation, which is at the heart of the report. The Spirit is not captive to the Church's institutional past, as both church history and any suitably dynamic pneumatology teach us. However, as my second point, and noting the Emerging Church's diversity as the report envisages it, I go on to identify challenges posed by mission in today's cultural context not only for the institutionally conservative but for the theologically-conservative-though-ecclesially-innovative constituency that has most eagerly embraced *Mission-Shaped Church*. My third and final point has to do with authority according to the report, in particular the key role it acknowledges for bishops enabling the mission. Might episcopacy be understood as more than a pragmatic addendum to our thinking about fresh expressions but rather more pneumatologically, integrally and holistically?

---

[63] Church of England Mission and Public Affairs Council, *Mission-Shaped Church: Church Planting and Fresh Expressions of Church in a Changing Context* (London: Church House Publishing, 2004).

Beyond institutional captivity

The report is a sustained invitation for us to think outside the box of the Church's accustomed institutional life. One key emphasis is church planting, understood as a fresh expression incarnated in a particular context. That context may be geographic, but it may also relate demographically to one of the various de-churched constituencies that the report identifies in contemporary Britain. It is important to note that such initiatives are not understood formulaically nor are they thought to be definable in advance of actual engagement between gospel and context. All of which is acknowledged as an advance on earlier approaches in England, shaped as they were by the much more doctrinaire Church Growth Movement imported from America.[64]

Apart from long-familiar geographic church plants, the report's examples of fresh ecclesial expressions include alternative worship communities, base ecclesial communities, café church, churches arising out of community activities or networks (such as schools), youth and seeker churches, as well as old forms striking new growth (such as a revival of the monastic ideal among the young, though entered into only for a season). Some common features in these various new expressions are the significance accorded to small groups as the locus for Christian formation, the likelihood that a church will not meet on Sunday morning, the connection to a particular network of people (including a resourcing body) and the post-denominational feel of the whole undertaking.[65] It is taken as read that such mission-shaped churches, of whichever expression, will be dynamic, relational and transformational communities of faith. Apart from that, what would be the point or from whence would come the impetus? Significantly, the ecclesial

---

[64] *Mission-Shaped Church*, Chapter 2, 16-28.
[65] *Mission-Shaped Church*, 43-44, and the examples throughout its Chapter 4.

vision celebrated in the report is explicitly, deeply theological and Trinitarian rather than merely pragmatic or faddish.[66]

All of this is alarming for many in the Church. For some of the more Catholic-leaning among us, this represents a bottom-up process of change that is contrary to belief in the apostolic mediation of God's grace from the top down, through the Church's hierarchy or else its official Councils. There is also our conviction that the Holy Spirit is preserver and protector as well as innovator and dismantler, reflecting a higher view of tradition than is found in other parts of our Church. For those of the more 'broad' Church, where the focus is on community and local custom rather than ideology, be it Catholic or Evangelical, this is a departure from the parochial model that has been the reliable symbol of God's incarnate presence in English life for a millennium and a half. For the clergy, too, all this brings challenges at several levels. They have not, by and large, been trained for this sort of ministry. It is not readily assimilable in terms of their accustomed expectations of remuneration, clergy housing, superannuation, parson's freehold, etc., let alone in terms of typical clergy career paths. And it is highly mission-oriented, which is a profile that many clergy, let alone many congregations, decidedly do not share (as the report obliquely but unmistakeably acknowledges).

Another key issue, which the report does not consider, is tension between the establishment nature of the Church of England and the missionary imperative. *Mission-Shaped Church* makes a virtue out of the necessity of establishment, viewing it positively as providing a mandate for missionary engagement with the whole nation. To some extent at least, the old wineskins remain suitable for new wine. But are establishment and radical newness compatible? Will the fresh expressions always remain the sideshow and not the main attraction? Will they be tolerated on the fringes but never be allowed to transform the whole

---

[66] *Mission-Shaped Church*, 81-82.

structure while the innately conservative, even reactionary pressure of establishment remains? Even in Australia, where Anglicanism was never established, the mindset perseveres. At least in our Middle-to-High traditions, we are an ethnic, British Empire Church determined as much by a cultural as a spiritual agenda. Caroline Miley has written devastatingly about this, with proof of her unerring aim provided by the affronted and defensive reviews that she received in Anglican diocesan papers.[67]

Since the Industrial Revolution, it was ill-fitting extremists in the Church of England, the Evangelicals and the Anglo-Catholics, who carried the missionary banner and not the establishment centre. *Mission-Shaped Church* recognises that today's mission endeavour, too, will issue not from the centre but from the innovative edges. Perhaps the best reading of the report here is that establishment is a given, bringing potential benefits in terms of social location, resources and goodwill upon which mission can draw, but it is not itself the source or the driver of mission. The new wine really does require new wineskins—that is, fresh expressions—recalling Jesus' teaching in Mark 2:18 to 3:6. This was certainly true in the missionary history of the religious orders, for instance, from the Desert Fathers to St Benedict, thence to the Cluniac Reform, then the Mendicant explosion under Francis and Dominic, evolving into modern form with the Jesuit movement and its 'contemplation in action'—from the desert to the Minster, transforming Europe, then outward to increasingly transform the world. Such structural evolution is envisaged in the report. This is not seen to be at the expense of the entire tradition, including the traditional orders of ministry and diocesan structures, but it is certainly transformative of all that.

Yet in the face of all such concerns, the report is nevertheless resolute in its belief that ours is a *Kairos* moment, and that God's

---

[67] Caroline Miley, *The Suicidal Church: Can the Anglican Church be Saved?* (Sydney: Pluto Press, 2002).

Holy Spirit is summoning today's Church to this new future. It is the Holy Spirit who releases this work, according to the report, also inspiring repentance from those who are resistant to it (p. 14). The Spirit is the source of this new thinking, for instance in the conscientious choice of non-Sunday worship as the norm for many new faith communities (p. 61)—flying in the face of much scriptural, symbolic and traditional warrant for worship on 'the Lord's Day'. The Holy Spirit is the enculturating force in the Church's mission, bringing the gospel alive (p. 86). Thus, the Spirit of Pentecost is God's perennial translator of the gospel message (p. 90). No doubt influenced by the theology of hope, the report understands the Spirit's work in bringing a foretaste of the last things (p. 89), favouring anticipation of the future rather than preservation of the past (p. 90).

This assessment is borne out by reflection on our Christian past. The Acts of the Apostles provides the most generally accepted early example of the Spirit driving both mission and emerging ecclesial structures in tandem. The conversion of the Gentiles and their incorporation within the structures of the early, Jerusalem-led Church is a classic instance of a Christian generation led into a new ecclesial paradigm, although we know the result in terms of misunderstanding, resistance and conflict. The Council of Jerusalem recalled in Acts 15—belatedly legislating to cope with the new Gentile mission—is of a piece with the Church of England process culminating in the report. And eventually, as we know, the earliest, Jewish version of Christianity disappeared entirely.

This represents the first of six paradigm changes that Hans Küng enumerates in his sweeping study of Christian identity from a historical perspective.[68] As the 'Jewish Apocalyptic Paradigm of Earliest Christianity' gave way (from Paul onwards) to the 'Ecumenical Hellenistic Paradigm of Christian Antiquity', as I

---

[68] Hans Küng, *Christianity: Its Essence and History (The Religious Situation of Our Time)*, trans. John Bowden (London: SCM Press, 1995).

Holy Spirit and Mission: Concerns about *Mission-Shaped Church* (2006)

have indicated, so in turn its more centralising development into the 'Roman Catholic Paradigm of the Middle Ages' was challenged by the 'Protestant Evangelical Paradigm of the Reformation'. Subsequently, gripped by the revolutionary scientific, political, economic and philosophical currents of modernity, the 'Paradigm of Modernity' arose in the Enlightenment, oriented to a new world of reason, equality and progress.

Three aspects of Küng's account resonate with what *Mission-Shaped Church* has to say about fresh expressions of Church today. First, each new paradigm brings a set of fresh Christian expressions as the gospel engages a new cultural context—from Hellenistic culture to medieval feudalism to the rise of a new commercial class in early modernity to the era of revolution, both political and industrial. Second, each paradigm shift involves a period of destabilisation, upset and conflict—just as in scientific paradigm change, before what Thomas Kuhn calls normal science can resume.[69] Third, each new stage builds on (and occasionally blends together) aspects of the ones before it, not requiring an entirely fresh palate to paint its new vision. Recovery of the past can be decisive in the present, as when Paul's vision was recovered at the Reformation (and again in the twentieth century, by Barth and the Ecumenical Movement), and when the Reformation influenced today's newly emerging Christian paradigm at Vatican II.

I daresay Küng would recognise many aspects of *Mission-Shaped Church* as expressions of the currently emerging new Christian paradigm, which he tentatively calls the 'Contemporary Ecumenical (or Postmodern) Paradigm'. It is plainly continuous with the great movements of God's Spirit in twentieth-century Christianity: the Ecumenical Movement (which challenged a divided, institutional understanding of the Church with the holistic, biblical imagery of Christ's body); the Liturgical Movement (which recovered a

---

[69] Thomas Kuhn, *The Structure of Scientific Revolutions*, 3rd edn. (Chicago: University of Chicago Press, 1996).

biblical emphasis on participation by all God's people, along with ancient appreciation of the formative role of liturgy, representing also a great impetus toward the enculturation of Church and gospel); the Charismatic Movement (a renewal of the Holy Spirit 'from below', at its best enriching and democratising both worship and Christian life throughout the mainline churches); and, perhaps more controversially for some, the various liberation movements (again, issuing 'from below' renewing the Church's faith, worship and witness among marginalised groups such as the Latin American and Asian poor, Western women, and African Americans. Indeed, *Mission-Shaped Church* includes so-called 'base ecclesial communities', which have their origin in Latin American Liberation Theology, as a viable fresh expression for today's West). Emphases from each and all of these movements are evident in the post-denominational, highly relational, experiential and culturally engaged fresh expressions celebrated in *Mission-Shaped Church*.[70]

Paul and the writer of Luke-Acts are clear that the agent of the first major paradigm change in church history was the Holy Spirit, and Paul's corpus can be understood as a sustained apologia for this new, global understanding of an inclusive Church. I argue by extension (and in critical accord with *Mission-Shaped Church*) that the Holy Spirit, who is leading us into all truth (John 16:13), consistently forms the mind of Christ in new cultural contexts.

Yet in the Church of England, in Australian Anglicanism and throughout mainline church life in the West, moroseness, nervousness, defensiveness and structural resistance confront such changes, as we have seen (and as our paradigm discussion leads us to expect). Here I am helped by the Greek Orthodox theologian Bishop John Zizioulas. He challenges the Western Church over

---

[70] I have written further on the Emerging Church in today's West: see Scott Cowdell, *God's Next Big Thing: Discovering the Future Church* (Melbourne: John Garratt Publishing, 2004).

its captivity to an institutional past from the perspective of the Greek Fathers and later Orthodox ecclesiology, adding to a proper emphasis on Christ and Christian origins an insistence on the Holy Spirit as both the ground of present ecclesial life and the presence of God's in-breaking future. 'Christ *in-stitutes* and the Spirit *con-stitutes*',[71] as Zizioulas memorably puts it, and hence we need not fear change in the Church if we are confident that its life in Christ *institutionally* is always and everywhere secured by the Holy Spirit *constitutionally*. Such a vision allows us to retain assurance, poise and engagement, and to welcome the fresh expressions, confident that God is leading the Church toward God's dream for it—dynamic and on-the-move, not static and paralysed.

No doubt Zizioulas is also challenging the ossified traditionalism and establishment Erastianism[72] of much Orthodox life, and not only various expressions of Western Christian captivity to past structures (the Scriptures or else Popes and Councils for conservatives; the Historical Jesus for liberals). We can certainly point to a preference for Platonic stasis over spiritual dynamism in Eastern Churches, despite their best theological instincts—though the Russian Orthodox Church under Stalin was the greatest Church of martyrs in the twentieth century, which amply demonstrates the presence of spiritual dynamism and eschatological joy at the very heart of its life despite any innate conservatism. Indeed, Orthodox experience during the Cold War shows how tradition can become the rallying point for protest against the demonic modern, apart from any reactionary motive. This demonstrates how tradition and Spirit can go together, as *Mission-Shaped Church* also clearly believes.

---

[71] John D. Zizioulas, *Being as Communion: Studies in Personhood and the Church*, (1985), (Contemporary Greek Theologians, 4. Crestwood, NY.: St. Vladimir's Seminary Press, 1997), 140.
[72] Erastianism is the doctrine of subjection of the Church to the power and agenda of the nation.

The Church is not a pre-existing mould into which the Spirit is poured, then. It is more like an evolving entity or a growing, changing body, with God's Holy Spirit as the inner principle of its ongoing life, maintaining continuity in change.

Beyond theological captivity

The report has been seized-upon with understandable enthusiasm by Evangelical Anglicans. Its post-denominational, non-traditional, culturally-attuned message encourages Evangelicals whose urgent commitment to mission is too often resisted by a hidebound institution. The eighteenth-century Church of England did, after all, fail to realise the treasure that God had planted in its field with the Methodist movement. At last, however, the innovative new ministries and church plants characteristic of energetic contemporary Evangelicalism have a chance to gain recognition and support within the Church of England. By and large, then, it is not the Evangelicals who blanch at the fresh expressions celebrated in *Mission-Shaped Church*.

However, there are significant challenges for Evangelical Anglicans in the report. While they are rightly encouraged when the report puts on notice much that is moribund in the Church's institutional and worshipping life, I suspect that challenges to favourite theological positions entailed by the new proposals have not been registered. It is not just institutional conservatism but also theological conservatism that *Mission-Shaped Church* cannot avoid challenging.

The main work of God's Spirit, according to the report, is to bring the gospel into compelling closeness with people's lives through enculturation. As I have suggested, such enculturation has marked the Spirit's work from the time of Paul's Hellenistic mission to more recent missionary initiatives: the Liturgical Movement, bringing the gospel alive through reinvigorated and enculturated worship; the Charismatic Movement, with its appeal to today's more informal, feeling-oriented culture in the West; and the various Liberation Theology base communities, with their emphasis on mutual dependence and authority arising 'from below'. Aspects of all these are evident in the fresh expressions of *Mission-Shaped Church*.

Among Evangelicals, much enculturation has to do with praise and alternative worship styles that abandon liturgy and its formality as alien and unhelpful. It also means adapting the Church to various concrete forms of life, often to niche or subculture markets: ethnic groups, university students, young families, surfers, the motorbike scene, the alternative music scene, etc.

Dave Tomlinson initiated a church plant in an English pub, called 'Holy Joes'. However, this priest and leader in the so-called Post-Evangelical movement found that with engaging the youthful pub culture came a resistance to pat answers and too-neat closure in matters of faith and life. So, while this new fellowship was Bible-based, it was not Evangelical in the sense of maintaining clear and familiar boundaries.[73] Patterns of evangelism, faith acquisition and conversion guaranteed to follow a traditional Protestant path from *notitia* (knowing) to *assensus* (assent) to *fiducia* (trust) cannot be relied upon. Among young people today, Evangelicals are discovering the role of belonging in the foreground of believing, with some advocating a more Catholic, catechumenal style of faith formation that blurs traditional emphases on conversion and declaration of faith in Jesus as personal saviour.[74] And traditional liturgical worship is not off the youth agenda by any means. There is evidence that authenticity in the context of worship

---

[73] Dave Tomlinson, *The Post-Evangelical* (London: SPCK, 1995).
[74] William Abraham, *The Logic of Evangelism* (London: Hodder & Stoughton, 1989); Robert E. Webber, *Ancient-Future Faith: Rethinking Evangelicalism for a Postmodern World* (Grand Rapids, MI.: Baker, 1999).

matters more than style or content among Generation X and Millennial Christians, so that praise or alternative worship styles are not necessarily perceived as more relevant to the real needs of these young people, even though they may be more culturally attuned.[75] It is clear that *Mission-Shaped Church* appreciates diversity and does not advocate a one-size-fits-all approach to mission. Evangelicals who welcome its message should appreciate that this engagement will stretch favourite Evangelical customs and theologies, just as it stretches many Middle-to-High Anglicans over institutional and liturgical matters closer to their hearts.

Here are more examples: one is reasonably obvious and receives brief mention, while the other is more subtle and I will dwell on it a little longer.

The first example of challenges that enculturation poses is already evident in the Roman Catholic Church, which embraced enculturation in the Liturgical Movement, and less officially in the Latin American Liberation Theology movements. The tolerant, democratic elements of contemporary culture, however, and the gender-equalising imperative that they bring, are proving harder for Rome to accommodate. Some if not all of this also challenges many Evangelicals. A typically hard line on gender and sexuality is

---

[75] See e.g., Shane Hubner, "'X' Marks the Spot? How Generational Theory can help the Emerging Church', *St Mark's Review* 193 (2003): 3-10, at 10; Colleen Carroll, *The New Faithful: Why Young Adults are Embracing Christian Orthodoxy* (Chicago: Loyola Press, 2002). On the enculturation of traditional liturgical worship in today's youth scene, see Tex Sample, *The Spectacle of Worship in a Wired World: Electronic Culture and the Gathered People of God*, (Nashville, TN.: Abingdon, 1998); see also Graham Cray himself, in 'The Eucharist and the Post-Modem World', in *Mass Culture: Eucharist and Mission in a Post-Modem World*, ed. Pete Ward (Oxford: Bible Reading Fellowship, 1999), 74-94. On the impact of Robert Webber and the renewal of liturgical thinking in a contemporary Charismatic context, see Dave Roberts, 'Charisma, Freedom and the Eucharist', in *Mass Culture*, 131-48.

one of the reasons why young people reject Evangelicalism,[76] and why a Post-Evangelical movement is now emerging.

The second example has to do with the penal substitutionary theory of atonement: that Jesus died in our place to satisfy God's wrath against sinful humanity. This central plank of Evangelical mission and apologetics retains great emotional power for those who are plagued by guilt. But anecdotal evidence suggests to me that this 'Latin' or 'objective' view, characteristic of Anselm, actually *functions* in a way closer to the 'humanistic' or 'subjective' view characteristic of Schleiermacher—that the extent of Christ's sufferings moves the heart to conversion.[77] That is, it is not the truth of the 'objective' view that convicts and compels as much as the subjective impact of such imagery working the conversion.

I am suggesting that many Evangelicals are actually converted by an experience mediated by the preaching of Christ's sacrifice rather than convinced by the actual, objective, sacrificial message of penal substitutionary atonement itself. Here is an instance of central Evangelical theological themes being accessed in a typically postmodern way, in a culture preferring feeling and experience to theoretical appeal and closure. In other words, many young people use Evangelical theology as software for accessing a personal reality of conversion and faith that is pre-theological and experiential. Graham Kendrick tips his hat to penal substitutionary atonement in the popular Evangelical hymn 'Shine, Jesus, Shine',[78] with

---

[76] Richard Holloway recalls how scandalised many of the young volunteers were at the 1998 Lambeth Conference, in *Doubts and Loves: What is Left of Christianity?* (Edinburgh: Canongate, 2002), ix-xi.

[77] These are terms used in the classic study by Gustav Aulen, *Christus Victor: An Historical Study of the Three Main Types of the Idea of the Atonement*, trans. A.G. Hebert, SSM (London: SPCK, 1931).

[78] Hymn #675 in *Together in Song: Australian Hymn Book II* (Melbourne: HarperCollinsReligious, 1999).

the words 'by your blood I may enter your brightness', but the experience of brightness does the converting work.[79]

Also, if enculturation of the gospel is central to *Mission-Shaped Church*, it is important to remember that it was in the cultural context of medieval feudalism that penal substitutionary theory captured the Western imagination. That particular enculturation of the gospel was perhaps inevitable before the rise of Nominalism and the modern, self-determining individual. It was what George Rupp, in a close historical study of atonement theories against their cultural and philosophical contexts, called 'Realist-Transactional'. This refers to an eternal transaction between God and humanity, brokered by Christ's sacrifice, though neglecting the means of its uptake. More likely to commend itself in a contemporary context, however, is the opposite position in Rupp's four-fold typology, which he called 'Nominalist-Processive', referring to atonement as a process of Christ's reconciling work continuing through a community of believers, 'raising the crucial question of whether ... a religious system is viable [today] if it declines to interpret as religiously significant man's [sic] increasing capacity to shape his personal and corporate life within the sphere of phenomenal existence'.[80]

So, enculturation of the gospel in today's context may require Evangelicals to jettison penal substitutionary atonement as a central plank of mission. It is increasingly criticised for its violent

---

[79] Bishop Bruce Wilson discusses this distinction between personal knowing and institutional believing, noting the gap between youthful Evangelical experience and the typical approach of Evangelical theological education. See his *Reasons of the Heart: A Vision for the New Millennium* (Sydney: Allen & Unwin [Albatross], 1998), 48-54.
[80] George Rupp, *Christologies and Cultures Toward a Typology of Religious Worldviews* (Religion and Reason, 10. The Hague: Mouton, 1974), 249.

and dysfunctional resonances, after all,[81] as well as being far from obvious in a culture that at bottom is now thoroughly individualised and historicised. This is not to deny the atoning grace of God in the life, death and resurrection of Jesus Christ, but it is to say that one venerable option for expressing this, much favoured by Evangelicals, may prove incompatible with enculturation of the gospel as *Mission-Shaped Church* understands it.

Charism and power

A big issue for fresh expressions is that of ministry and authority. According to many Evangelicals and Charismatics, one of the moribund institutional hangovers from yesterday's Church is a ministry structure that stifles mission. For some, the whole structure of ministry needs to change, with emphasis on bottom-up entirely replacing the older Catholic model of top-down. The suggestion is that God's Spirit works uniformly through the body of Christ and is not mediated institutionally through suitably authorised leaders. Why bother with continuity in patterns of ministry, then? Why not dispense with existing orders and structures in favour of an adaptable, independent congregationalism with a very flattened authority structure? Surely this is a plain instance of how enculturation of the Church in today's culture might look. These are some of the voices that *Mission-Shaped Church* seeks to keep within the Anglican fold.

Behind these concerns is a key issue in corporate life today, and that is adapting hierarchical and centralising institutions to a more decentralised environment in which bottom-up influence

---

[81] It is challenged nowhere more sharply than by James Alison: see 'Unpicking Atonement's Knots', in *On Being Liked* (London: Darton, Longman & Todd, 2003), 17-31.

is valorised.[82] In the business world, there is pressure on firms to become more dynamic, flexible 'learning organisations' if they are to survive and thrive in global, postmodern conditions.[83] Likewise, church planters and other advocates of fresh expressions seek to move beyond yesterday's mistakes to ensure success in mission. I see two problems with a bottom-up approach to ministry, however.

One is that such a view is contrary to the Bible. In the New Testament, there are clearly various sorts of prophets, teachers and apostles who lead a ministering community, in a genuinely collaborative vision that nevertheless entails diversity in ministerial gifts and roles. As Paul can talk about different gifts of the Holy Spirit for the building-up of Christ's body, including his own ministry of apostleship (1 Corinthians 12:27-30), so Peter Carnley can talk about 'a different realm of the gifts of the Spirit'[84] manifest in ordained ministry—not at the expense of the body, nor only as a representative expression of the body's omni-giftedness, but as a special thing that the Holy Spirit underwrites, alongside a range of other ministries, contributing to the total ministry of that body.

The other problem with a solely bottom-up model emerges in light of Church history. Structured order arose for a reason, and rapidly from the first century on. It guarded the gospel and enabled mission at a time of conflicted internal self-definition and externally inflicted trauma for the Church in antiquity. Such Church order remains as a sign, agent and guarantee of ecclesial faithfulness to this day. Of course, it can go too far, as many believe to be the case with Roman Catholic understandings of the Petrine ministry, or within Anglicanism (which should know

---

[82] See e.g., Alistair Mant, *Intelligent Leadership*, 2nd edn. (Sydney: Allen & Unwin, 1999), 34-38.
[83] See e.g., Peter M. Senge, *The Fifth Discipline: The Art & Practice of the Learning Organization* (Sydney: Random House, 1992).
[84] Peter Carnley, 'Lay and Ordained Ministry', in *Reflections in Glass: Trends and Tensions in the Contemporary Anglican Church* (Sydney: HarperCollins, 2004), 156-180.

Holy Spirit and Mission: Concerns about *Mission-Shaped Church* (2006)

better) whenever the laity are denied the ministry that should properly be theirs. Nevertheless, despite pushing the envelope of institutional flexibility, *Mission-Shaped Church* remains convinced that the Holy Spirit ensures proper leadership in the Church, and that Anglican order and structure is adequate to the fresh expressions that it champions.

In particular, the report recognises a crucial role for bishops in mission. Not as missionary bishops of the Celtic, or else nineteenth-century Anglo-Catholic sort (which may in fact constitute an oversight), but certainly in terms of authorising, encouraging and protecting the Church's fresh expressions.[85] Experience has taught that without episcopal leadership, in particular brokering the changes in custom and structure that fresh expressions regularly demand, church plants and other mission initiatives struggle to succeed. It appears, then, that the gift of authority that God gives to bishops through the Holy Spirit, according to our ordinal, is indispensable if tomorrow's Church is to emerge in the midst of today's Church without losing continuity with yesterday's Church.

Apart from this pragmatic effect, however, and apart from its venerable status as an early and resilient emergence from the range of New Testament ministries, can we offer further warrant for episcopal order? And can we thus relieve the minds of those who believe that any such top-down ministry can be no longer a work of the Spirit in our day? Here I am indebted to my colleague at St Mark's National Theological Centre in Canberra, Stephen Pickard, for the beginnings of a new theology of ministry that affirms the traditional threefold order in general and the episcopate in particular as a viable emergent life-form in the Spirit,

---

[85] *Mission-Shaped Church*, 135-43.

powerfully linked to how God works in the world for creation and redemption.[86]

Pickard goes beyond suggestive but not ultimately compelling attempts to base a theology of complementary ministries in the Trinitarian diversity-in-unity of God's own being, seeking a firmer basis for the collaborative ministry that is absolutely essential in the Emerging Church. He looks to priest/biologist Arthur Peacocke writing on emergent complexity in nature, and how influence is conveyed not only bottom-up but also top-down in natural systems. Theology of God's action in the world now recognises both the sort of influences that arise from parts of a system to affect the whole, but also whole-part effects. Think of how introducing a single diseased individual can infect a whole population—the contagion moving from part to whole within the system. But think also of how a tiny change in the ambient temperature can lead to a phase change, from icy crystal to liquid to gas, with the behaviour of every molecular part influenced by this change to the whole.

So, if God were to institute change within the natural world, action at the quantum level is one option (i.e., expanding from a point of origin hidden in quantum indeterminacy to produce a large-scale, visible effect), while altering a whole system to produce changes in whichever desired target portion is another possibility. We are now far clearer about the latter option with the advent of chaos theory, exploring how behaviour throughout a whole physical system can suddenly change, with unexpected appearances of order where all was chaos, and vice versa.[87]

By extension, Pickard follows some recent thinking on systems theory and corporate leadership to propose a ministerial correlate.

---

[86] Stephen Pickard, 'Healing the Wound: Collaborative Ministry for Mission', *St Mark's Review* 199 (2005), 3-11.
[87] These options are widely canvassed in recent theological literature. See for instance my own contribution in *A God for This World* (London and New York: Continuum, 2001).

Holy Spirit and Mission: Concerns about *Mission-Shaped Church* (2006)

God guides and transforms the Church through bottom-up as well as top-down means. The episcopate enables and creates the conditions for creative growth at lower levels, just as creativity at those lower levels influences the exercise of *episcope*. Pickard understands the orders of ministry as 'irreducible, intrinsic and interdependent', commending 'a dynamic ontology of order' in which 'the vitalities of the ministries are embedded *within* the system',[88] allowing a flexible response to opportunities and threats from the environment—just the sort of thing *Mission-Shaped Church* requires. For Pickard, 'This means that such ministries are intrinsically related in a "mode of togetherness" such that they raise each other to the fullness of the ministry of each. As the ministries are so inter-related they become participants in God's own energetic ordering of the church for the world. To this extent the ministry and the ministries can be genuine mediations of God's own holy order'.[89]

Thus we have the sort of equality, flexibility and dynamism that advocates of bottom-up models seek, while preserving the potential good effect of top-down structure, held together in an energetic complementarity that is holistic to the point of being organic, retaining the role of the individual along with the structural diversity of office. Here a whole range of contemporary cultural emphases finds a home while continuity with both Scripture and the wisdom of Church tradition is preserved, all within a dual focus on creation and redemption.[90] This constitutes a pragmatically minded pneumatology of ministry allowing the Church to focus effectively on mission.

As we noted earlier, however, church history strongly suggests that the Holy Spirit of God is regularly served but never confined by ecclesial structures. Pickard's organic account recognises that

---

[88] Pickard, 'Healing the Wound', 8.
[89] Pickard, 'Healing the Wound', 8.
[90] Pickard, 'Healing the Wound', 9.

new forms arise under the pressure of circumstances, which may in time prove to be vigorous and sustained developments. Or else they may not. Here I think of John Wesley, whose missionary movement was not ultimately able to be preserved within Anglicanism (to our great shame), though he was 'arguably, the greatest saint, the greatest witness to Jesus Christ, produced by the eighteenth-century Church of England—the last place you'd expect to find fools for Christ's sake'.[91] Or of General William Booth, in the nineteenth century, who produced a fresh expression of Church with the Salvation Army, responding to a missionary need that the 'proper' Churches were not meeting. And, 'although it has no sacraments, we could not for a moment deny that it receives and transmits divine grace'.[92]

It is certainly true that Methodism and Salvationism influenced other Churches, including the Church of England, to greater missionary endeavours. Accordingly, the separate identity of Methodism and Salvationism may one day no longer be required, with history remembering them as influential though temporary reform movements in the wider Church. But their emergence and flourishing, if only for a season, is a reminder that the Holy Spirit will not only develop and transform our structures but also go around them should the demands of mission be overlooked or resisted.

---

[91] Rowan Williams, 'John Wesley', in *Open to Judgement: Sermons and Addresses* (London: Darton, Longman & Todd, 1994), 203 & 202-06.
[92] John Macquarrie, *Principles of Christian Theology*, rev. edn. (London: SCM Press, 1977), 422

5

Baptismal Ecclesiology and its Enemies (2006)

> *The Church is the community of the baptised, grounded not just in the agendas and dynamics of every other human group as understood by sociology and anthropology. It is a body with a purpose, based on God's call to a people through the everlasting covenant—a claim that is visibly signed and sealed in baptism. Hence every baptised Christian has a vocational calling within the Church's wider mission of knowing, worshipping and serving the God of Jesus Christ. Other names for this are 'every member ministry', 'total ministry' and, more recently, 'ministering communities'. I commend this approach, especially since it is widely resisted. This was a Keynote Address at the National Living Stones Conference and a Diocesan Ministry Day jointly held at Newcastle Grammar School on Saturday 12 August 2006, in my last year as Rector of St Paul's, Manuka, in Canberra. It appeared as 'Baptismal Ecclesiology and its Enemies', in* Into the World You Love: Encountering God in Everyday Life, *ed. Graham Garrett (Adelaide: ATF Press, 2007), 202-10. It is reproduced by kind permission of ATF Press.*

Baptismal ecclesiology emerged from the Church's great spiritual ferment of the mid-twentieth century, as heir of at least four major Christian movements. First, it is indebted to the Biblical Theology Movement, which recovered a vision of the Christian life as a distinctive calling in response to God's revelation in Jesus Christ—a revelation not reducible to the bourgeois values and social conformity of so-called Culture Protestantism. Second, it is indebted to the Ecumenical Movement, which taught us so much about our commonality as Christians, with the mutual recognition of each other's baptism as a powerful sign and pledge of growing unity. Third, it is influenced by the Liturgical Movement, which transformed Roman Catholic, Anglican and some mainstream Protestant traditions by recovering the common liturgical heritage of the ancient undivided Church, helping congregations around the world to discover liturgy as the centre of Christian life and imagination. Hence the recovery of baptism as a venerable mystery of inclusion into Christ, alongside the growing centrality of the Eucharist in Anglican thought and practice. Indeed, baptismal ecclesiology can equally be seen as a Eucharistic ecclesiology, announcing and enabling God's call to all the baptised who are sent out from the liturgy week by week 'to love and serve the Lord'. And, fourth, baptismal ecclesiology is influenced by the Charismatic Movement, which emphasised the life-changing, joyful birthright of every Christian in the outpouring of God's Spirit, making us all into witnesses. While the Charismatic Movement has regularly downplayed water baptism in favour of a second event, a baptism in the Holy Spirit, which represents a distinctive and controversial aspect of Charismatic theology, nevertheless Charismatic emphasis on the increasing democratisation and inclusivity of the Church's ministry is relatable to baptismal ecclesiology.

Thanks to more holistic reflections on the human person, not least under the influence of Feminist and Liberation Theologies, along with the avalanche of Trinitarian reflection in Western theology since roughly the end of the Cold War, ministry is coming to be understood less individualistically and more relationally.

This is not to deny the special ministry of the ordained in serving and gathering the community of faith, nor the calling of each Christian to be Christ's witness in their individual life. But it is a timely reminder that the ministry task belongs to the community as a whole and not only to its individual members, whether lay or ordained, with or without an 'official' ministry.

The ministering communities model is growing legs in the more remote parts of Australian Anglicanism. Conditions of economic contraction, drought and depopulation are challenging the viability of parishes (and, indeed, dioceses) in regional Australia. Ministry in the remote regions of Anglo-Catholic dioceses used to be the preserve of Bush Brotherhoods, with often younger priests living together under temporary vows of poverty and celibacy (five years was a normal commitment), with the support of local 'lay readers'. Today's model, now that straitened conditions have returned in regional churches, emphasises the giftedness and calling of each local congregation of baptised Christians. One member of that congregation might be raised up to the priesthood after suitable training as part of a team ministry grounded in the life of that remote community while supported by the diocese.

Baptismal ecclesiology is not just for those geographic areas where more conventional ministry models can no longer be sustained, however. Even a large city parish with stipendiary and associate clergy needs to evolve into a ministering community, in which the baptised are called to a more self-consciously ecclesial and missional life. This is a calling to enhanced theological self-awareness, to Christian maturity and to greater spiritual seriousness than we have tended to expect from Anglican congregations in the past, at least in the non-Evangelical traditions of our Church.

But we can surely be forgiven if a mood of unease or even scepticism emerges at this point. 'The theory is all well and good, but what about the practice?' We have a Church that often thinks of itself in anything but baptismal or Eucharistic terms, despite the 'official' centrality of these sacraments for its ongoing life. And this will not be fixed by techniques or programs that merely scratch the surface. Rather, it is a matter of a counter-cultural worldview needing to commend itself to Christians who are culturally captive to a different vision. Modern Western culture writes a poorer script for the Church than baptism and its resultant ecclesiology of ministering equals commends to us. It is my aim in what follows to set out the dominant imaginative reality of modern Western culture against which baptismal ecclesiology simply does not compute, and then suggest some things that we will have to do to get on board with the new thing that God is already bringing to birth in our midst—a mature, vocational Church of ministering communities emerging in fulfilment of the baptismal promise.

I

What are the key aspects of modern Western culture that make the notion of a ritually shaped Church characterised by organic, necessary, vocational belonging so foreign to us, and where did they come from?

A strong case can be made that the roots of our modern vision are to be found in the late-medieval period. The cosmos of the medieval imagination was hierarchical, certainly, with political orders reflecting the vertical hierarchies extending from earth through the angelic orders to heaven. But it was a holistic vision, and God's presence was richly mediated through all the dimensions of life in the world. A new philosophy called Nominalism changed this imaginative world and made the Reformation possible. The profoundly integrated cosmic order, represented in the Church, was one in which all God's people held encompassing vocations. This gave way under Nominalism to a more individualistic understanding of the human person and a similar picture of God remote from the world. Hence, we became individual worshippers of an individual God.

To be sure, the Reformation changed much in the Church for the better. But it also changed our idea and experience of the Church. Gone was the mediation of God's presence throughout the Church and its sacraments echoing God's presence throughout the life and natural happenings of our world. Each believer's direct contact with God precluded the need for such mediation, so the Church became secondary and derivative. While common prayer remained the Anglican norm, nevertheless the Church, like the society, was beginning to be imagined on a social contract basis. Margaret Thatcher famously declared the idea of society to be a fiction, but the roots of her opinion were in sixteenth and seventeenth century social contract theories of the state enshrining individuality as the primary human reality.

The same imaginative currents that gave rise to modern individuality further separated human subjects from the world of which they were part, heightening the mood of isolation characterising Western modernity. Early in the seventeenth century, Cartesian philosophy represented the most radical separation of humanity from the rest of the world to date, with mind and thought removed from the realm of causes in the natural realm—this was a separation that only began to break down late in the nineteenth century with the rise of scientific psychology.

The thinking individual made famous by René Descartes' dictum 'I think therefore I am' came to relate to the world in a highly instrumental way. The resultant triumphs of Western science and technology demonstrate their downside, though, in the appalling environmental harm we are doing to our world, along with the psychological damage we have done to ourselves—imagining ourselves to be so sovereign and detached that the strain has proved too great. Our brave new world has brought us an isolation that our medieval forebears did not experience. They fundamentally misunderstood astronomy, for instance, yet looking up at the stars they were reassured by the richness of a God-filled cosmos to which they were integrally linked. Among moderns, however, even a great Christian spirit like Blaise Pascal, on looking up into the night sky, was terrified by the vast, cold emptiness that confronted him.

Isolated from one another and from our world, we took comfort in a new scientific worldview that emphasised rational control and new-fangled forces of nature that were imposed by law rather than flowing from God's loving embrace of the world through the within of things. God became even more remote thanks to this new scientific cosmology and was allowed only occasional interventions from outside a closed natural order, while control came to typify the culture of modernity.

Part of that controlling mindset was a fundamental distinction between rational, sober, managing values on the one hand and all that confronted us in a frequently irrational, undisciplined world on the other. Thus, the ill-fitting other was to be controlled. Roman Catholicism, which had retained an integral vision of Church and sacrament, was seen as the primitive anti-type of modern, rational Protestant divinity. This mood of modern Western superiority continued well into the twentieth century, with primitive cultures, Catholic religion and the foreign more generally, along with the feminine and wild nature, all consigned to the realm of 'otherness'. Only recently in the various liberation movements, from feminism to post-colonialism to animal liberation, has 'the other' emerged with its own claim beyond the controlling Western agenda. Indeed, the seeds of Western modernity's decline are in this drive to make a world according to our own lights. The severing of worldview from reality that began in Western philosophy with Immanuel Kant in the eighteenth century eventually led to today's radical pluralism, where reality is whatever you want it to be. This is the epitaph of modernity's approach to the world, which favoured objectivity and control over embrace and contemplation.

The idealising of ordinary life, which began in the spirituality of the Reformers and their rejection of clericalism and monasticism, and with the Puritans' detached, instrumental worldliness, is now entrenched in secular form, providing the characteristic imaginative and moral scope of Western life. We can recognise it as the so-called plain man's creed consisting of the work ethic, conventional moral virtue, home and family, all smiled upon by a benignly remote deity.

This plain man's creed is a paean to the reassuring modern order, and if such personal faith manifests itself in ecclesial form, it can only ever be a matter of externals. Accordingly, worship and sacraments are at best dress-up pageants projecting outward the stable world existing within pious individuals. And of course, such pious individuals living proudly according to Christian principles would allow no claim by the Church on their obedience, since faith is a private matter between the individual and God. Hence the struggle in mainstream Australian Anglicanism, for instance, to commend weekly churchgoing, financial stewardship, participation in Christian education or taking responsible roles in the parish's life and ministry, let alone any understanding of ministry that is universal, essential and urgent.

Baptismal ecclesiology, I believe, founders upon this invincible, detached, purely internal and non-sacramental, moralistic individualism, according to which the Church and its worship simply cannot register as the generative, encompassing, authoritative context of Christian life. The struggle of the Roman Catholics to enforce discipline since Vatican II and *Humanae Vitae*, rightly or wrongly, nevertheless shows that everyone nowadays is a religious individualist really—even those whose religious software package of choice remains the Roman Catholic Church.

II

If the chief enemy of baptismal ecclesiology is the characteristic religious temper of modernity, then the solution is to challenge and transform this religious temper. As for the means of achieving this, my central insight is that this is a divine task before it is a human one. God's Holy Spirit brings the new thing to birth in every age. While we are involved, it is as participants in something

God is doing rather than as sole agents of the transformation. Hence my concern about the culture, or more correctly the *cult* of managerialism that is on the rise as mainstream Australian Anglicanism considers its future. I argue that managerialism is a sickly child of modernity—a last bastion of its controlling, over-simplifying spirit. And while aspects of management theory can usefully inform church leadership as it pursues a spiritual and theologically informed way forward, we will not strategically plan our way out of trouble. God will lead us there, and while management is the tool, spiritual leadership will be the guiding reality. Hence my commitment to the ordained ministry and the importance of wise and mature episcopal oversight in the enabling of genuine vocational cohesion among the baptised, recognising that God works top-down through the hierarchy as well as bottom-up from the laity, with lay and ordained ministry influencing and constituting each another.

I locate the chief work of imaginative transformation in the area of liturgy and the encouragement of lay people to grow in faith and discipleship. My *aide memoir* for what matters most is *liturgy, laity and leadership*. The imaginative power of the liturgy is a guiding insight of the twentieth-century Liturgical Movement of which I am a devotee, though I recognise that the liturgical vision that we celebrate needs help to come alive. We can all testify to the fact that participation in word and sacrament for a lifetime can fail to unpick the imaginative knots of individualistic, rationalistic and consumeristic thinking. Hence, theologically informed preaching, with parish discussion and study groups, are needed to support the impetus toward prayerful, liturgical inhabitation of an alternative worldview among the people of God.

Hence, I declare my hand as an unashamed champion of theological education as a must for every parish and a fundamentally self-definitional priority for every diocese. Our theological colleges, though inevitably few in number, will need to be prayerful, communitarian, and deeply orthodox as well as culturally savvy—on the model of what Dietrich Bonhoeffer did in the Finkenwalde Seminary of the Confessing Church—if they are to have a transforming affect on the whole people of God.

What I did not argue in *God's Next Big Thing*, though with hindsight I recognise I should have, is that small communities of intense discipleship and devotion will play a crucial role in fostering a baptismal ecclesiology—as indeed they always have, since the time of the Desert Fathers. While concern has been raised about some religious institutes, such as Opus Dei and the Neo-Catechumenal Way within the Roman Catholic Church, nevertheless a vowed life lived with strong communal undergirding is possible today without needing to be counter-cultural in a fearful or controlling way. Here I think of the various third orders or oblate groups of our well-established religious communities. But let us not underestimate resources available right under our noses: parish home groups, Cursillo, and the Catechumenate—which of course at its best is not a program but simply the Church being the Church in the most naturally inclusive and liturgically-integrated form of evangelism imaginable.

What we need is to embrace what the Spirit of God is doing in the Churches, building an organic sense of community and Christian life that is vocational. The right practical emphases for us to pursue will be those and only those that honour this spirit, rather than perpetuating the isolating, impoverishing individualism of modern Western culture. The enemies of baptismal ecclesiology are chiefly imaginative ones. What we need in our Church is scarcely conceivable when the culture we inhabit dominates the Christian imagination. So, our task is discerning where the Holy Spirit in the Church is challenging that culture, liberating that imagination, and putting in our best efforts there.

6

An Abusive Church Culture: Sexual Abuse and Systemic Dysfunction (2008)

> *I suggest that something is missing from attempts to diagnose and treat the scourge of clergy sexual abuse. I judge these responses, while laudable as far as they go, to be insufficiently systemic. They identify and address the symptom without inquiring after a deeper malaise in the Church. This extends to theological failures in the way God is understood. Abuse in the Church goes with belief in an abusive God. I offer a theological critique, reimagining God's wrath and judgment as good news not bad. This essay was my contribution to the Australian Anglican Doctrine Commission's collection of responses to the abuse issue, as requested by the national church. It was partly motivated by experience of a vexatious complaint procedure mounted by a parish antagonist. Such procedures, put in place to address sexual abuse, were soon being used to harass clergy who had simply offended the wrong gatekeeper. This particular case was eventually dismissed, though such justice is sometimes denied, and someone gets scapegoated. Michel Foucault's insight is thus confirmed: that institutional power seizes every opportunity to extend itself, including via supposed correctives. Published as 'An Abusive Church Culture? Clergy Sexual Abuse and Systemic Dysfunction in Ecclesial Faith and Life', St Mark's Review 205 (2008): 31-49, this essay appears here by kind permission. I updated it mildly some years later for an international publication, but here I stick to the 2008 original.*

I was initially led to my conclusions about abuse in the Church by family systems theory, which helped open my eyes to a deeper understanding of Scripture and its collective understanding of sin and salvation. Systems theory is a psychological discipline that explores the systemic dynamics of relationships, discovering standard patterns of provocation and reactivity. Hence the commonplace acknowledgment that oldest, youngest and middle children face distinct challenges based on their relative position in the family. We have also come to recognise certain widespread family roles, such as the over-functioning 'good daughter' who compulsively adopts the role of mediator in a conflicted family, or else the 'black sheep of the family' whose chronic poor judgment, misbehaviour or self-destructiveness plays out the unacknowledged and unresolved denials, hurts and aggressions of the whole family. Such individuals are known as 'the designated patient', through whom the system expresses its sickness. Healing the disordered family system depends upon the diagnosis of its true condition. Challenging dysfunctional participants and naming the systemic disorder as a whole go together in righting a systemic wrong. The designated patient is not the only one with a problem, nor are they necessarily the optimal starting point for treatment.

An abusive church culture?

Family systems theory is now being applied more widely. It helps in diagnosing and treating unhealthy corporate and workplace cultures, which can maintain themselves in dysfunction over time even if all the players change. Now the widespread reality of church conflict is being analysed using systems theory,[93] helping us

---

[93] See e.g., Peter L. Steinke, *How Your Church Family Works: Understanding Congregations as Emotional Systems* (Washington: The Alban Institute, 1993); Edwin H. Friedman, *Generation to Generation: Family Process in Church and Synagogue* (London and New York: Guildford Press, 1985); Michael H. Crosby, *The Dysfunctional Church: Addiction and Codependency in the Family of*

understand the parish that cannot keep its clergy, for instance, or the priest who is chronically pastorally accident prone, or the run of clergy family disasters that plague particular congregations—like the Australian parish that in four successive incumbencies left no Rectory family unscathed, with depression, two divorces, and a suicide.

All this can seem fanciful to some, who properly insist on the responsibility of each individual before God for repentance and amendment of life. If the parents eat sour grapes, must the children's teeth be set on edge (Jeremiah 31:29; Ezekiel 18)? Yet the systemic, holistic nature of both physical reality and human identity is now well established throughout the natural and human sciences. Similarly, Bible and tradition affirm that sin is a primordial disorder woven into being human both individually and collectively. The old and the new Adam are both collective realities. The whole people of God as well as its individual members are called to repent, just as the corrupting influence on individuals of the disordered whole is a constant of prophetic testimony, from the prophets of Israel to the prophets of the Reformation to today's Feminist Theology and Liberation Theology.

The Epistles approach disorders of faith and life in the earliest churches by ministering theologically and spiritually to the whole community, and not just denouncing individual wrongdoing. Their household codes (Ephesians 5:21-6:9; Colossians 3:18-4:1) mandate transformation of individuals through transformed understandings of the household and its relationships, as well as seeking to influence households through altering the behaviour of their individual members. Our struggle is not with flesh and blood so much as with powers and principalities in the heavenly places, which represents New Testament wisdom about the systemic nature of evil understood as a system that co-opts

---

Catholicism (Notre Dame, IN.: Ave Maria Press, 1991); David B. Lott, ed. *Conflict Management in Congregations* (Bethesda, MD.: The Alban Institute, 2001).

An Abusive Church Culture: Sexual Abuse and Systemic Dysfunction (2008)

individuals, neither reducible to individual acts of wrongdoing nor separable from them. It is necessary, in announcing God's judgment, to proclaim the gospel to the angel of a church, not only to wrongdoers within it (Revelation 2-3). That is, the Book of Revelation mandates a ministry to ecclesial culture and not just to individuals.

These insights have led me to question how clergy sexual abuse is understood by the Church. I have come to wonder whether the priest who abuses is in fact the designated patient acting-out the abusive dynamics of a larger system in the Church. Consequently, it concerns me that the increasingly widespread acknowledgment of systemic factors in producing abusive Church environments is not reflected in our current modes of response. Specifically, it is disingenuous at best and sinister at worst for the Church to limit its response to addressing individual behaviour, as the Codes of Good Practice and their attendant complaints procedures do. Seeking only to identify and discipline individual abusers, as if that alone will address the problem comprehensively, is to misrepresent and trivialise a more complex reality, and to risk creating scapegoats. Of course, scapegoats often draw attention to themselves precisely because of disordered behaviour, and may well need to be disciplined, but neither truth nor justice is served by loading all our sins and burdens onto them, thereby denying a wider problem in ecclesial faith and life.

Further, I suggest that these new institutional arrangements on the Church's part, with codes, tribunals and a new pitch of clergy discipline, covering much wider issues than sexual abuse, are themselves potentially if not actually abusive. Under cover of a genuine crisis of sexual abuse, detailed codes of behaviour governing every aspect of ministry are now applied in many dioceses, with clergy being brought before investigators, some of whom are ex-police officers, and before committees and tribunals, based on complaints received from parishioners and members of the public that have nothing whatsoever to do with sexual abuse.

Even undergoing such investigation can incur stigma and guilt by association, hence risking irreparable harm.

So, for instance, parish conflicts that have nothing to do with sexual abuse, of the sort once handled by bishops pastorally or, if serious, by the mechanisms of benefice avoidance canons, are now the bread and butter of these new committees of discipline. In the worst cases, disaffected parishioners are effectively assisted to harass disfavoured clergy by official means. Clergy have been brought undone by such processes, complaining with some justification of having been abused by the Church.[94] Such a state of affairs serves the prince of lies, not the prince of peace.

Australian voices

The systemic nature of the Roman Catholic Church's abuse problems is now the subject of a growing literature.[95] An Australian book by former Sydney Auxiliary Bishop and national clergy abuse crisis frontman, Geoffrey Robinson, goes to unprecedented lengths (indeed, Bishop Robinson decided to retire before writing it).[96]

---

[94] See e.g., Louise Greentree, 'Confusing Abuse with Misconduct', *Marketplace* (12 December 2007): 7 (Author's Note: this was Australia's national Anglican newspaper, sadly long defunct).

[95] For a powerful discussion of the American Catholic Church crisis, see Donald Cozzens, *Sacred Silence: Denial and the Crisis in the Church* (Collegeville, MN.: Liturgical Press, 2002). Serious psychological work on Roman Catholic Church culture and clericalism has been done by the German priest, theologian and psychotherapist Eugen Drewermann, at the cost of official censure. His works are not yet translated into English, so I am indebted to a comprehensive overview by Matthew Beier, *A Violent God-Image: An Introduction to the Work of Eugen Drewermann* (London and New York: Continuum, 2004).

[96] Geoffrey Robinson, *Confronting Power and Sex in the Catholic Church: Reclaiming the Spirit of Jesus* (Melbourne: John Garratt Publishing, 2007).

Bishop Robinson concentrates on immature patterns of relating between hierarchical levels in the Church, with the papacy not properly grounded in a relationship of respectful mutuality with the bishops, and the clergy regularly dominating the laity. This state of affairs is supported by a 'creeping infallibility' which, in this era of fast communications, makes the papacy ever more obviously in control—also a detached and self-protective authority structure in the Vatican Curia that monitors and disciplines clergy and theologians who raise awkward questions, so the Church as a whole finds it difficult to acknowledge error officially. This loyal son of the Church is no advocate of anything-goes liberalism, which he sees as an overreaction to past excesses. Rather, he advocates the development of mature relationships and mutual accountability in his Church, with the Peter-figure uniquely placed to lead by example.

Significantly, Bishop Robinson links failures in Church culture to distorted beliefs. One aspect is the way that sexuality has been demonised and repressed, as in the imposition of celibacy on priests who have not received celibacy as a gift and calling from God. The underlying issue is God's portrayal in Australia's traditional Irish Catholic culture as a God of disapproval and judgment, of obedience and rule, rather than a God of love, who by a mix of tenderness and firm vocational leading draws human beings into the fullness of their own being in Christ.

In Anglicanism, biblical testimony to the goodness of human sexuality has been honoured to some extent, with clerical marriage from the sixteenth century representing a key turning point for the Western Church.[97] However, Anglican rejection of clerical celibacy probably had more to do with a growing Protestant distaste for what David Hume called the monkish virtues than with any really positive affirmation of human sexuality—which the legacy

---

[97] See Muriel Porter, *Sex, Marriage and the Church: Patterns of Change* (Melbourne: Dove, 1996).

of Greek philosophy had helped to problematise for Christians, overcoming the earthiness of embodied Old Testament faith.

I judge that Anglicanism remains ill-at-ease in bringing sexuality, spirituality and psychological maturity together. In Australia, it also struggles with widespread patterns of unhealthy relating between clergy and laity, as Muriel Porter concludes.[98] Caroline Miley gets it right about a mood of resistance in Middle-to-High Australian Anglicanism to necessary spiritual growth and attitudinal change.[99] Aspects of Evangelical Anglicanism have received similar critical attention from writers such as Muriel Porter and Chris McGillion,[100] who point to patterns of authority and aspects of belief recalling the ones identified by Bishop Robinson as problematic for Roman Catholicism. A challenge of this sort has been registered in the Diocese of Sydney, following a controversial Open Letter by the Revd Keith Mascord about aspects of diocesan culture that he and many of his respondents found abusive.[101]

The cult of managerialism and abusive culture in the Church

At least part of the blame for abusive attitudes in the Church—especially regarding the discipline of non-abusing clergy who are nevertheless deemed to be errant—can be attributed to the managerial culture that is increasingly annexing the ecclesial imagination in Australia

---

[98] Muriel Porter, *Sex, Power and the Clergy* (Melbourne: Hardie Grant Books, 2003).
[99] Caroline Miley, *The Suicidal Church: Can the Anglican Church be Saved?* (Melbourne: Pluto Press, 2002).
[100] Muriel Porter, *The New Puritans: The Rise of Fundamentalism in the Anglican Church* (Melbourne: Melbourne University Publishing, 2006); Chris McGillion, *The Chosen Ones: The Politics of Salvation in the Anglican Church* (Sydney: Allen & Unwin, 2005).
[101] (Author's Note: there was an Open Letter website at the time, now long defunct. However, the text of Keith Mascord's 2007 Open Letter to the Diocese of Sydney can be found online at http://www.jmm.org.au/articles/18984.htm [last accessed July 2022]).

and throughout the West. Managerial thinking, reducing the gospel to a commodity that the Church provides to spiritual consumers, is at the root of a lot of evangelistic talk, with sustained attention given to 'client preferences' in worship and catering for whichever 'niche market'. Likewise, the culture of strategic planning and human resources management now determines how we evaluate ministerial effectiveness and hence treat our 'staff'. I have written elsewhere about the will to power that infects this latest version of modernity's characteristically controlling mindset, and how this cult of managerialism is inimical to a properly theological understanding of the Church, its leadership and its mission.[102]

Managerialism flourishes in the Church because its instrumental attitude towards people and its two-dimensional approach to the three-dimensional business of spiritual leadership sits well with aspects of Christian faith as practised. The Conservative Protestant God who imputes salvation impersonally, with personal transformation and the formational context of the Church deemed to be secondary and derivative, is well-suited to managerial culture,[103] as is the commodification of the gospel under Liberal Protestant influence, seeing Christianity primarily in terms of resources for crafting personal meaning.[104] Both seriously compromise gospel and mission. Managerialism dismisses the Christian conviction that people matter as people, replacing an organic understanding of Church and mission with an industrial and economic one.

---

[102] Scott Cowdell, *God's Next Big Thing: Discovering the Future Church* (Melbourne: John Garratt Publishing, 2004), 191-227. See also Stephen Pattison, *The Faith of the Managers: When Management Becomes Religion* (London: Cassell, 1997); Richard H. Roberts, *Religion, Theology and the Human Sciences* (Cambridge: Cambridge University Press, 2002).

[103] John Milbank, 'Stale Expressions: The Management-Shaped Church', *Studies in Christian Ethics* 21, no. 1 (2008): 117-28.

[104] Bernd Wannenwetsch, 'Inwardness and Commodification: How Romanticist Hermeneutics Prepared the Way for the Culture of Managerialism—A Theological Analysis', *Studies in Christian Ethics* 21, no. 1 (2008): 26-44.

This state of affairs is widely experienced by clergy as abusive and destructive of vocation. God the bond of love was increasingly replaced by an authoritarian, arbitrarily willing God from the fourteenth century onwards, who is now best served by managers rather than shepherds. This case is strongly argued by Richard H. Roberts, who dons the prophet's mantle in condemning the typically dominating, performance-orientated agenda of human resources management as a post-democratic, post-human project.[105]

In light of this insight, I have come to see that clergy Codes of Good Practice, and their increasing deployment against clergy who are not sexual abusers, represent a characteristic example of how power-focused managerial culture will always seek more control over staff. The goal of this trend is towards a compliant and inoffensive body of clergy who endorse 'management priorities'. The recipients of these controlling attentions are not necessarily the child abusers and sexual predators who should be dealt with, or even those clergy who demonstrate serious pastoral liabilities, but are regularly found among those more independent-minded clergy who will not conform themselves to the required superficial and submissive pastoral profile. To some further reflections on problems of belief underlying dysfunctional Church culture I now turn.

An abusive God?

Let me be clear at the outset: I am not saying that Christian orthodoxy is blighted by an abusive God, though many modern critical voices—feminist, liberationist and environmentalist, to name a few—testify to the regularly poisonous legacy of misapplied orthodox Christian belief. We have given our God a bad name.

---

[105] Richard H. Roberts, 'Personhood and Performance: Managerialism, Post-Democracy and the Ethics of "Enrichment"', *Studies in Christian Ethics* 21 no. 1 (2008): 61-82.

An Abusive Church Culture: Sexual Abuse and Systemic Dysfunction (2008)

At the heart of Western imagination, a deep-seated cultural and religious conviction has established itself that sees God as opposed to our embodied and limited nature, so that a disapproving, sexless perfectionism is widely held to be the Christian norm. Many internalise this disapproval thanks to harsh methods of child-rearing widely applied until recent decades in the West,[106] projecting it onto God thereafter. God functioning as the superego on an internally repressive mission is nothing to do with a God understood according to the gospel, however—a God whose love issues in imaginative and moral transformation, rather than a god of will imposing a dry, fragile obedience that sucks the *jouissance* out of life. Atheism is a suitable reaction to such a false god and is often the necessary first step in a life of faith illuminated by a different God, the real God, through the gospel.[107]

A dangerously mixed message about God's love in tandem with divine disapproval is involved. The gospel is invoked to deal with the burden of sin, but regularly supplanted by the law when it comes to living out the Christian life. The gospel is certainly gift and task, indicative and imperative, but even as a task it is always a gift, and being able to acknowledge the gift-like nature of all Christian life as grace and affirmation—even those aspects involving judgment and transformation—would go far toward removing the mood of life-denying negativity that many associate with the Church. This touches deep issues in the way we imagine human persons before God, and whether salvation is formal and forensic or else more deeply personal and transformative in the cause of human wholeness—not the repression but the healing and fulfilling of our actual selves.

---

[106] For the far-reaching harm this can do, see Alice Miller, *For Your Own Good: Hidden Cruelty in Child-Rearing and the Roots of Violence*, 2nd edn., trans. Hildegarde and Hunter Hannum (New York: Farrar, Straus, Giroux, 1984).

[107] For a fuller discussion of these matters, see my book, *A God for this World* (London and New York: Continuum, 2000).

The price of preferring a repressive dualism to a liberating holism in our theology, ethics and practice is a Church in which flat, unimaginative, conflicted, false selves are overrepresented, manifesting a widespread Christian inability to accept the shadow side of our human nature. Former Church of Ireland priest and now family therapist Jeremy Young could no longer bear this awful version of faith and left the Church. Among his Christian patients, he regularly identifies the 'prison symptoms' of anger, blame, guilt, self-hatred and depression.[108] Young zeroes in on the growing market for authoritative religious certainty in Western Christianity as a key symptom of our inability to live at ease with the incompleteness and regularly unresolved nature of life—with our inherently limited human nature, in fact—subjecting ourselves instead to the type of god that establishes our certainty and worth at the expense of a weak and despised 'other' upon whom all that we cannot face in ourselves is projected.

With this range of psychological insights, we are in the territory recently mapped to great effect by the French American theorist René Girard and his theological interpreter, the English Catholic priest James Alison. At the heart of his comprehensive account of human culture, Girard places the mechanism of human meaning-creation by scapegoating, which serves to quieten the escalation of violence.[109] The meaning that humans make for themselves, in every culture and religion, is what Girard calls the false sacred and, like Karl Barth, he sees the gospel as the critique of such religion. The real sacred is affirming, inclusive and non-violent, whereas the false sacred subsumes the individual into collective processes of cultural creation that are typically violent and exclusive.

---

[108] Jeremy Young, *The Cost of Certainty: How Religious Conviction Betrays the Human Psyche* (London: Darton, Longman & Todd, 2004).
[109] See René Girard, *Violence and the Sacred*, trans. Patrick Gregory (Baltimore and London: The Johns Hopkins University Press, 1977).

An Abusive Church Culture: Sexual Abuse and Systemic Dysfunction (2008)

A widespread sense that the Christian God is abusive is due to the penal substitutionary theory of atonement. It is not my intention to reject this venerable theory, which can be traced back to St Paul, but it is necessary to interpret it, ensuring that it serves rather than undermines the gospel. The cross of Jesus Christ, rather than the price paid to an abusive God, is better understood as God's Trinitarian act reaching out to humanity through Jesus—a sacrifice outing and overcoming the sacrificial mechanism of every false sacred reality.

James Alison dismisses what he calls the Aztec view of atonement. He points out that it is *God's* lifeblood poured out on the cross while we humans—and our culture, and our religion—adopt the role of wrathful deity. If we need blood to be spilled before we can abandon our wrath, or if self-harm is necessary before the depth of our grief can be accessed, then our God says 'I will give my blood', 'I will let myself be assaulted', 'I will pay to help you break through'. But it is our requirement, not God's. Hence an abusive god-image is overcome by the God disclosed in Jesus as loving, transforming and non-violent.[110]

Jesus takes away the sin of the world, but not as the ultimate human sacrifice to an angry god. Rather, the cross demonstrates how far our loving God is prepared to journey into the far country to meet us and, through the death of God the Son, to do away with the universal psychological disorder of sacrificial, false sacred religion. The Evangelical tradition needs to recover this more Trinitarian understanding of the cross as Jürgen Moltmann[111] and, more recently, Peter Adam[112] remind us, so the death of Jesus in

---

[110] James Alison, 'An Atonement Update', in *Undergoing God: Dispatches from the Scene of a Break-in* (London: Darton, Longman & Todd, 2006), 50-67.
[111] Jürgen Moltmann, *The Crucified God: The Cross of Christ as the Foundation and Criticism of Christian Theology*, trans. R.A. Wilson and John Bowden (London: SCM Press, 1974).
[112] Peter Adam, 'Trinity Essential to Understanding the Atonement', *The Melbourne Anglican* (December 2007): 17.

our place to save us can be reclaimed from the mistaken albeit widespread conception of God as abusive.

Divine judgment without divine abuse

At this point, it is important to acknowledge the concern of those who believe that such arguments understate the reality of sin and misrepresent how the God of the Bible deals with it. Many, especially Evangelical Protestants, insist that a God without wrath toward the sinner, who lacks a righteousness fit to redress the evils of history, is neither biblical nor effectual. I want to endorse the biblical doctrine of judgment while ensuring that we do so in a properly biblical way. We must remember that if there is a God of wrath in the Bible, then this is the same biblical God we know to be a loving God. If there is divine punishment for sins, it will be administered in a way that has nothing to do with typically human desires to get even and pay back the evil. If there is divine justice, it will be a restorative justice. And if it has a retributive dimension, then that will serve as it does in the best expressions of restorative justice. These lead offenders to confront their wrongdoing as a necessary step on the way to their eventual repentance and the restoration of relationship. If our God punishes, the clue to imagining the nature of God's punishment will be Jesus' nonviolent demeanour on the cross, rather than that of the vengeful mob that put him there.

Some will rightly counter that there is real vengeance in the Bible—not only in the Old Testament but also in Jesus' teaching. The Old Testament witness to divine violence is not uniform, however, and it is regularly challenged by other accounts of divine mercy. Is the foundational Judaeo-Christian testimony to God's oneness—to God's consistency, undividedness and covenant faithfulness—to be trusted? Could it be that God has a conflicted personality, like many abusers (i.e., not all bad, perhaps, but certainly bad enough)? Is the God of the Bible more like

Jesus, or more like the Destroyer of the Egyptians, of Sodom and Gomorrah, of the Canaanite tribes? And as for Jesus, is the Synoptic apocalyptic Christ the last word on judgment in the Gospels? I look to John's Gospel for an answer here.

The Gospel of John presents a view of divine judgment as the flipside of revelation. The light and truth revealed in Jesus shows up the darkness and lies of this world. Judgment is the exposure of sin and evil, of false divinity and structural betrayal of the abundant life that Jesus brings. Jesus is the agent of God's judgment (John 5:22, 27, 30; 8:16), so God's judgment cannot be inconsistent with the rest of Jesus' liberating project. Jesus' mission of judgment is to bring the truth of God, while at the same time to reveal evil and confound its agents, 'so that those who do not see may see, and those who do see may become blind' (John 9:39b). In this passage, from John's account of Jesus and the man born blind, it is to be noted that a secure religious establishment is revealed to have gotten God completely wrong, and in this it is judged by Jesus.

The nature of Jesus' judgment is evident in the way his own passion is portrayed by John as God's great revelation of the true nature of good and evil. The punishment that Jesus underwent, rather than any punishment that Jesus might inflict on others, is declared decisive: 'Now is the judgment of this world; now the ruler of this world will be driven out'—this is a judgment that when rightly understood is seen to be attractive, not repulsive—'And I, when I am lifted up from the earth, will draw all people to myself' (John 12:31).

Importantly, the ultimate nature of judgment is not properly understood in advance of Jesus' ministry nor of God sending the Holy Spirit to aid the Church in a time of violence and persecution, according to John 16. In such a time, it would be easy for the Church to arrogate righteousness to itself alone, loading the sin and the vengeful judgment craved by wounded human egos onto its enemies. But just as sin and righteousness need to be rescued from misunderstanding by Jesus, so too the Church is invited to re-evaluate judgment: 'And when he [i.e., the Advocate] comes, he will prove the world wrong about sin and righteousness and judgment...' (John 16:8-11). It is his own ministry of judgment and liberation into which the risen Jesus incorporates the Church when he pours out the Holy Spirit, reassuring them that 'If you forgive the sins of any, they are forgiven them; if you retain the sins of any, they are retained' (John 20:23). It would not do for us to mistake this commission and invitation for a vengeful theology of judgment, which the whole Johannine arc of teaching on judgment appears to set aside.

Charles Wesley seems to have understood judgment along such Johannine lines as revelation rather than vengeance, according to his well-loved Advent hymn, 'Lo, He Comes with Clouds Descending'. The judgment of light upon darkness will be felt suitably keenly when the truth about God, Christ and humanity is revealed publicly at last in its fullness. A modern translation brings this out even more clearly.

> Every eye shall now behold him
> robed in awesome majesty;
> those who have betrayed and sold him,
> pierced and nailed him to the tree,
> deeply shamed before him,
> deeply shamed before him,
> deeply shamed before him
> shall the true Messiah see.[113]

---

[113] #263 in *Together in Song: Australian Hymn Book II* (Melbourne: HarperCollinsReligious, 1999). (Author's Note: readers familiar with the hymn will recall the older translation, which has "deeply wailing" instead of "deeply shamed before him". I use the newer version because it makes clearer what judgment brings, according to my interpretation, which is shame as the first step in conversion rather than despair over the likelihood of damnation—that judgment is about transforming grace, not violent wrath.)

And one of the things they will see is a vision of judgment very different from what we humans inflict on one another.

What form of punishment might be involved if this is the nature of judgment and if, contrary to the false sacred, our God is not in the business of payback? Perhaps we could extrapolate from John's Gospel, concluding that punishment comes with the fruits of living in darkness, so that God's punishment for those who on account of their sin are revealed to be spiritually blind is experienced in the actual living-out of their disordered lives. Could this view of God's punishment—as woven into the pains and burdens of a sinfully deluded life—be what Jesus means by saying that misguidedly pious religious leaders 'have already received their reward' (Matthew 6:1-6)? Those who condemned the man born blind in John, Chapter 9 did not at that stage recognise their fault. But perhaps living with the consequences of flawed attitudes and stubborn choices, in a life of anxiety, emptiness and bitterness, is the way that people come to their senses. There is, as I have suggested, a place for an element of retributive justice as part of the journey that equips people for experiencing restorative justice.

Further extrapolation could lead us to imagine eternal damnation as *self-selected* alienation from God—an outcome with which God would concur, though without it being God's own vengeful punishment of the sinner. This is the sort of hell that C.S. Lewis imagined in *The Great Divorce*,[114] with some of the inmates thinking it was really heaven, and which they could have left at any time to go to heaven had they wished.

There is an obvious problem with this attempt at a non-violent account of divine judgment and punishment, however. If God's punishment is experienced as the cost of living under sin's tyranny, what of those more sinned against than sinning, and especially the victims of sexual abuse whose suffering is logically entailed by

---

[114] C.S. Lewis, *The Great Divorce* (London: Geoffrey Bles, 1946).

sinners remaining and acting in the darkness that God's judgment has revealed? Could my attempt at a more positive account, seeking a scriptural route beyond a violently punitive god, actually make things worse for victims of abuse? I suggest not, and invoke the traditional Christian conviction that, without liking it, God nevertheless allows human sin and its consequences as the price of human free will. But God does not stand back and leave us to our fate. By helping us bear and heal life's wounds in the present, also through the promise to redeem and transform them into glory in eternity, God helps victims find a way beyond their suffering. The fact that faith abides for so many victims shows that they know God to be neither the cause of their suffering nor a passive bystander as they undergo it but, rather, that God is their partner in bearing it and their hope of moving beyond it.

Victims of human sin and violence, including sexual abuse, bear a terrible burden as God's judgment is revealed in sin's bitter outworking. Only God's incarnate solidarity with the victims of abuse in God's crucified Son, promising the liberation and healing of victims through the resurrection and the outpoured Spirit of New Creation, makes faith possible in the face of such human evil. Likewise, the self-loathing and alienation of many abusers, or else their empty megalomaniacal isolation—all of which they may stubbornly choose to maintain eternally—shows that the God whose light reveals our darkness in judgment is also punishing human sin. Not as an active punitive agent, however, but as the stubborn force of love against which we pray and hope that all evil will eventually batter itself into submission.

Such an understanding as this, following hints in John's Gospel and elsewhere, is not only reasonable and credible. It is also *necessary* if we are to claim back divine judgment as part of the good news. Otherwise, widespread misapprehension will continue to greet our presentation of the gospel. This has been the case throughout the West since the Enlightenment, which opted for tolerance, universalism, humanism, and providential deism over a religion that seemed obsessed with sin and sacrifice.[115] Thanks to that obsession, the Church helped prepare the ground for its own rejection throughout today's West. This was a profound theological and spiritual failure that we can no longer afford. Indeed, unless the Christian imagination begins to be freed from this error, all our earnest talk about mission will remain largely ineffectual.

Abuse, the clergy and the Church

I am suggesting that the emotional root of abuse in the Church is located in God's portrayal as the disapproving enemy of human ordinariness, and especially of human sexuality—a God committed to overshadowing and punishing us rather than journeying with us through human depths of which God has no fear to the fullness of our human life with God. Clergy formed in such a toxic theological and spiritual environment, and the culture of immaturity, resentment and abuse that it fosters, are more likely to punish in others the softness, the weakness, the childlike, the feminine, that they have been prevented from accepting and honouring in themselves.

Here is the resentment of a thwarted self that Friedrich Nietzsche identified. He extolled the Greek divinities as swaggering, life-affirming bullies, favourably comparing them with paltry Christianity—a religion for losers, making do with a slave morality that breeds a Christian emotional underground of repressive rancour. Nietzsche is right about the rancour, and the failure of a religion that infantilises people, with 'ascetic priests' dispensing pastoral escapism rather than helping people grow to emotional

---

[115] On the particular problem that the juridical-penal model of the atonement became for the Enlightenment mind (and continues to be for many unbelievers today), see Charles Taylor, *A Secular Age* (Cambridge, MA. and London: The Belknap Press, 2007), 78-79, 650.

maturity.[116] But he gets the cause wrong. It is not that Christianity has killed the real sacred, which he believes to be violent and self-assertive, in favour of a pallid imitation. Rather, the false sacred, in the person of an abusive (false) god, has entrenched a bitter and defeated attitude in the Church, which emerges in resentful, hard done by, abusive behaviour of all sorts. The real sacred has nothing to do with this at all, however. The God of Jesus Christ does not rob us of authentically human life but is its great champion and guarantor. Rather than a dominating divine individual creating a race of cowering, vengeful human individuals, in a dynamic that was correctly identified by Nietzsche, we have a God of love and relationship whose will is to build a Church of mature, emotionally healthy, confident and accountable human mutuality.

Our response to abuse

As well as contributing to the cause of abuse, dysfunctional Church culture is also evident in aspects of its preferred treatment. I have indicated that closing ranks against sexually errant clergy and scapegoating them is an inadequate and in fact quite disordered response. Owning-up to the emotional harm encoded in beliefs, practices and structures is necessary in addition to the properly firm, just and transparent treatment of those who have offended, so the Church as a whole can move beyond psychological immaturity in sexuality and relationships of power.

Importantly, it is not acceptable for churches to assume that their beliefs and structures are preserved infallibly from distortion so that sin adheres only to individual Christians. In the sixteenth century, the Reformation pressed on the Roman

---

[116] Friedrich Nietzsche, *On the Genealogy of Morals* (1887), trans. Douglas Smith (Oxford: Oxford University Press, 1996), especially 2/22 (at 72-73), 3/11 (at 97), 3/15 (at 104-05).

Church this claim of error in faith and morals, while the Roman Church at the Council of Trent only partially accepted it. As for Protestant Churches subsequently, the belief that all corruptions were purged at the Reformation dies hard, so that Protestant beliefs and structures are regularly declared to be sin free, in a way that demonstrates little difference from the spiritual arrogance that Protestantism regularly condemns in Roman Catholicism. Whenever a Church, be it Roman, Protestant or Anglican, seeks its institutional preservation by hiding its sin and dysfunction, like any corrupt business or government, it demonstrates a theological and spiritual loss of nerve. Such churches plainly prefer lies and self-deception over judgment, repentance, and conversion, all of which are significant marks of authentic faith among the people of God.

One sign of this repentance is that greater maturity of relationship is encouraged between clergy, bishops and laity for both Anglicans and Catholics. With this must come a greater freedom to name the deep problems openly, rather than more-or-less fearfully playing along with the false optimism and the managerial superficiality with which deep issues are often addressed. The pastoral ministry needs to be reclaimed from today's widespread ecclesial agenda of institutional survivalism.

In responding to abuse, we must take care not to deepen our perceived hostility towards human sexuality. But we must also avoid the overcompensation of refusing to challenge further sexual deregulation. We see quite enough of that today in response to culture's obsession with and commodification of sexuality—though, strangely, this comes at the expense of the sparkle that a healthily inhabited sexual nature can bring to one's whole range of human relationships. With the sociologist Anthony Giddens, I am simply advocating 'the flowering of Eros in communicative love and friendship'.[117]

A further challenge faces us now that proper, loving and joyful physical relating with children is increasingly off-limits in the wider society. I have in mind the sort of physical contact that once seemed so naturally and properly a part of ministry, as when children take the priest's hand during a social gathering, or stretch out their arms to be picked up during the informality of a typical peace greeting in the Parish Eucharist. Detailed rules now govern all clergy interaction with children. This concern arises in tandem with society's growing sexualisation of children—a seeming disparity resolved by attending to the unrivalled power in today's West of the commodity form. According to sociologist Zygmunt Bauman, human persons are increasingly commodified in the West. This is true for children, too, and it works in a particular way. As parents and other adults increasingly keep their distance from children, for fear of risking abuse allegations, children are rendered increasingly socially isolated. Thus they become the unbonded, free-floating, more easily programmable consumers of commodities that the global economy most needs them to become.[118] Here the Church ought to be able to tell a different story, modelling a genuine and joyful community of free, emotionally healthy adults and deeply loved, integrated children.

Conclusion

In this discussion, I have linked unhealthy and immature approaches to relationships and authority in the Church with a widespread, harmful image of God accompanying a set of beliefs, practices

---

[117] Anthony Giddens, *The Transformation of Intimacy: Sexuality, Love and Eroticism in Modern Societies* (Stanford, CA.: Stanford University Press, 1992), 167ff.

[118] Zygmunt Bauman, 'On Postmodern Uses of Sex', in *The Individualized Society* (Cambridge: Polity, 2001), 220-37, especially 232-36.

An Abusive Church Culture: Sexual Abuse and Systemic Dysfunction (2008)

and structures widely perceived as hostile to human thriving. The result for many is a Church that is turned inward, anti-life, and in denial about its own crisis while continuing to claim the moral high ground. Some individuals within the Church's ordained ministry become abusive, just as children subject to abuse can become abusers themselves. Institutional failures to respond in the past, and the abusive deployment of more recent disciplinary means designed to solve the problem, risk perpetuating rather than healing the abuse. Clergy who abuse and victimise others emerge not from a vacuum but from the Church's culture. Only by attending to that culture, and the spiritual distortions that it accommodates, can we cut the nerve of victimisation and abuse.

7

Baptism in Australia: 'Civil Baptism' and the Social Miracle (2009)

> *Leading adults to baptism through the Catechumenate and preparing practising Christian parents for the baptism of their children has counted among my chief joys as an Anglican priest, and these baptisms at the Easter Vigil or Sunday Eucharist are always satisfying. But what about what I call civil baptism? What to make of parents expecting the private baptism of their children when their connection to the believing, worshipping Church is often a family memory at best, or an alien imposition at worst? I was invited to contribute a chapter to an ecumenical volume on liturgical enculturation in the Australian context and took the opportunity to find the best theological warrant I could for this practice. In so doing, I found myself thinking more generous thoughts. This was published as 'Baptism in Australia: Secularisation, "Civil Baptism" and the Social Miracle', in* Christian Worship in Australia: Perspectives on Liturgical Enculturation, *eds. Stephen Burns and Anita Monro (Sydney: St Pauls Publications, 2009), 155-66, and appears here by kind permission.*

The public mandate of the Church of England as established Church for a nation, serving the whole community and not only its gathered congregations, creates an expectation that baptism should be available for all comers, no questions asked. But while Anglicans have regularly seen themselves as a *de facto* religious establishment in secular Australia, this nation has never established any church. Australian Anglicanism has no wider accountability beyond its own members and its guiding sense that Christianity should have an integral role in society. Civil baptism continues, however, with Anglican clergy called upon to minister the sacrament apart from clear signs of explicit faith and the likelihood of continued regular church involvement, making what pastoral headway they can with parents. I am sure that, *mutatis mutandis*, Roman Catholic, Uniting Church and Lutheran clergy face similar challenges when essentially post-Christian Australians, retaining an ancestral connection to their churches, come expecting civil baptism.

Seeking a shared horizon of meaning with such parents, and helping to unpack the hopes and dreams awoken by their baby's arrival, rates among my hardest ministry challenges and has often left me feeling pastorally and theologically inadequate. I am always glad to minister God's promised gift of new birth to these infants, while sharing the gospel and hopefully offering a positive encounter with the Church to the strangers who gather. Still, Jesus' Parable of the Sower makes me wonder if all this sowing will lead to a harvest.

However, in preparing these reflections, I have come to a more positive assessment of civil baptism. I have discovered just how integral baptism was to the Christian society of pre-modern Europe as an eirenic, unifying force quite Christian in its intent, though lacking the doctrinal specificity and ecclesial distinctiveness that one might hope for in the gathered churches of more secular times. Today's civil baptism, with its typical emphasis on celebrating togetherness and social 'coming out', is more continuous with the norm of Christendom than I had imagined. I had to admit, too, that self-conscious doctrinal specificity is hardly the measure of things in today's typical gathered congregation. Reflection on language use—and liturgical language in particular—has also influenced me, revealing the relationship-building function of language in addition to the referential and performative aspects that I had previously recognised.

Baptism still unifies people, as in pre-modern Europe, though with some loss of doctrinal clarity and content. The sacraments are, as Louis-Marie Chauvet argues, 'the word of God at the mercy of the body'. This is a Vatican II-type insight, about the necessary immersion of theology and liturgy in the lived life of our world. My mistake had been to share today's widespread ecclesial overreaction to secularisation and to step back from the world, overestimating the presence of Christ in full doctrinal clarity for gathered congregations at the expense of Christ's wider presence in the world.

In what follows, I consider civil baptism in the context of Western secularisation and typical church responses to it, compared with pre-modern baptism, noting also some pertinent Australian factors. I conclude with a theological, pastoral and missional reflection aimed at improving our practice of civil baptism.

Civil baptism in retrospect

Postmodern Westerners live in a secular age, marked typically by the disembedding of religious belief and practice from communal belonging. Modernising societies differentiate internally, distributing their core functions around various agencies, which include a newly separate thing called religion. Individual allegiance becomes more problematic in such conditions, as a privatising turn away from God at the centre of public reality accompanies the collapse of shared public meaningfulness.[119] Faith becomes a choice, even

---

[119] José Casanova, 'Secularisation, Enlightenment and Modern Religion,' in *Public Religions in the Modern World* (Chicago and London: The University of Chicago Press, 1994), 11-39.

for serious practitioners, while belonging to a religious tradition is an increasingly conscious, intentional matter.

As a result, the gathered congregation emerges self-definitionally from wider society. This is a reaction against Enlightenment trends de-emphasising doctrinal distinctiveness in favour of a universal ethic focused on work, family and wealth creation, with Christian belief volatilised and its pieties redirected to the world of everyday affairs.[120] No ecclesial institution or credal confession is granted authority over the priorities of secular life. Those who pursue religion in explicit form must do so privately, on the margins of 'normality'. Some churches push back, becoming increasingly intentional and self-conscious. Their newer liturgies, including those of baptism, emphasise the explicitly theological, ecclesial and volitional nature of Christian identity, calling for more than was once typical of believing and belonging.

In that bygone world of Christendom, baptism was the foundation of a Christian society. There was no separation in the 'social miracle' of pre-modern European Christianity between social commensality and religious rites, as historian John Bossy establishes in his discussion of the Late Middle Ages.[121] Only later did new secular rites of social cohesion emerge with the rise of civility, and with Christianity becoming a separate 'ism' centred on a distinctive, gathered Church. So, baptism in the Christendom era was more ethnic, more folk-oriented, than anything a newly intentional, boundary-conscious Church in the postmodern West might insist on. What is more, the pre-modern social miracle grounded in baptism was conceived in a fully Christian way as the outworking of Christ's peace by strengthening the bonds of Christian society. Surely this is the fruit of Christ's doctrine

---

[120] Charles Taylor, *A Secular Age* (Cambridge, MA. and London: The Belknap Press, 2007), 221-69.
[121] John Bossy, *Christianity in the West 1400-1700* (Oxford: Oxford University Press [Opus], 1985), 14-19.

and practice, if not its comprehensive declaration. So, ironically, a more folky and more communal understanding of baptism represented not the absence of Christian commitment but, rather, its society-wide manifestation.

Let us now attempt to clarify the kinds of beliefs and attitudes that today's non-churchgoing families seek to express through civil baptism, representing a new take on those pre-modern, socialising trends. The French sacramental theologian Louis-Marie Chauvet identifies the primary motivation for what I call civil baptism in terms of conformity to the surrounding milieu rather than explicit doctrine and church belonging. He correlates the common motivations of un-churched parents bringing their children with the unspoken God-images and understandings of religion that these entail. He identifies a 'God' of status quo and tribal belonging with a 'religion' of bourgeois social integration standing behind such expressed motivations as 'it's always been done in my family', 'we want the child to be like everybody' and we intend that 'the child will receive good principles'. There is also the God of arbitrary sovereignty and a religion of prudent self-regard behind motivations such as 'if anything bad should happen to the child' and 'we want to give the child every possible chance'. Chauvet also acknowledges an unfocused and often nostalgic sense of something sacred and transcendent being involved.[122] But, like the folk sentiments that still bring non-churchgoers to midnight Mass at Christmas, this is surely more a matter of being offered a space to reach out towards mystery than actually nailing down that mystery in the bright light of doctrinal conviction.[123]

---

[122] Louis-Marie Chauvet, *The Sacraments: The Word of God at the Mercy of the Body* (1997), trans. Madeleine Beaumont (Collegeville, MN.: Liturgical Press [Pueblo], 2001), 180.

[123] David Martin, 'The Political Economy of Baptism' and 'Believing without Belonging: A Commentary on Religion in England', in *Christian Language and its Mutations: Essays in Sociological Understanding* (Theology and Religion in Interdisciplinary Perspective. Aldershot, UK. and Burlington, VT.: Ashgate, 2002), 145-56.

I am helped here by England's 'atheist priest', the philosopher of religion Don Cupitt, who identifies what he calls a new religion of life in everyday speech. His careful attention to the proliferation of life idioms in current English usage convinces him that, for most English people, doctrinally and ecclesially authoritative religion has been replaced by an ironic and optional spirituality of everyday living without consolations beyond this life. Cupitt regards people as characteristically content to make the best of things, doing whatever is possible—as professionals and performers do—to improve and brighten the human lot, while not being fazed by the mysterious and the unknown, leaving self-conscious engagement with *theoria* to gloomy and obsessive Romantics. This represents a further radicalising of the Enlightenment 'turn towards the world'.

For Cupitt, the transcendent is now merely the 'It' that marks the boundary of intelligible speech. In this spirit, it is not necessary to dismiss religion in the mode of militant atheism but simply to draw on its services (should you wish) for achieving your own goals. So, church weddings evoke beauty and the reassuring weight of traditional commitments and values, while the Christian funeral, despite retaining old-fashioned language of eschatology and *memento mori*, now universally becomes 'a celebration of the life of...'.[124]

Though Cupitt does not discuss baptism, it is clear by extension that a structured opportunity to affirm many good things in life—joy at the newness and gratuitousness of life revealed in a birth, of being together, and of the newborn's coming out into the wider life of society—is reason enough for baptism, with any reference to God being a symbolic way of talking about all that without remainder. Clearly the social miracle is now expected to happen without the deep interweaving of God throughout social

---

[124] Don Cupitt, *The New Religion of Life in Everyday Speech* (London: SCM Press, 1999), *The Meaning of It All in Everyday Speech* (London: SCM Press, 1999) and *Kingdom Come in Everyday Speech* (London: SCM Press, 2000).

life. But God language and liturgical practice remains as a resource that many still turn to for help in achieving this deepening of mutuality and enhancement of life.

For Cupitt, and his radically postmodern understanding of language, there is no problem using traditional worship to create a space or a mood without ascribing any metaphysical truth or doctrinal weight to the language used. This approach undoes an older, realist account of language as truthful to the extent that it correctly mirrors external reality so that, following the so-called linguistic turn in philosophy from the mid-twentieth century, the meaning of words comes to reside chiefly in their context and use.

The philosopher J.L. Austin distinguished the familiar, plain and direct *locutionary* meaning of words from other aspects of language use, explicating the 'something more' that emerges whenever humans communicate. There is also a *perlocutionary* meaning referring to the performativity of some utterances through the changes they effect simply by being stated in the right context (e.g., 'You are under arrest', 'I declare this new bridge open', 'I absolve you from all your sins in the name of ...'). A third aspect of language that Austin defines, and the one that most illuminates the practice of civil baptism, is its *illocutionary* use, which has to do with language use establishing relations between various subjects in the exchange.[125]

I suggest that illocutionary uses underpin the group cohesion and other shared expectations of family and friends who bring children for civil baptism. At the locutionary level, a certain account is being given in the words of baptismal liturgy, with a theological and ecclesial focus. However, at the illocutionary level, the words of the rite serve as carriers of a potentially different

---

[125] J.L. Austin, *How to Do Things with Words* (Oxford: Clarendon Press, 1962). The ever-present reality of this 'other level' of illocution behind even objective technical language (e.g., a dry scientific presentation also being the scientist's bid for peer recognition) is noted in Chauvet, *The Sacraments*, 79.

meaning, expressing the hopes and expectations of those who bring the child in love and hopefulness but apart from explicit faith. There is a sense that for them, at least at the locutionary level (i.e., that of strict doctrinal reference), the liturgical words go in one ear and out the other. But at the illocutionary level, it is a different story. A secular echo of Europe's pre-modern social miracle is taking place.

Indeed, it seems that the illocutionary not only overmasters the locutionary but can even annex the perlocutionary, when performative utterances that a baptismal regenerationist believes will secure the child's salvation achieve a different effect for others present—as the declaration of a new name and a new relationship to the family, the community and the world. This account of language shows how the same words can mean and achieve different things, depending on who you are and where you stand in the baptismal performance. For this reason, it is possible—though potentially galling for *habitués* of the locutionary use, like theologians and liturgists—to see how wave after wave of young un-churched parents can 'make promises they have no intention of keeping' and do other things that those wary of civil baptism accuse them of doing, all apparently in good conscience.

Of course, the locutionary meaning is very important, and much worthwhile scientific and legal-evidential labour is devoted to untangling objective from subjective. However, the very fact of this perennial struggle shows how potentially unhelpful the specific wording is for understanding what is actually going on. And—let it be said—this can be as true for the unchurched as it is for the 'churched'. It is not as if the locutionary use is *actually* favoured at the expense of the illocutionary even by churchgoers. I had long discerned that lay religious sensibility and a theologian's account of Christian life typically differ. Herein lies the theologian's particular challenge in the pulpit, in parish leadership where quite divergent priorities can emerge between priest and people, and in pastoral ministry where articulate theology is revealed regularly to have little obvious place in lay self-understanding and the practice of lay ministry. I had appreciated the regular disjunction between guiding spiritual instincts and their articulation,[126] also the often limited uptake by a faith community of its guiding narrative.[127] But the English sociologist Martin Stringer really brought this home to me by laying bare the deepest motives evident in a wide range of today's regular Christian worship contexts.

Stringer studied the worship of four Manchester congregations: Baptist, Pentecostal, Roman Catholic and Anglo-Catholic. Through careful embedded reflection and interviews over time, he found significant commonality in the lived reality, beneath obvious 'official' differences. He concluded that in each case, worship functions for its participants by creating a space for significant experiences to be recovered by repetition and memory—whether it be an orienting narrative (Baptist), conversion (Pentecostal), abiding in a communal tradition (Roman Catholic) or a sense of community evoked by liturgical occasions (Anglo-Catholic).[128] I am tempted to conclude that liturgy mediates Christian identity and belonging without its language working chiefly in a referential way *for churchgoers as well as for non-churchgoers*—indeed, probably for all but theologians and liturgists. So, why would I have thought that practising Christian couples bringing children for baptism had a significantly different or superior theological understanding from those who do not share their church connection? Perhaps the

---

[126] Robert N. Bellah, et al, *Habits of the Heart: Individualism and Commitment in American Life* (1985) (Berkeley, CA. and London: University of California Press, 1996), 81.
[127] George A. Lindbeck, *The Nature of Doctrine: Religion and Theology in a Postliberal Age* (Philadelphia, PA.: Westminster Press, 1984), 100.
[128] Martin D. Stringer, *The Perception of Worship: The Ethnography of Worship in Four Christian Congregations in Manchester* (Birmingham: The University of Birmingham Press, 1999). For a similar warning see Chauvet, *The Sacraments*, 184.

only one in either baptismal context with a locutionary theological approach to the proceedings was *me*, while both churchgoing *and* non-churchgoing parents approached the baptism of their children chiefly in socially inclusive, non-doctrinally explicit, illocutionary ways.

The Australian context

Does anything distinctively Australian need to be added concerning civil baptism? A well-loved Australian poem of 1893, first appearing in *The Bulletin*, is highly suggestive. By A.B. 'Banjo' Paterson, it is called 'A Bush Christening'.

> On the outer Barcoo where the churches are few,
>   And men of religion are scanty,
> On a road never cross'd 'cept by folk that are lost,
>   One Michael Magee had a shanty.
>
> Now this Mike was the dad of a ten-year-old lad,
>   Plump, healthy, and stoutly conditioned;
> He was strong as the best, but poor Mike had no rest
>   For the youngster had never been christened,
>
> And his wife used to cry, 'If the darlin' should die
>   Saint Peter would not recognise him'.
> But by luck he survived till a preacher arrived,
>   Who agreed straightaway to baptise him.
>
> Now the artful young rogue, while they held their collogue,
>   With his ear to the keyhole was listenin',
> And he muttered in fright while his features turned white,
>   'What the divil and all is this christenin'?
>
> He was none of your dolts, he had seen them brand colts,
>   And it seemed to his small understanding,
> If the man in the frock made him one of the flock,
>   It must mean something very like branding.

So away with a rush he set off for the bush,
    While the tears in his eyelids they glistened–
'Tis outrageous', says he, 'to brand youngsters like me,
    I'll be dashed if I'll stop to be christened!'

Like a young native dog he ran into a log,
    And his father with language uncivil,
Never heeding the 'praste' cried aloud in his haste,
    'Come out and be christened, you divil!'

But he lay there as snug as a bug in a rug,
    And his parents in vain might reprove him,
Till his reverence spoke (he was fond of a joke)
    'I've a notion,' says he, 'that'll move him.'

'Poke a stick up the log, give the spalpeen a prog;
    Poke him aisy - don't hurt him or maim him,
'Tis not long that he'll stand, I've the water at hand,
    As he rushes out this end I'll name him'.

'Here he comes, and for shame! Ye've forgotten the name–
    Is it Patsy or Michael or Dinnis?'
Here the youngster ran out, and the priest gave a shout–
    'Take your chance, anyhow, wid "Maginnis"'!

As the howling young cub ran away to the scrub
    Where he knew that pursuit would be risky,
The priest, as he fled, flung a flask at his head
    That was labelled 'Maginnis's Whisky'!

And Maginnis Magee has been made a J.P.,
    And the one thing he hates more than sin is
To be asked by the folk who have heard of the joke,
    How he came to be christened 'Maginnis'![129]

---

[129] Online: https://www.bushverse.com/andrew-banjo-paterson/a-bush-christening/ (last accessed August 2022).

Baptism in Australia: 'Civil Baptism' and the Social Miracle (2009)

Three things strike me about baptism according to this delightfully scurrilous poem: the bush christening is understood primarily in relational terms; it is stripped of theological, liturgical and denominational distinctiveness; and it celebrates social assimilation for the Irish, all making it a clear example of the social miracle.

First, note that recognition and belonging—relational considerations—are the chief explanations given for the baptism, with only the mother concerned that 'If the darlin' should die Saint Peter would not recognise him'. There is the overheard motive of making the boy 'one of the flock'. But the crucial thing is the conferring of a name, both in the priest's articulated goal for the act—'As he rushes out this end I'll name him'—and in the farcical climax, where all is nearly lost for want of a name (and any name will do, because what clearly matters here has nothing to do with individualism). The canny young rascal was right that baptism did indeed 'mean something very like branding'. Here the explicitly theological could not be more occluded in favour of baptism strengthening social life—and also perhaps establishing a wider belonging beyond the painful remoteness of the pioneer family's existence.

This leads to my second point, about the lack of all theological and ecclesial niceties. Australian church historian Ian Breward names 'the ecumenism of need' that characterised church life in early Australia. Co-operation between non-established denominations and the efforts of many civic-minded Christians played a key role in nation building, through strengthening the bonds and institutions of a new society.[130] The churches' contribution included civilising and reforming public manners, and today's continuing lack of an integral role for theology in Australian church and university life recalls this very Enlightenment-flavoured, non-doctrinal and certainly non-critical understanding of Christianity carried over

---

130 See Ian Breward, *Australia: 'The Most Godless Place Under Heaven'?* (1988) (Adelaide: Lutheran Publishing House, 1991), 15, 37, 87.

from the period of modern Australia's origins. We see from the poem that differences in faith and order seem to matter little, with the minister of baptism first named as 'preacher' (perhaps recalling the Methodist circuit riders who roamed outback Australia preaching and baptising), then 'praste' (i.e., an Irish Catholic priest) and then 'his reverence' (which has a distinctly Church of England respectability about it). Or perhaps this non-differentiation is meant to assert denominational equivalence? There is also the lack of any liturgical aspects of baptism, with no evidence of the water being used—indeed, a knock on the head with a whisky flask may have been the 'matter' of the sacrament—nor any mention of the three-fold name. Nothing theological seems to be on anyone's mind in the poem.

My third point has to do with the social miracle as it applied to Australia's Irish after a troubled start in the convict era.[131] The poem's language and accent affectionately establishes its Irish focus: 'divil', 'praste', 'aisy', 'Patsy or Michael or Dinnis' and 'spalpeen'. This last reference, meaning scamp or rascal, is particularly notable in light of how Maginnis Magee ends up—as himself a magistrate, a J.P., with little he 'hates more than sin'. In keeping with the independent and nationalist tenor of *The Bulletin*, this satirical poem should not be read as in any way anti-Irish. The whisky priest is surely a friendly caricature poking more or less gentle fun at Irish stereotypes. The truth is that nineteenth-century Irish priests in Australia were often every bit as morally serious as the strictest Protestants, thanks to the influence of Jansenism, while the Irish diaspora brought the largest influx of free settlers to Australia's colonies, with many Protestants and free-thinkers as well as Catholics. Maginnis Magee J.P. represents all the Irish descendants among jurists, writers, churchmen, Governors and eventually Prime Ministers

---

[131] See Patrick O'Farrell, *The Irish in Australia* (Sydney: The University of New South Wales Press, 1986).

who sealed Ireland's triumphant contribution to the reinvention of Britishness in Australia. Paterson's 'A Bush Christening' presents baptism as a non-theological, non-ecclesial, down-under version of the social miracle—especially regarding the formerly marginalised Irish.

Civil baptism: a theological, pastoral and missional conclusion

From a Catholic perspective, this recalls the Vatican II-inspired engagement between Christ and culture, recognising that Christ and his Kingdom are at work in the world apart from their articulate acknowledgment and the Church's official presence. So, treating cultures seriously and respectfully is mandated for pastoral ministry and proclamation, because God goes ahead of us and we are always likely to find ourselves on holy ground as we advance into God's world. But the gospel imperative remains, as we further honour culture by believing in the possibility of its transformation in Christ.

From a Protestant perspective, this is the duality of geography and eschatology named by Eugene Peterson. Pastoral work should only proceed from deep engagement and investment in the local culture and the lives lived within it, while its eschatological dimension challenges everything in locality and culture that seeks to usurp God's place. Peterson points to Jonah's journey far into Nineveh, concluding that only Jonah's immersion in that city's life gave him the authority to declare God's coming judgment on it.[132]

In their pastoral reflections on this theological assessment of Christ and culture, both Chauvet and Peterson acknowledge the risen Christ going before us, as he went ahead of his disciples in the mission to Galilee. Both writers are driven to a posture of humble expectation, open to the human weight and spiritual potential

---

[132] Eugene H. Peterson, *Under the Unpredictable Plant: An Exploration in Vocational Holiness* (Grand Rapids, MI. and Cambridge, UK.: Eerdmans, 1992), 117-53.

of pastoral encounters, knowing too that their own pastoral input is not Christ's first or even key entry into the situation. Peterson becomes a listener and learner first and foremost,[133] while Chauvet raises the possibility of ecclesial outsiders who bring children for baptism becoming agents of conversion for the Church's representatives. He refocuses pastoral emphasis away from articulate performance in presenting a polished position, anticipating the Godly dynamic that will play out in these pastoral interviews even if the Church's representatives experience them as awkward. God is best served by forbearing witnesses, confident that the Word is at work in the midst of human mess and incompleteness. We pastoral agents are reassured that while Paul might plant and Apollos water, it is up to God, not us, to give the growth (1 Corinthians 3:6-8).[134]

---

[133] Peterson, *Under the Unpredictable Plant*, 123-28, discussing the impact on him of James Joyce, *Ulysses*, with its cumulatively moving account of Leopold Bloom and the minutiae of his daily life in a dreary Dublin.

[134] Chauvet, *The Sacraments*, 187-99.

8

Church and Faith as if Easter Makes a Difference (2012)

> *This short piece provides a succinct theological rationale for my view of the Church and how faith relates to belonging within the household of faith. I offer a Catholic version of so-called postliberalism. Once again, you see me trying to articulate a third way beyond what I regard as unprepossessing contemporary alternatives—a road less travelled. It was published as 'Faith built on belonging, not debate', The Australian Financial Review (Easter, 5-9 April 2012): 'Review', 1 and 9. For its appearance here, I restore the title it was submitted under, the original paragraph breaks, and I add references. No permission was required to reproduce it. I remember this piece fondly, not least because Fairfax paid me a dollar a word to write it!*

In his short story 'Bells in the Morning', set in 1945, Richard Yates has two GIs dug in along the Ruhr in a morning mist. All the church bells start to ring, and they think for a brief moment that the war might be over. Until one remembers someone saying the previous week that it had been Good Friday. To which the other glumly responds, 'Son of a bitch. Easter Sunday'.[135]

Faith built on Jesus' death and resurrection once changed the world. It overcame the violent fatalism of Rome's Imperial

---

[135] Richard Yates, 'Bells in the Morning,' in *The Collected Stories of Richard Yates* (New York: Picador, 2001), 399-403, at 403.

religion via a radical new social movement called the Church. Yet those fictional GIs are typical of the many who today find Christian faith remote and uninteresting. Likewise, any kind of church involvement beyond what the social niceties demand strikes most Westerners as inconceivable.

Christian faith and the beliefs articulating it makes most sense when embodied in a community. In the same way that learning a foreign language becomes more vital and engaging when one goes to live among native speakers. A lot that seemed difficult comes more easily from the inside. Yet mainstream Western churches regularly fail to excite and compel even their own dwindling membership. Their occasional claims for success often rest on repackaging aspects of the good life as our society conceives it, or else providing a safe haven for the anxious and the nostalgic.

A movement in theology and Christian ethics called postliberalism is helping to identify these problems and to picture a way forward. It offers a third way beyond today's impasse between Christian conservatives and fundamentalists, on the one hand, and so-called liberal or progressive Christians on the other. These two poles are familiar to us from wider society's culture wars in America and to some extent in Australia. Yet for postliberals, these flaccid alternatives represent the shrivelling of Christian imagination. As mirror doubles locked in mutual reaction, theological conservatives and liberals are equally culturally captive. Religion plays for each the essentially privatised, individualised role that modernity scripts for it, while the truth of faith is cashed out in one or other of modernity's standard coinages: rationalism or romanticism.

Postliberalism finds its inspiration in three major sources. Chiefly, there is the Bible, understood as a narrative universe into which believers are progressively drawn. This approach, also known as narrative theology, retrieves biblical interpretation from the sterile debate over propositional factoids into which it has typically descended among theological conservatives, liberals and anti-Christian sceptics alike.

Scripture comes alive in communal reflection on real-life issues. Consider the so-called base ecclesial communities of Latin America, closely associated with Liberation Theology. Gatherings of Catholic peasants who might otherwise have been radicalised by Marxist ideology found an alternative identity and empowerment. Biblical reflection on the economic injustice and political violence that blighted their lives fostered a countervailing sense of dignity and poise as God's beloved people. Their movement constituted a non-violent social revolution.

A second source is the Church's traditional liturgies. Baptism and Eucharist reinforce an alternative vision of what matters most in life. They rattle the cage of today's ruling mindset, which is 'look good, feel good and make good'. Here is an alternative to worship as a non-threateningly amateurish, old-fashioned exercise in nostalgic reassurance, as certain traditionalist conservatives like it. Or else to confecting the laboured relevancy that many liberals along with conservative Evangelicals prefer, which risks turning Sunday worship into a lacklustre outpost of the personal services sector. Postliberalism might encourage us instead to think of the Eucharist as revolutionary theatre. It confronts every ultimately toxic version of human thriving with the public enactment of God's vision for humanity.

Postliberalism's third source of inspiration is the Church's historic communities of radical discipleship, notably Catholic monasticism and Anabaptist congregationalism. Monasticism began as a countercultural alternative to decadent currents in the newly Christianised Constantinian Empire. Originally, monks and nuns withdrew to the desert, devoting themselves to Scripture and liturgy, prayer and work. Their life together was marked by solitude, simplicity and mutual respect. Later, the baton passed to St Benedict along with his Cistercian and Carthusian inheritors. Through their mission, ministry, architecture, land management, agriculture and learning, these numerous monasteries helped to 'refashion' Europe, as John Henry Newman put it.

Of course, monastic communities often failed to fulfil their potential as public witnesses to the way of Christ. So, at the radical end of Europe's Reformation, Anabaptist communities took up Christianity's foundational challenge to live differently in the world. Their Mennonite descendants among the so-called peace churches, including the Amish, inspire postliberals today. The late American Christian pacifist John Howard Yoder, whose best-known book was *The Politics of Jesus*, provided a formative postliberal voice from the Mennonite tradition.[136]

Postliberal champions of more intentional Christian living respond chiefly to the condition of American Christianity. They want to disentangle faith and Church from the religious civic-mindedness, moralistic rationalism or else romantic individualism into which it has regularly descended throughout American history. One particular concern is to retrieve the banner of Evangelical Christianity from the Moral Majority and its successors. While individual freedom, so-called family values and related obsessions of the American Christian right carry great political weight, it is not Christ but American culture that effectively sets this agenda. The gospel is co-opted for socio-political duty, leaving little scope for churches to challenge the prevailing groupthink of adversarial moralism.

Duke University ethicist Stanley Hauerwas is the main postliberal advocate for Christian communities living their faith more intentionally. Hauerwas challenges America's conservative churches that if they crave political influence, they should first become more attractive examples of the Christian values they profess. He challenges liberal churches, whenever they define their mission as helping to make the world a better place, to start by being good churches. This approach reveals the influence of moral philosopher Alasdair MacIntyre, whose virtue ethics calls for

---

[136] John Howard Yoder, *The Politics of Jesus: Vicit Agnus Noster* (Grand Rapids, MI.: Eerdmans, 1972).

'communities of character' as the basis for producing transformed individuals and influencing wider society.[137]

A Catholic advocate of such thinking is the veteran German New Testament scholar Gerhard Lohfink. He resigned his Tübingen professorship in 1986 to live and work in a new religious community of priests and lay people called the Integrierte Gemeinde. Such movements are multiplying in Europe. Worth a visit are the Comunità di Sant' Egidio, based in Rome's Trastevere, and the Fraternités monastiques de Jérusalem, based at the historic Church of St Gervais in the 4th *arrondissement*.

Lohfink is convinced that the Church will keep dwindling, its faith sinking further into implausibility, unless such communities of compelling witness can nurture a rebirth. In his book *Does God Need the Church?* he writes, 'What the Church needs before anything else is itself to be a concrete society that makes faith visible as a way of life, different from neo-paganism'.[138]

If postliberal thinking began to gain ground, what are some ways in which the churches' habits and preoccupations might change? So-called family values would no longer be an excuse for retreat into the nuclear family and protective individualism, or serve as a stick to beat those we disapprove of. Rather, congregations where belonging and identity are re-imagined would help forge the relational values on which wider civic engagement can be rebuilt. In a departure from left-Christian rhetoric, the Church's prophetic witness would move beyond its committee reports and media quotes from bishops' Easter sermons. Rather, congregations and dioceses would demonstrate publicly what living differently with respect and solidarity actually looks like.

---

[137] Alasdair MacIntyre, *After Virtue: A Study in Moral Theory*, 2nd edn. (Notre Dame, IN.: The University of Notre Dame Press, 1984).

[138] Gerhard Lohfink, *Does God Need the Church? Toward a Theology of the People of God*, trans. Linda M. Maloney (Collegeville, MN.: Liturgical Press [Michael Glazier], 1999), 273.

The Church would show how to abide more critically and less anxiously in late-capitalist culture. Christians would learn to let go of today's preoccupations with security and relative social position, which in turn fuel obsessions with wealth and consumption. Christian congregations would take the lead in modelling social alternatives. Beyond today's cult of managerialism and its curse of corporate downsizing, Christian employers would show how to deal more humanely and collaboratively with employees. This is because they had learned to share God's justice and compassion through themselves being loved and valued in a Christian community.

Instead of simply protesting Australia's bipartisan political set against asylum seekers, Christian congregations would model a different, non-anxious response to 'the other'. This comes naturally to those who learn in word, sacrament and communal belonging that grace, gift and acceptance stand at the heart of God's reality. Beyond today's defence of fixed positions on women's ordination as priests and bishops by the Church's patriarchal conservatives and their feminist critics, new questions would emerge. We would ask ourselves how best to foster Jesus' practice of radical inclusion, which led New Testament churches beyond antiquity's culture-defining distinctions between Jew and Greek, slave and free, male and female. How best to model Jesus' culturally confronting practice of leadership by taking the towel of a slave? So, churches might well come to women's ordination but by a different route.

Instead of being mired in set-piece debates about human sexuality, congregational life involving people of differing sexuality would help to reposition this hot-button issue. Such conflicted positions tend to soften once they wear the faces of beloved and trusted fellow travellers. Rather than contending over objective rights or wrongs on same-sex marriage, for instance, the question would shift. It would become one of learning to live together in communities that explore and commend the Christian virtues of fidelity and solidarity. Encouraging the formation of Christian households marked by generosity and hospitality, able to form children's moral imaginations accordingly, would become more important than policing the makeup of those households. None of this is helped when a necessarily communal exercise in patient openness and mutual discovery is reduced to black-and-white abstractions.

Postliberalism is not just a practically oriented movement. First, it was an intellectual one, theorised by Yale University Lutheran theologian George Lindbeck in his 1984 book, *The Nature of Doctrine*.[139] Lindbeck redefined Christian belief as the grammar and syntax of a living language in the Church. It was not a made-up language like Esperanto, however, but a real, vibrant and evolving language of the sort found in communities of native speakers. Compared with conservative Christianity's regular emphasis on objective believing, Lindbeck sees coming to faith as more like learning this new language and its accompanying cultural practices. Compared with liberal Christianity's characteristic emphasis on one's own personal truth and experience, for which Christian belief and practice might provide helpful resources, faith for Lindbeck is more like hardware than software.

Here the philosopher Ludwig Wittgenstein and cultural anthropologists like Clifford Geertz point the way. They show how beliefs need to be understood through the forms of life that accompany them. Such a 'thick description' of faith represents an improvement on the pointless too-and-fro between today's 'new atheists' and Christian fundamentalists over the truth or otherwise of Christian beliefs. Brothers under the skin, Richard Dawkins and his fundamentalist opponents are prisoners of the same meagre modern rationalism when it comes to comprehending Christian truth claims.

---

[139] George A. Lindbeck, *The Nature of Doctrine: Religion and Theology in a Postliberal Age* (Philadelphia, PA.: Westminster Press, 1984).

This is not to reduce the content of Christian belief to purely regulative principles, however, as radical Wittgensteinian philosophers of religion such as R.B. Braithwaite, Peter Winch and D.Z. Phillips advocate. What it does mean is that we cannot understand the cross of Jesus, say, apart from knowing the power of forgiveness in an actual community that practises it. Or really believe in Jesus' resurrection without having been shown that Easter faith overcomes evil, cynicism and the weight of a stifling past.

At a time when many are seeking something to make churchgoing more invigorating and Christian belief more engaging, postliberal insights issue a timely challenge to the churches. Easter faith and worship have more going for them than many conservative and liberal Christians imagine, let alone those who Friedrich Schleiermacher called the cultured despisers of religion.

9

The Eucharist Makes the Church (2013)

> *This is a* cri de coeur *on my part for a more integral conception of the body of Christ. I have been advancing a theological and spiritual view of what being the Church actually means at a time when alternative ecclesial agendas are taking hold in Australian Anglicanism—either militant social conservatism or else wokeness, and, of course, the provision of personal services to individual consumers, while a number of bishops want to be more like corporate managers. This previously unpublished piece was given as two lectures at the St James Institute, Sydney, on Saturday 2 June 2013.*

There is a crisis of identity and purpose in the Australian Anglican Church today that defies easy solution. I am not referring to the fallout over clergy sexual abuse, though this excruciating development does help to explain the problem we face. Which is that the Church in general and the Eucharist in particular have become optional extras in living a good life, even for living the Christian life, and widely derided options at that. Hence a glaring failure of spiritual vision, compassion, and pastoral leadership on the part of abusers and Church leaders is matched by a new pitch of scapegoating rectitude directed toward the whole Church by its cultured despisers. We are paying the price for our Church's longstanding fascination with respectability and for claiming the moral high ground, since our institutional feet of clay and our share in the ordinary traffic of human ill will, folly and misery have now been fully exposed.

Such respectability was what church and worship were all about according to my suburban 1960s and early-1970s Queensland childhood—though winds of change had by then begun to blow throughout the Western world in the direction of moral autonomy and the exhilaration of being able to choose how our lives are to be lived. Church as a valued part of community life, a marker of respectability, and even a badge of social status is now, by and large, limited to rural communities in Australia, if it survives at all.

A 'leading layman', as certain distinguished persons are sometimes referred to, once told me that he came to church for the music and to keep his wife happy—but he was in his 70s; no-one under 50 would think like that anymore. The former Scottish bishop and now atheist, Richard Holloway, paints an unsparing picture in his memoirs of this increasingly bygone attitude to churchgoing, offering little more for many than a sense of connection with the past and a vague feeling of something transcendent.[140] For a time, the Church suited Holloway's own romantic and melancholy temperament, but eventually the dysfunction displayed by many of his fellow Anglicans (the clergy especially) got the better of him. A lot of psychological and spiritual immaturity clings to the Church still—such people seem to hang on in there while many more confident and healthy-minded people have had enough and have moved on.

The Canadian theologian Gary Badcock interprets today's mass exodus from the Church, explaining why so many have opted out since the personal and social benefits once associated with the Church are now recognised as being more widely available: 'the hungry sheep look up, remain unfed, and have decided in the hundreds of millions that they can find the same thing (and

---

[140] Richard Holloway, *Leaving Alexandria: A Memoir of Faith and Doubt* (London: Canongate, 2012), 153.

it is the same thing) in more convincing forms from the other available consumerist alternatives that equally serve the end of individual flourishing: popular culture, environmental activism, uninhibited sex, the fulfilment of career ambition, politics, or even crass materialism'.[141]

For those healthier-minded ones who stay with the Church, there may be no clear sense of why they have stayed, and no strong likelihood that their belonging would survive anything much in the way of provocations or setbacks. Even the real, genuine believers who are trying to make a go of following Christ, with a clearer sense than their parents may well have had about what being a Christian means, are typically less clear about the place, the necessity and the authority of the Church in their Christian lives.

Religious consumerism

The reality is that our postmodern Western culture of choices rather than givens, of optional obligations and personal agendas, is a world of consumers, yes, and sometimes of joiners—as long as whatever you join provides you with worthwhile benefits—but it is no longer a world of unquestioned belonging. In matters of religion, things are no different. For example, the second-generation immigrant youth chooses to embrace radical Islam because it provides him with a clear sense of identity for the first time in his life, since he belongs neither to his ancestral culture nor fully to that of his adopted country. So, even fundamentalists are really shoppers in the spiritual marketplace.

The young Christian fundamentalist, too, has essentially chosen a product—one that will help him or her to negotiate the difficult transition from adolescence to adulthood, whereupon

---

[141] Gary Badcock, *The House Where God Lives: Renewing the Doctrine of the Church for Today* (Grand Rapids, MI.: Eerdmans, 2009), 335-36.

another lifestyle product could very well take its place. Even for serious adult Christians, their Church and parish affiliation falls under the sway of consumer forces. And increasingly, the choice is not just which denomination, which congregation, or which style of worship, but whether churchgoing is necessary at all for my 'spiritual needs' to be met. This is akin to the question of whether marriage is necessary for my 'relationship needs' or even my 'sexual needs', so called, to be met—as if sexual needs and relationship needs, like 'insurance needs' or even 'motoring needs', are best addressed by shopping around. But this is the extent of our belonging in postmodern Western culture, which even for Christians can mean that today's agenda of consumer-driven therapeutic individualism trumps any properly theological and spiritual account of belonging to the Church and participating in its central act of worship.

Let me offer a clarifying metaphor, from the now ubiquitous language of computing: that of hardware and software. The *hardware*, the basic agenda of our lives, is our set of personal needs, while these needs are met by various forms of *software*. Just choose whichever package or app is compatible with your priorities. For your software needs in the personal realm, seek out the Church if you like, or whichever other provider of personal spiritual services—from a 'wilderness experience', to a theatre or Musica Viva subscription, to a spa retreat.

As for our 'worship needs', if we have those, these might be met by a traditional Eucharist but increasingly it will be anything but that: a 'public Christian gathering' for Evangelical teaching and fellowship, or a Pentecostal praise event, or one of the proliferating fresh expressions that typify today's Emerging Church movement. A variation of this state of affairs, perhaps its precursor, is the original Protestant instinct that personal faith in God constitutes the hardware and Church constitutes the software; or else, that word and gospel are hardware while worship forms and habits are software. As long as you have a smart phone, there are myriad software resources in the app store from which you can choose. Likewise, we hear that as long as you are a Christian, then where you worship, how you worship and, increasingly, whether or not you worship are entirely up to you. Because, of course, these are essentially software options that are secondary, interchangeable and, by extension, disposable.

Software Church, optional Eucharistic app

This state of affairs is represented in every stripe of Australian Anglicanism, though the most obvious examples are Evangelical ones. Let me offer some vignettes, to illustrate aspects of the problem.

Evangelical

Today's push in some Evangelical circles for so-called lay administration of the Lord's Supper is at least in part to ensure that the word and preaching retain their Protestant supremacy over sacrament and cult, which are tolerated for the sake of obedience to Christ's ordinance rather than embraced enthusiastically as foundational practices. Even the older Evangelical commitment to Matins and Evensong is waning as prayer book worship ceases to be the Evangelical norm. A priest friend in Tasmania informed me that the clergy gathered with their bishop for a few days could not get organised to say Evening Prayer together let alone celebrate the Eucharist, though they did manage a scratch clergy rock band for a session of praise songs. An Anglo-Catholic priest-musician in my own diocese, whose efforts at introducing some contemporary Catholic hymnody represented something entirely new at a Clergy Conference, was thanked by an Evangelical clergyperson afterwards with the words, 'I don't normally go in for Holy Communion, but that was very nice'.

Anglo-Catholic

Lest I seem to be harsh about Evangelicalism, we can find similar issues arising within Anglo-Catholicism. There is a preference for high-culture performance in some Anglo-Catholic showpiece parishes, and in some places for antique forms of the liturgy, often celebrated with the full panoply of elaborate ceremonial. These preferences can make Anglicans of this persuasion dismissive of a more mainstream 'Family Eucharist', for instance, with its signs of communal welcome such as the presence of boisterous children and folksier, less formal music. In other words, the quality of their worship experience comes first while the actual inclusive ecclesial miracle of the Eucharist itself is disdained whenever it appears in unacceptable garb. Latin Mass Catholics have their own version of this, when they refuse to participate in vernacular rites.

Conservative Anglo-Catholics risk annexing the Eucharist to their own project of ecclesiastical self-definition, so that their preferred form of worship becomes a mark of their specialness and distinctiveness rather than a call to repentance and God's invitation into a wider Eucharistic fellowship. Anglo-Catholicism can be a peevish and anxious movement, after all, especially when the properly bold spirit of 'Forward in Faith' yields to a mood that the aforementioned Richard Holloway once wryly called 'backwards in despair'. It is not properly Eucharistic for Anglo-Catholics to huddle together in their beautiful shrines, dreaming of what might have been. Properly Catholic Christianity is more outward looking and world affirming, also ecclesiastically confident enough to welcome other Christian expressions with grace rather than anxious disdain.

Broad Church

Most Anglicans are neither Evangelical nor Anglo-Catholic, and this broad Anglican middle also manifests various forms of a

The Eucharist Makes the Church (2013)

'software church' attitude, as evident in its Eucharistic habits. There are legacies of the older respectable community group approach to Anglicanism that congregate in our Broad-Church middle, according to which the Church is not especially concerned with doctrine or discipleship, while the Eucharist is a habituated gathering without notable implications for distinctive Christian identity let alone mission. This low-temperature, middle-of-the-road Anglicanism is neither a Bible reading fellowship, nor is it marked by Eucharistic devotion, nor is it missional in its self-understanding, beyond perhaps a well-intentioned helping profile in the local community.

A major parish where I once served exemplified this attitude when Australia Day fell on a Sunday and an official commemoration was to be held with the Governor-General present, and with a marquee set up in the grounds for a champagne breakfast to follow. Our role was to provide Choral Matins instead of the normal 10.00am Sung Eucharist, and my advertising, both in the newspaper and in house, emphasised that Holy Communion would still be celebrated in the regular 8.00am timeslot for those who wanted it. The result was that not one regular worshipper from the large 10.00am congregation came to the 8.00am Eucharist, so that one whole congregation missed Holy Communion for a week in favour of Matins served with chicken and champagne. Does this not indicate that a social agenda and the bare habit of churchgoing are primary while Eucharistic belonging is secondary?

In another example from the broad Anglican middle, I take my life in my hands and comment on the rising habit of receiving communion by intinction—of dunking the Eucharistic Host (i.e., the consecrated wafer) into the chalice, or into a specially-provided 'dipping chalice', rather than sipping from the common cup—in response to so-called health needs.[142] In that same former parish, up to three-quarters of parishioners were eventually receiving communion in this way—including most children, who had been taught by their parents to receive by intinction contrary to how I had prepared them for their First Communion. Likewise, I regularly see Broad-Church clergy communicating by intinction, even if as president of the Eucharist I have been the only one to receive the chalice before them. Where is the devotion, recollection and reverential awe of earlier Catholic discipline in receiving the Blessed Sacrament, such that what was once known as the medicine of immortality can nowadays primarily be viewed as a health risk? Thus, we see the spirit of 'Let all mortal flesh keep silence' turning into 'keep that thing away from my child'.

I daresay that personal, inward communion with God is the primary reality here and the Anglo-Catholic's proper reverence for Christ's real presence in the sacrament means little or nothing. My chief concern with the practice of intinction, however, is that it has anti-ecclesial as well as anti-Eucharistic overtones. I fear that preferring intinction not only involves seeing the common cup as an imposition rather than a blessing but also the fellow Christians with whom it is shared. Rather than providing the context for our Christian belonging and, indeed, our salvation, the Eucharist and its elements are thus made subject to the sovereign, choosing, modern individual will, much as any other consumer product. I have been known to tell congregations that 'the Communion Host is not a "Scotch Finger" biscuit that you dip in your tea', though with little discernible change to communion practice ensuing.

---

[142] (Author's Note: this was written long before COVID-19 and the quite proper restrictions on use of the chalice that were imposed in response, including giving communion in one kind only or—in places that way inclined—by using individual cups.)

Fresh expressions

A further vignette has to do with the latest fruit of our institutional anxiety in contemporary Anglicanism, the Emerging Church movement and its fresh expressions of worship. The missionary, Eucharistic Church has always reached out to win converts for Christ and has incorporated new believers into the Eucharistic community through catechumenal formation and subsequent baptism with the laying on of episcopal hands in confirmation. Today, however, a variety of new ways of doing church commend themselves to increasingly managerial bishops.

The pastoral and missional worth of new, so-called church plants aside, I am concerned when new Christian groups emerging from special interest gatherings of youth, young mothers, students, immigrants, etc., are kept practically and in fact structurally isolated from the parish church and from other Christians who abide locally. These fresh expressions are regularly viewed as new churches in their own right, though they may not involve the Eucharist.

I have guarded sympathy for 'Messy Church', for instance, designed to welcome parents with young children into a maximally child-friendly gathering based on play and craft with a biblical theme, including hospitality and prayer. One of my most talented former students is using Messy Church to help renew her parish in the Diocese of Grafton, though she views it as a steppingstone to people joining the Eucharistic community (i.e., as a form of pre-evangelism) rather than an alternative to joining that community, since it is not obviously a type of gathering amenable to the Eucharist. Unless, of course, it is a 'Messy Eucharist'. Which means, what?—that it is friendly, fun, inclusive, not typically boring and 'churchy'; or might it also mean that soft drink and cake are served along with the more predictable Eucharistic elements?

So, if we are to have the Eucharist, must it be 'Eucharist plus', offering inducements that will give things a lift? Though, as mentioned earlier, a version of this same attitude is also found among Anglo-Catholics when they insist on glorious music and the perfection of ceremonial if the Eucharist is to be tolerable—on obsessive compulsive church, if you like, rather than messy church.

Eucharist before baptism

The final vignette that I offer has to do with what for me is a worrying Episcopalian trend that is finding its way into Australian Anglicanism of every stripe—though, admittedly, it is most typically found in the broad middle of our Church. I refer to the belief that restricting Holy Communion to the baptised, let alone to the confirmed or to others who have been officially admitted to Holy Communion, represents an intolerable example of un-Christlike exclusion. On occasions where a lot of unfamiliar faces are present, this approach leads to invitations from the priest such as 'this is the Lord's table, anyone who desires God's mercy is welcome', where once we said something like, 'baptised communicant members of whichever Christian Church are welcome to receive communion today'—which is what I still say. The Eucharist is certainly valued according to the newer view, along with its role in making the Church a welcoming fellowship. The significance of baptism is not necessarily being questioned, either, though Christian initiation is being seen as a ritual of commitment that comes later, once a person has been drawn to Christ through the Church and its Eucharistic fellowship. Nevertheless, I have serious misgivings.

One example of this approach is an Episcopalian church like no other in San Francisco called St Gregory of Nyssa.[143] A lively and diverse congregation gathers at St Gregory's in a dedicated place for hearing the word, for prayer, preaching and the sharing of stories.

---

[143] Visit https://www.saintgregorys.org for the full picture (last accessed August 2022).

The Eucharist Makes the Church (2013)

They then do a special dance together to encircle the altar, which is right by the main door, whereupon all join together with the presiding priest in reciting the whole consecration prayer. After Mass, the congregation remains where it is and coffee is brought out immediately to the altar, from which it is served. During the week, the local poor and homeless are generously fed in the same worship rotunda, including use of its altar, whereby Christ's radical call to hospitality and sharing is certainly given concrete expression. One of the lay leaders at St Gregory's, Sara Miles, has written a book about her conversion to Christ through the generosity of this place, called *Take This Bread: A Radical Conversion*.[144] Her baptism, in a font situated in an attractive space outside the church, followed after a further time of preparation and was very meaningful for her.

I do not doubt that God is at work in whichever order we do things, though I am concerned when baptism is seen as a barrier to inclusion rather than the richest blessing of inclusion, and when sharing in Christ through Holy Communion is not preceded by the renunciation of our former sinful life and by our public embrace of the cross in baptism. There is togetherness expressed here, certainly, but it risks becoming a form of togetherness minus the cross of Christ, as English Catholic theologian James Alison warns.[145] No celebration of natural belonging is ever reliably free from groupthink and herd behaviour, unless it is leavened by the costly and transformative encounter with Christ that baptism represents, which the Eucharist goes on to celebrate and cement—a form of belonging beyond what comes naturally, if you like.

The actual state of our Church membership today, with its spectrum of beliefs, stages of Christian maturity and hence levels of 'convertedness' present in the same gathering, can make the logic of restricting communion to the already initiated hard to

---

[144] Sara Miles, *Take This Bread: A Radical Conversion* (New York: Ballantine, 2007).
[145] James Alison, *Broken Hearts and New Creations: Intimations of a Great Reversal* (London and New York: Continuum, 2010), 87-88.

justify. It would have been much easier when slaves, Roman soldiers, prostitutes and tax collectors were quite obviously being brought from darkness into light through baptism during the three centuries before Christianity became the Roman Empire's official and respectable religion. It seems incongruous not to offer communion to a potential spiritual seeker who turns up one day while those who happen to have undergone infant baptism yet rarely attend receive communion with no questions asked. But the answer surely lies in calling all of us to a higher standard rather than swelling the ranks of half-converted worshippers by carelessly admitting new ones unprepared.

A better welcome before baptism would be provided by taking the trouble to meet and befriend newcomers, with an appropriate regular process in place to gently but intentionally lead them on a journey of increasing familiarity. This would involve mentoring, habituation to worship, and opportunities to discuss faith and life matters that are open to the newcomer's questions. The significantly lay-led Catechumenal process is ideal for this, though a regular friendship and exploration group for newcomers would be a good start. Involvement in such conversations and relationships can stretch the regular congregation members who take part with the priest. It creates the remarkable situation in which ordinary Anglican parishioners actually talk together about 'religion'. But this requires some organisation and pastoral effort from the priest, unlike simply inviting everyone to receive Holy Communion holus bolus and making out that this represents inclusion and welcome.

A venerable alternative

What I am advocating is that we come to understand Church and Eucharist as hardware, not software, even though this possibility will sound odd to contemporary ears. Further, I want to re-establish the early Christian expectation that Eucharistic gatherings constitute and define the Church, rather than representing some sort of afterthought or optional extra to Christian believing and belonging. This primacy of the Church for the Christian life and the Eucharist for the Church's life is what we find among the New Testament churches and in the undivided Catholic Church of East and West during the first Christian millennium, before a number of philosophical, social and political changes in the Late Middle Ages began to undo this organic, Eucharistic bonding of life in the Western Church. I sketch this much more foundational vision of Church and Eucharist for the Christian life in what follows, along with its decline, then offer some reflections on where we see signs of its revival throughout history and again today.

The body of Christ in the New Testament: an integral vision

Our conception of Christ's body has become less integral than that of the New Testament churches. This may not seem obvious, given Protestant emphasis on New Testament texts and teachings above Catholic and Orthodox emphasis on the Eucharist and its cult of worship—the so-called externals of religion—which are deemed to be relatively less important than the word (hardware and software again). Yet the Eucharist lies at the heart of Christian self-understanding according to a range of New Testament witnesses.

I begin with Paul, chronologically the first New Testament writer, and his multivalent image of Christ's Body. From Paul to late-medieval Christianity, the body of Christ referred to Jesus himself, but also to the Church as his body, as well as to his body distributed in the Eucharist itself. This rich and complex image broke down, as we shall see, introducing a split into Christian imagination between Christ and his Church, and between the Church and its Eucharist. We have been considering some contemporary manifestations of that imaginative split in the different expressions of Anglicanism today.

Paul's key insights here are found in 1 Corinthians 11-13. His main teaching on the organic body of Christians with Christ as its head is in 1 Corinthians 12, while the love needed to bind that body together is memorably set out in 1 Corinthians 13, as every attendee at Anglican weddings will have heard. But the nub of it is in 1 Corinthians 11, where Paul talks about the tradition of Eucharistic worship—handed down to his first-generation Church from Christ at the last supper—as actually forming the Church. Hospitable sharing rather than self-indulgent and distracted banqueting is commended, and an end to the cliqueyness that this represents, with those who neglect the lesser members of Christ's body at the Eucharistic meal warned that 'all who eat and drink without discerning the body, eat and drink damnation against themselves' (1 Corinthians 11:29).

Now, which 'body' is referred to here? Certainly the Church as Christ's body, which we neglect by preferring our own clique and our own prerogatives over respect for fellow Christians who may differ from our preferred norm, but also surely the Lord himself in the faces of other Christians—and why not the Lord himself in the Eucharistic elements, too, who Paul recalls as having said, 'this is my body that is for you'; 'This is the new covenant in my blood' (1 Corinthians 11:24-25)? Paul makes no meaningful distinction between these interwoven uses, nor did the ancient Church Fathers in the subsequent age of the creeds, nor indeed were they separated throughout the whole first Christian millennium.

In the first written Gospel, from the next stage of Christian sacred writing after Paul's letters, Mark gives us a more compact account than Matthew and Luke did in their subsequent elaborations of Mark's text. But at the heart of this earliest Gospel, in Mark 8, well before the climactic last supper is set out in Mark 14, we find a Eucharistic narrative about the nature of Christ's Church in the multiplication of the loaves, also that single loaf which the troubled disciples in their boat were told by Jesus would be sufficient. Here, as throughout the Gospels, we are dealing with

The Eucharist Makes the Church (2013)

experiences of the earliest churches that have been written back into the story of Jesus with his disciples. The miraculous feeding with manna in the wilderness, which sustained Israel in its desert journey, is here repeated by Jesus, the new Moses, in the midst of his Church, the new Israel. Later in the boat, Jesus remonstrates with his disciples over their failure to understand that the one loaf in their midst is sufficient, because from such a loaf Jesus feeds a multitude (Mark 8:16-21). The Church in our own time has also failed to understand Christ's sustaining presence in our midst through the Eucharist that makes the Church.

Jesus contrasts this bread with the yeast of the Pharisees and Herod (Mark 8:15), which, of course, refers to the violence and exclusion directed towards Jesus himself and subsequently towards his Church in many places. This juxtaposition is made more explicit in Matthew's version. Matthew 14 gives us Herod's horrific banquet, at which the head of John the Baptist is served up on a platter, as a counterfoil to Jesus' feeding of the multitude that follows. Thus, Matthew gives us an engaging image of the coming Kingdom of God, showing how the Church and its Eucharistic logic differs from the sort of uneasy and often violent togetherness that the world offers, symbolised by Herod's banquet. Luke does not give us the feeding of the multitude, but from the middle of Luke 11 and through Chapter 12 he does give us Jesus' teaching about the violently maintained boundaries of the older religion, set against the alternative that fearless insidership in Jesus' resurrected body can bring.

In the Book of Revelation, that great and inscrutable testimony to the triumph of Jesus and his Church, we should note that the angels and saints, gathered around the heavenly throne of God and the slain lamb (e.g., Revelation 5:6-14; 7:13-17; 19:1-8), recall the liturgical gatherings of early Christians around the bishop and the altar at the Easter Eucharist, with the newly baptised catechumens robed in white. Indeed, as American Catholic theologian Paul McPartlan points out, the key to the Book of Revelation is provided by the fact that the troubled seer in exile on Patmos has his vision splendid when he is 'in the spirit on the Lord's day' (Revelation 1:10), the day of the Eucharist, which places his vision of the triumphant Church in a Eucharistic context.[146]

In Hebrews 12:18-24, we have a similar word of encouragement to the persecuted Church,[147] in which again the sort of religious togetherness that ultimately has blood on its hands is contrasted with the new creation in Jesus Christ. Right after mention of the Godless Esau, who sold his birthright for the wrong sort of meal, we have an extraordinary image of the right sort of meal, with heaven opened and God's new creation on full view. The point is that together in Christ, in the Eucharist, we the baptised are participating in nothing less than a new and different way of doing the world and re-imagining its future. It is one of the most imaginative and stirring passages in the New Testament and deserves to be quoted in full, recalling that this is a Eucharistic gathering with Christ present in the midst of a new humanity.

> You have not come to something that can be touched, a blazing fire, and darkness, and gloom, and a tempest, and the sound of a trumpet, and a voice whose words made the hearers beg that not another word be spoken to them. (For they could not endure the order that was given, 'If even an animal touches the mountain, it shall be stoned to death.' Indeed, so terrifying was the sight that Moses said, 'I tremble with fear.') But you have come to Mount Zion and to the city of the living God, the heavenly Jerusalem, and to innumerable angels in festal gathering, and to the assembly of the firstborn who are enrolled in heaven, and to God the judge of all, and to the spirits of the righteous made perfect, and to Jesus, the mediator of a new covenant,

---

[146] Paul McPartlan, *Sacrament of Salvation: An Introduction to Eucharistic Ecclesiology* (Edinburgh: T&T Clark, 1995), 9.
[147] McPartlan, *Sacrament of Salvation*, 4.

and to the sprinkled blood that speaks a better word than the blood of Abel.

I mention three other examples, from the third and fourth Gospels, that demonstrate the weaving together of Christ himself and the Eucharist in the formation of his Church. Luke offers us the road to Emmaus narrative, in which the risen Lord prepares his disciples' minds by expounding the Scriptures, though they only recognise him in the breaking of the bread. That encounter provides them with the impetus to return to Jerusalem where their Eucharistic discovery shared with others contributes to the birth of resurrection faith (Luke 24:13-35). John's Church begins in the upper room of the last supper on the day of the resurrection, where the Spirit is poured out (John 20:19-23). John 21 gives us a meal by the shore where the bread and fish, which are given by the risen Jesus to his disciples, are widely recognised to be Eucharistic signs, tied to the disciples' miraculous draft of fish which represents the Church's mission.

In these New Testament vignettes, Christ himself present in the Eucharist constitutes the Church as his body—as a new version of humanity, empowered for a world-transforming mission. There is no sense in which the Eucharistic gathering is any less central and formative an encounter with Christ than the equally important beliefs, writings, prayer and fellowship of his disciples that are also mentioned, which many Protestants would regard as more significant. Paul McPartlan puts these elements in chronological perspective.

> Week in, week out, Christians gathered in local communities to celebrate their faith in Christ our Saviour. They had not yet finalised the formal creed to express that faith in words; they were still exploring it in worship. They had not yet even finally decided which books should be included in the Bible and honoured as truly inspired. That did not happen until the year 382, in the time of Pope Damasus ... when a

council in Rome gave a complete listing. All of these things were still to come, but the weekly rhythm of the Eucharist in the local churches was already beating, underpinning the Church's developing life.[148]

Sundering the body of Christ

The Church of the first Christian millennium, from the New Testament period then on through and beyond the age of Fathers and official creeds, was a Church of contrasts and conflicts yet it retained significant spiritual and structural bonds. Early struggles with heretical teachings and schismatic movements led necessarily to the tightening of doctrine, discipline, worship and the structures of ministry, including an important emerging role for communion with the Bishop of Rome that demonstrated one's desire to stay with the whole body of Christ, even in dispute. East and West were still part of the one Church, though very different historical forces in the Eastern and Western Empires of Constantinople and Rome led to the divergence of two increasingly different visions of Church and Eucharist that eventually split in the eleventh century. Still, the local Church remained at the heart of Christian imagination, expressed structurally in the diocese gathered around its bishop. The communion of dioceses together, manifest in the various councils of bishops, such as the most famous one at Nicaea in the year 325, represented something more organic than a mere federation, though the universal Church was inconceivable apart from its expression in the local Church. Maintaining orthodox faith in Christ in communion with your bishop meant sharing in the one Eucharist—and indeed there was only one Eucharist, the bishop's Eucharist, before larger dioceses and the parish system with a resident priest in each locality became a necessary

---

[148] McPartlan, *Sacrament of Salvation*, 34.

The Eucharist Makes the Church (2013)

development from the fourth century, when the whole Empire became officially Christian.

In sum, it was a Church that had not yet divided by mutual excommunication into Roman and Eastern, let alone Protestant strands; it was a spiritual fellowship between Christians and God 'in contrast to juridical approaches that over-emphasise the institutional and legal aspects of the Church', as American lay Catholic theologian Dennis M. Doyle explains, going on to describe a Church that 'places a high value on the need for visible unity as symbolically realised through shared participation in the Eucharist' and which 'promotes a dynamic and healthy interplay between unity and diversity... between the Church universal and the local churches'.[149]

Our Christian story in today's West emerges from the collapse of this vision along the trajectory of Roman Catholic and then Protestant or else Anglican denominationalism. A number of related factors led to the Western Catholic Church becoming progressively institutionalised, centralised, hierarchicalised, and its Eucharistic ministries bureaucratised from the Early Middle Ages. Here are some of the most important ones.[150]

The return of imperial rule in the West, after the Dark Ages, came in the ninth century when Charlemagne became Holy Roman Emperor, setting the scene for power struggles between Pope and Emperor over the control of Europe. These included the Investiture Controversy, about who had the right to appoint clergy and bishops, leading to the Gregorian reforms that centralised papal rule in the eleventh century. Such struggles, as necessary as

---

[149] Dennis M. Doyle, *Communion Ecclesiology: Visions and Versions* (Maryknoll, NY.: Orbis, 2000), 13.
[150] I am grateful here to the discussion in Richard R. Gaillardetz, *Ecclesiology for a Global Church: A People Called and Sent* (Theology in Global Perspective. Maryknoll, NY.: Orbis, 2008), 94-99.

they were, made the Church more a worldly centre of power and less of a Eucharistic fellowship rooted in spiritual communion.

Another ninth-century development saw a breakdown in the significant conjunction of first-millennium themes around the concept 'body of Christ'. As we have seen, this multivalent image linked Christ himself with his Eucharistic body and his ecclesial body in a very integral and participatory way. But with the Eucharistic theology of Paschasius Radbertus in the ninth century and Berengar of Tours in the eleventh, the long-accepted sense of Christ's body present in the Eucharistic bread and wine became *more physical and objective*. As a result, the laity actually receiving Holy Communion in the Eucharist became rarer. It was regarded as less significant than viewing the Body of Christ lifted up by the priest at the elevation, with the practice of regular reception of communion proving harder to sustain. Attempts to reassert the spiritual dimension of Holy Communion led to compromise under Lanfranc and Thomas Aquinas whereby the bread and wine were understood to change objectively, though by a process that they declined to over-specify called *transubstantiation*. This new objective emphasis on the Eucharistic elements apart from their faithful reception continued to grow in Roman Catholicism. In *Unam Sanctam* (1302), Pope Boniface VIII formally distinguished between Christ's 'true body' in the Eucharist and his 'mystical body' in the Church. The Eucharist thus became an end in itself—a mystery to be lived ecclesially became a miracle to be believed in.[151]

A further development, from the twelfth century under the influence of Gratian, saw the rise of canon law modelled on Roman law to a position of dominance in church life. It was not long before popes were chosen from among canon lawyers rather than monks, theologians and pastors as formerly. A Church of integral

---

[151] McPartlan, *Sacrament of Salvation*, 37-38 (using an image drawn from Henri de Lubac).

Eucharistic belonging was becoming instead the institutional arena in which Christ's body was displayed in Eucharistic form before an increasingly passive laity, literally making a spectacle of society's new power relations.[152] The Eucharistic cult of the Late Middle Ages, with its non-communicating High Masses, and its exposition of the Blessed Sacrament to bless crops and ensure the fertility of livestock while warding off plagues and disasters, served the same purpose for God and the Church that the spectacle of public executions later served for exhibiting Royal power, as memorably set out by Michel Foucault at the start of his classic *Discipline and Punish*.[153]

A related factor was the decline of Christian Neoplatonism. This development of Plato's philosophy later manifested itself politically in a feudalistic view of society, with being and authority devolving from God down a great chain of being to the lowest orders—linking society together, if you like, from above through within. In the Late Middle Ages, Neoplatonism yielded to Nominalist philosophy. Grand idealistic schemes of being, its categories and its distribution gave way to a more individualistic conception of each thing and each person. Here we find the necessary shift that enabled modern science to get going, as attention began to focus on things in themselves rather than speculation about their abstract natures. These abstract natures, in particular the Platonic forms, came to be seen merely as names—*nomina*. A new metaphysics usually accompanies a new political philosophy, and this Nominalist worldview supported individualism. The sovereign emerged with a more nakedly independent power out

---

[152] Catherine Pickstock, *After Writing: On the Liturgical Consummation of Philosophy* (Oxford: Blackwell, 1998), 140-64. On what he interprets as a curse of legalism in Western Catholicism that was inherited from Roman law, and its implications for the body of Christ, see also Arthur Michael Ramsey, *The Gospel and the Catholic Church* (London: Longman, Green and Co., 1936), 165-70.

[153] Michel Foucault, *Discipline and Punish: The Birth of the Prison*, trans. Alan Sheridan (London: Penguin, 1977), 3-31.

of the feudal nexus of belonging that had linked kings to nobles to peasants—and bishops to clergy to laity—in the great chain of being.

It was in this climate that democracy advocates like John of Paris and Marsilius of Padua challenged monarchy, while canon lawyers started talking about the Church primarily in terms of individuals linked to Christ rather than the mutual abiding in Christ and in each other that had been typical of first-millennium views on Church and Eucharist. The communion of churches familiar from the first millennium thus became a corporation of believers, in a view of the Church that retains widespread currency to this day. The Anglican *Book of Common Prayer* with its definition of the Catholic Church as 'the blessed company of all faithful people' represents this thinking, which characterised the Protestant Reformation. As the great mid-twentieth century Catholic theologian, Cardinal Henri de Lubac, concludes, 'Having stripped it of all its mystical attributes, [Protestantism] acknowledged in the visible Church a mere secular institution; as a matter of course it abandoned it to the patronage of the state and sought refuge for the spiritual life in an invisible Church, its concept of which it had evaporated into an abstract ideal'.[154]

And hence to our familiar modern world, in which the welcome blessings of democracy and freedom, science, bureaucratic expertise, and what the French call *laïcité*, none of which we would necessarily want to do without, come at the expense of imaginatively sundering Christ from his Eucharist and from his Church. These—the Eucharist and the Church—have now become things that we opt into or out of, rather than the very nexus in which our identity as Christians is grounded.

---

[154] Henri de Lubac, *Catholicism: Christ and the Common Destiny of Man* (1947), trans. Lancelot C. Shepherd and Sister Elizabeth Englund, OCD (Tunbridge Wells: Burns and Oates, 1950), 75-76.

Re-weaving the body of Christ in our time

One effect of the sixteenth-century Reformation was that Protestantism became defined by an anti-Catholic animus, while the anti-Protestant bias of militant Roman Catholicism returned the favour, from the Council of Trent onward. The relatively High-Church Anglicanism of Richard Hooker, the great apologist of the Elizabethan settlement, was neither Puritan nor papist, however, and it restored key elements of the early undivided Church, including its reverence for the Eucharist as something participated in rather than objectively displayed.[155]

Only with the mid-twentieth-century *nouvelle théologie* of Henri de Lubac,[156] which recovered the ancient roots of Catholic tradition beneath many later accretions—along with Roman Catholic reawakening to the Bible in preaching and scholarship, also the recovery of a whole people of God and body of Christ view of the Church thanks to ecumenically-minded theologians like Hans Küng[157]—did Roman Catholicism begin to recover some of the earlier holistic wisdom that was being obscured by its reactionary, anti-modern and anti-secular currents.

The Second Vatican Council in the 1960s cemented these healthier trends,[158] recovering the Eucharist as an organic, participatory event rather than a spectacle of ecclesial power only infrequently accompanied by lay reception of communion. The laity had been used to bringing private devotions such as the Rosary to Mass,

---

[155] Richard Hooker, *Of the Lawes of Ecclesiastical Politie* (Books 1-4 published in 1593; Book 5 in 1597) (London: J.M. Dent & Sons, 1907, in 2 vols).
[156] See de Lubac, *Catholicism*.
[157] Hans Küng, *The Church* (1967), trans. Ray and Rosaleen Ockenden (London and Tunbridge Wells: Search Press, 1968).
[158] See especially the Vatican II document *Lumen Gentium*, 'Dogmatic Constitution on the Church', online at http://www.vatican.va/archive/hist_councils/ii _vatican_council/documents/vat-ii_const_19641121_lumen-gentium_en.html (last accessed August 2016).

rather than participating fully in the liturgy as has become the expectation more recently.

In the hands of Edward Schillebeeckx,[159] in tune with the earlier Anglican theologian O.C. Quick[160] and followed later by John Macquarrie,[161] Christ himself came to be seen as sacramental and the Church by extension, so that its sacraments, especially the Eucharist, became key manifestations of the Church's being rather than performances and services delivered by the agents of a bureaucratic institution.

The Liturgical Movement of the mid-twentieth century, and its Anglican version the so-called Parish Communion Movement, or else the Parish and People Movement, ensured that the Anglican and Roman Catholic norm is now a community Eucharist around the altar in a purpose-built building using a rite that draws us far more closely together, and closer to the worship of our early Christians forebears, than has ever been the case. The ecumenical movement, too, is returning us to this communal ecclesiology, with even mainstream Protestantism increasingly offering a weekly Sunday Eucharist. Our various denominational structures must now demonstrate that they can foster such a communal ecclesiology if they are to be theologically and spiritually credible.

In many places, the Church's worship, theological education and missional rhetoric is recovering the ancient simplicity of abiding in Christ's Body, now that Christendom is a thing of the past and that being Christian is no longer identified with respectability and good citizenship. Our Church's big challenge

---

[159] Edward Schillebeeckx, *Christ the Sacrament of Encounter with God* (London: Sheed and Ward, 1963); *The Eucharist*, trans. N.D. Smith (London: Sheed and Ward, 1968).
[160] O.C. Quick, *The Christian Sacraments* (London: Nesbit, 1927), 105.
[161] John Macquarrie, *A Guide to the Sacraments* (London: SCM Press, 1997), Chapter 4: 'Christ as the Primordial Sacrament', 34-44.

today is to take this vision so seriously that our Eucharistic community truly manifests Christ's Body in the world, as a desperately needed alternative to consumerism and to a worsening global culture of dog eat dog.

10

The Church of the Apostles, Seattle (2013)

> *Having included a piece about fresh expressions of Church earlier in this volume, conveying guarded enthusiasm and naming some concerns, here is my reflection on one fresh expression about which I am entirely enthusiastic and have no concerns. It proves that everything I regard as important in ecclesial and Eucharistic belonging can find striking contemporary expression, in a way that attracts and wins over the young. I am also pleased to include it as proof that I do not pine for the old fashioned. Commitment to the Church and liturgical tradition can return as a powerful postmodern option that by no means represents a nostalgic or reactionary retreat. This little piece was posted on a regular blog, called 'From the Canon Theologian' which I used to write for our diocesan website during the episcopate of Bishop Stuart Robinson.*

One of the good things about travel is the chance to visit art galleries and see 'in the flesh' the great paintings that you have only known as reproductions in art books. The same applies to churches. On a recent trip to the United States, I was able to look in on some magnificent modern church buildings, as well as worship with a variety of impressive faith communities. On the West coast, I was delighted to revisit the inspiring Roman Catholic Cathedral of the Angels in Los Angeles, also spending time in the fine Chapel of St Ignatius at Seattle University. Here are newly minted Catholic worship spaces where ancient and

The Church of the Apostles, Seattle (2013)

modern themes cohere beautifully and movingly. Surely, modern church architecture and the reordering of older church buildings enlivened by the best, most up-to-date liturgical thinking about our ancient faith is something that Australian Anglicanism needs to be more involved in.

But my most memorable visit was to a community rather than a building, though the worship space and the liturgy they created were conceived with the same gospel intelligence for manifesting ancient faith in a contemporary context. I refer to COTA in Seattle, the Church of the Apostles, which is an eleven-year old joint Episcopalian-Lutheran congregation (the Episcopal Church and the Evangelical Lutheran Church—not the conservative, Missouri Synod Lutheran alternative—are in full communion, which allows mutual recognition of ministries, joint ordinations, Eucharistic hospitality, etc.).

COTA meets in a rambling urban space called Fremont Abbey, though we attended in high summer when numbers were down and the 5.00pm Sunday Eucharist was being held in the basement, where it is cooler. Here is church for the urban species, as one of their music CDs refers to the largely Millennial congregation—though there were older people present, including a few aging hippy types. The vibe was funky West coast grunge, but nothing über-cool or affected. COTA felt like the real thing. Let me tell you about this moving and engaging act of worship.

A dark space was lit by a wide scattering of candles, clusters of which marked out various points of focus. There was a Eucharistic table covered with a woven green cloth, a draped lectern for reading and preaching, and a prayer station off to the side with a half life-sized icon crucifix propped up among comfortable cushions for kneeling or sitting cross-legged in front of it. The music group was on one side and the *son et lumière* guys were busy throughout on the other. The wall behind the altar was a screen on which graphics were projected, including labelled sections of the liturgy, words for songs, and the dictionary definition of a potentially unfamiliar reference from one of the Bible readings (in this case, to a plumb line—apparently not a familiar concept to Millennials). An older lay woman with beads and long grey hair preached. Self-described as a social activist, she connected the Old Testament and Gospel readings from the lectionary with the progressive social agenda of this inclusive, inner-urban community. That said, it was a far 'whiter' gathering than I had seen elsewhere in America, compared with some Anglican Cathedrals I visited (for instance, the entirely multi-racial congregation at the Episcopal Cathedral of St John in Los Angeles).

COTA's music is distinctive, drawn in part from other contemporary ancient-future churches like the Scottish Late Late Service. I noticed that they follow the Lutheran custom of sitting for the hymns. The quality of the music was outstanding: meditative in tone, personal in focus and intended to be transforming. KJ, the young female music director, sang and played like an angel. Her music was hip but not self-consciously so—a bit like Taizé, and a bit like Roman Catholic liturgical music drawn from contemporary monastic sources. There was a CD for sale of Morning and Evening prayer settings in the house style, to assist people in praying the offices at home or during their daily commute.

This is a seriously prayerful church. Indeed, in the middle of the Eucharist, there is a segment called 'Open Space' during which people are invited to have eight minutes of time out. You can sit and listen to the music, pray before the icon crucifix in its dedicated corner, place a lighted prayer candle in a sand tray, or go upstairs to walk a prayer labyrinth.

There was a barbecue dinner to follow, with the food brought forward at the offertory and placed on the altar. Ivar Hillesland, the Pastor, was in his shorts and thongs, as it was a very hot night,

The Church of the Apostles, Seattle (2013)

but he put on a priest's stole for the Great Thanksgiving.[162] The Eucharistic Prayer he used was unfamiliar to me, but it was as sonorous and dignified as it was contemporary in language and imagery. Ivar's manner at the altar was devout and recollected. There was a sense of occasion about this celebration, though nothing theatrical. The Eucharistic bread and wine tasted really good. Notices given out before the final blessing included an invitation for anyone who was interested to gather for meals over two nights at someone's house to design COTA's new logo.

Seattle has been called the 'none zone', where more people per capita put 'none' in surveys about their religious affiliation than anywhere else in America. It is also a potentially depressing place—regularly cold, grey, wet and blighted with a high youth suicide rate. Young people gravitate to Seattle, where a few make IT fortunes while many others struggle to find their way. In the midst of this, COTA is a sign of hope and orientation. It stands for gospel vibrancy, culturally savvy excellence in worship, traditional scriptural and sacramental life in a fresh context, multi-generational community, and an ecumenical vision that honours past traditions in thoughtful engagement with the present. There is a sense that these traditions are inhabited and owned at COTA, rather than representing merely a buffet of options into which people might dip while their *raison d'être* comes from elsewhere (therapeutic individualism, for instance).

Visiting COTA was great for me. I found an authentic fresh expression, exhibiting an 'Evangelical Catholicism' that managed to combine doctrinal orthodoxy with something youthful, authentic and edgy. Our Church has a future because Jesus Christ and his gospel have a future. All praise to COTA in Seattle for demonstrating that our ancient faith is fit to sustain the future Church.

---

[162] See more details online at https://www.apostleschurch.org/about (last accessed July 2022) (Author's Note: as at July 2022, Ivar was still the Pastor at COTA.)

11

Two Cheers for the Parish (2015)

> *This previously unpublished piece was a lecture given at St James the Less Anglican Church, Mount Eliza, Victoria, on 13 October 2015, arranged by the then Vicar, Fr Shane Hubner. I presented a theological vision of parish life, against a range of sub-optimal current alternatives. There was a push against traditional worship in the parish at the time, which I wanted to challenge. I took the opportunity to reiterate my recurring theme: that the Church is a particular sort of thing, with a well-established* raison d'être, *and it is not for us to turn it into something else.*

I have been asked to speak about the parish style of Christian community and its future, because, of course, parishes face a lot of challenges today. Still, I believe in the parish way of being Church: two cheers for it, I say. I will tell you why I think two cheers are appropriate, and what might turn my confidence into a full-throated three cheers. To set the scene for my reflections, let me tell you about a day out that my wife and I had a few months ago in Houston, Texas, when we visited two very different chapels.

Houston, we have a problem

The first was the Rothko Chapel, famous among modern art enthusiasts.[163] Mark Rothko, the mid-20th century minimalist

---
[163] Online at http://www.rothkochapel.org (last accessed August 2022).

Two Cheers for the Parish (2015)

painter, was noted for his large canvasses containing no representation at all—just large dark surfaces, differently shaded borders, and varied textural finishes. In the silent, spare, empty octagonal space of the chapel—non-denominational of course—big Rothko paintings occupy all the walls, catching the shifting sunlight from skylights above. As you sit quietly, the mood changes with the paintings, which sometimes appear flat and expressionless and sometimes glowing. They are intended to evoke something sublime, but beyond any sort of representation at all. These are religious paintings for a spirituality without content or doctrine—only mystery, and a sense of bare transcendence suggesting itself to the patient and attentive.

Mark Rothko speaks for a typical modern experience, albeit one with several manifestations. People today are not typically crass materialists or purely hedonistic pleasure seekers, as some churchmen suggest. Many ordinary people claim a sense of there being more to life than can be weighed or measured. They find it in music and dance, in exhilarating sport and risky outdoor adventure, in love and sex and friendship, in being creative and in celebrating the creativity of others. It's found, too, in the ethical demands that so many ordinary decent people stick fast to, and where would we be without them?

Some people try to access this sense of mystery and transcendence through the spiritual practices that are available to us nowadays from many religions, while most seem content to sense the mystery and to honour it by living as well as they can. The limiting case of this modern sensibility is on show at the Rothko Chapel in its leafy Houston suburb.

A short walk from the Rothko Chapel is St Thomas' University, a Catholic college run by a religious order called the Basilian Fathers. On their campus is an architectural masterpiece called the Chapel of St Basil.[164] It's like a big white concrete tent with a

---

[164] A Google search will reveal many striking images.

Greek-looking golden dome. You go in through an open flap, and inside it's all modern. But there are still the familiar markers of the people of God gathering to share and continue a story and a journey together. There is the font, where human life stories become stories of God with us. There is the altar, where God with us takes shape in the midst of God's people. And there is the place of the word, with the Scriptures open to summon God's people in their journey of knowing, loving and being converted. There are the pews where God's people take their place by right in a community at once divine and human, with statues to remind them of the saints who stand with God's people in the Eucharist: St Basil, and, of course, the Blessed Virgin Mary. On the wall are modern stations of the cross, to draw the imagination beyond the self and into the mystery of God as Christ has embodied that mystery plain to see. There is deep silence, and mystery, as in the Rothko Chapel, but in the Chapel of St Basil it is a storied silence, and an embodied mystery—the sublime is not without representation.

Also nearby is one of America's great museums of modern art, the Menil Collection, and there in a gallery of surrealists I saw a painting that helped me appreciate the difference between those two chapels that had been playing on my mind. It was by Giorgio de Chirico, he of the mysterious statues with their wrong-way shadows, and a spooky sense of something hidden. The picture was called 'Metaphysical Interior with Biscuits', with various abstract objects in the background and a box of biscuits open in the foreground.[165] The artist was playing off the mysterious and the un-representable against the recognisable and the everyday, and I immediately thought of the Eucharist, where the depth of divine mystery is reliably pressed into our hands Sunday by Sunday.

---

[165] Online at : https://www.menil.org/collection/objects/4296-metaphysical-interior-with-biscuits-interno-metafisico-con-biscotti (last accessed August 2022).

Here was the difference between those two chapels: in one the mystery is evoked, but in the other the mystery is present, and it is represented, though of course never exhausted. We Christians with our parishes, our churches, our worship gatherings and our sacraments are in touch with the mystery in a way that is accessible and transformative. We have the metaphysical interior, but we also have the biscuits. My point is that for all the sublimity, mystery and obligation that many modern Westerners feel and acknowledge, which the Church ought to respect, nevertheless in Jesus Christ, in his sacraments and in his Church, what is unnamed and unfocused becomes communal and urgent. And it is this reality that issues in the stable, habitual dynamics of parish life. Can we hold onto it, or are we in danger of losing it? And if so, what might help us get it back?

Are we capable of parish life anymore?

I have mentioned the unfocused sense of transcendence that many people have, though the Church claims more than this. But, of course, many Christians in our pews are not so different from the wider public, though perhaps they value the reassuring mood that churchgoing provides, along with friendship and support. The Church is something attended in response to habit or perhaps in search of something missing in life, but it is rarer for our people to say confidently that they *are* the Church, and that through the parish and its worship they come to know the living God.

Long experience of a lukewarm Church in the era of Christendom, when the institutional Church was caught up in the Empire, the Nation State and their agendas, led some saints to distinguish an invisible Church from the visible Church. Eventually, in the modern West, a private Christian life with God but separate from the gathered sacramental fellowship of Christians became conceivable, and such an understanding of being Christian is now widespread.

Even churchgoers can separate the most important aspects of life with God from the regular habits of worship together, without taking the corporate reality of Christian life as seriously as God takes it. Which reminds me of St Paul's warning, in 1 Corinthians 11, about the dangers of eating and drinking the body and blood of Christ together without discerning the body, and how the health of the Church is badly affected by this failure. The widespread malaise in our local fellowships is perhaps the result of this same failing in our own day: we have not taken the importance of belonging together in Christ seriously enough, and have been content to use the Church as a resource or a meeting place without sensing the central importance of actually being the Church together. The fundamentally isolated modern Christian for whom churchgoing is optional can struggle with ordinary parish Christianity—its habits, its obligations, its everydayness. And our parish life is often sick and unattractive as a result.

As with Goldilocks and her porridge, there is a too-hot and a too-cold solution to all of this. The too-hot one is the fundamentalist escape from a common, shared world of meaning into a kind of ghetto of the mind—into a sectarian way of being Christian. Christ is against culture, according to this view, and calls Christians away from the world. There is no compatibility here with the ordinary mixed bag of Christians distributed right along the spectrum of conversion that we know to be typical of parish life. So, the sectarian, too-hot alternative means disrupting and overturning the parish if not simply abandoning it for something deemed to be more Christian.

Then there is the too-cold option. It takes various forms, but all of them tend to identify Christ with culture. When I was young, it was middle-class suburban respectability—the sort of thing that Barry Humphries has spent a lifetime trying to get over. More recently, as a tightly wound and rule-governed model of society has given way since the 1960s, a culture of therapeutic individualism has taken over. Where once church commended itself rather smugly as a marker of social respectability, now it has to sell itself in the marketplace of service provision. The American sociologist Robert Bellah, in *Habits of the Heart*, traces this transformation in his own country, with the Church catering to the fellowship needs and desire for meaning of middle-class society.[166]

Yet communities of personal support, if that is what parishes are becoming, are fragile, since people's expectations are so high. It is like marriage today, to which people bring higher-than-ever expectations. The amount of conflict and breakdown in our marriages is matched nowadays by the amount of conflict and breakdown in our parishes, because we need and expect so much for ourselves from institutions that were conceived in quite different terms.

So, what we are often left with in parish life is something that the writer of 2 Timothy 3 was also familiar with: holding an outward form of godliness while denying its power. We see this problem play out in the lack of mature regard that Christians ought to have for one another, between clergy and laity, and between bishops and their clergy. Anyone who has been around parish life cannot help witnessing a range of behaviours and attitudes that are incompatible with Christian maturity. The letters of Paul and others in the New Testament warn against just these problems, so they are not new.

We witness dysfunctional agendas flourishing, with some who are anxious and controlling seeking to rule the roost, and aided in this by others who lack the confidence and sense of responsibility to challenge them. We see un-self-awareness, stiff and unvarying self-presentation, and symptoms of co-dependency, with some preferring self-advancing sycophancy while others favour adolescent-style rebellion. We see the widespread abusiveness

---

[166] Robert N. Bellah, et al, *Habits of the Heart: Individualism and Commitment in American Life* (1985) (Berkeley and Los Angeles, CA.: University of California Press, 1996).

that forces lay people out of the Church, and clergy out of the ministry, involving a terrible cost to the little ones whom God cherishes. And we find institutional cover-ups. The agility and curiosity and confidence that Malcolm Turnbull wants for our nation is what many of us want for our parishes, but there is evidence that lassitude and paralysis are more typical.

The distinctive Christian habitus of the parish

Between the too-hot and too-cold solutions, what might Goldilocks find in the parish? I suggest that a just-right solution is there if we want it. I refer to Christian life together under the guiding star of Christ's incarnation: God in Christ blesses our world by abiding in it, experiencing its joy and sadness from within, knowing habit and discipline, laughter and conflict, all revealing God's patient investment. Here we have the earthly city opening its heart and mind to the heavenly city, and the heavenly city drawing near to the earthly city. Here, in a global world of fast-moving winners and slow-moving losers, we rediscover the local, with a range of people we would not normally encounter.

Such an approach to Christian life and fellowship once came far more naturally than it does for us in the third Christian millennium. In the first millennium, being Christian was a far more integral reality. Our faith, our life and our worship were woven together in ways that seem very foreign today. Christ's body was not divided. Christ himself was present in his body the Church, and present in his body and blood on the altar—one Christ, one integral body. And that integral abiding manifested itself in the parish system, as a Roman Empire of provinces and jurisdictions was matched by a Church of dioceses and parishes. If no place or person was meant to escape the Emperor's power, so no place or person could escape God's grace.

The Anglican version of traditional Catholic parish polity emphasised this local belonging of Christians even more. We were not a confessing Church as the Protestants tended to be. We were the traditional Church of the English people that had undergone some key reforms, yielding a result that was quite distinctive.

The identity of the reformed Church of England was found in the way it lived and prayed together locally, with a common form of life shared by the laity and their newly-married clergy, and with a common form of prayer intended to keep a range of doctrinal perspectives together in the one tent. It was not an ideological version of Church. Central to the Elizabethan Settlement of 1559 was the Queen's refusal 'to make windows into men's souls'. Instead, if we could pray and live together that was a sufficient mark of our Christian seriousness.

Dietrich Bonhoeffer said that 'He who loves his dream of a community more than the Christian community itself becomes a destroyer of the latter, even though his personal intentions may be ever so honest and earnest and sacrificial'.[167] The Anglican parochial system at its best is faithful to this prophetic challenge, in which the actual Church is what matters and not anyone's preferred ideological version of the Church—a warning that Evangelicals and Anglo-Catholics at their best have always respected.

But that was then. What about now? The challenge comes when we find ourselves inhabiting a flawed and disappointing institutional Church, or a parish that exasperates us. Many lay people give up on the parish and many clergy never stay long enough to eventually be known and trusted and finally make a lasting impact. As I said earlier, we are all easily disillusioned with our church experience as it is. But there is something about this situation that is good for us as Christians, so that it is worth opening our hearts and minds to others and to God even in the face of dissatisfaction and setbacks. In other words, there is something

---

[167] Dietrich Bonhoeffer, *Life Together*, 5th edn. (1949), trans. John W. Doberstein (London: SCM Press, 1954), 17.

about the parish that presents us with just the challenges we need to grow in faith and maturity—if we let it. We are not always right, and everything does not have to go our way. It is more important to honour the deep bonds of oneness in Christ that are declared at the font and the altar than to be right at the expense of someone else having to be wrong. I am not saying that there are no rights and wrongs. What I am saying that there is a right and a wrong way to go about disagreeing, and that having to work out this right way is good for us and for the Church. You could say that the parish is like a gymnasium. It can help us to develop strong Christian muscles through having to work with opposing forces.

For anyone who might want to protest at this point, 'what about the gospel, what about the truth?' the answer is that there is plenty of gospel truth in the attitude that I commend. The gospel is centred on God's unbreakable faithfulness, made flesh and sealed with blood in Jesus Christ. When we stick together and honour one another's baptism, which the parish version of Christian community properly entails, then we are being witnesses to this gospel.

Rowan Williams, the former Archbishop of Canterbury, was always struggling to commend this vision of sanctified togetherness in the face of many who wanted a purer, less compromised Church—whether they were zealous Evangelicals, affronted Anglo-Catholic traditionalists, or equally vehement and affronted gay rights activists. Dr Williams' steady, dogged perspective was widely criticised, even mocked, but then that is what happens to prophets when they speak God's word out of season.

In his essay 'Nobody Knows Who I am Till the Judgment Morning', Rowan Williams pointed out that we only become ourselves through our struggle with the other, and with the unsympathetic grain of reality.[168] Everyone who has ever honed

---

[168] Rowan Williams, 'Nobody Knows Who I am Till the Judgement Morning,' in *On Christian Theology* (Oxford: Blackwell, Oxford, 2000), 276-89.

Two Cheers for the Parish (2015)

a craft in the face of difficulty knows this as a general truth, but some of us can testify to it as a truth of parish life as well. My decade as Rector of two parishes has shaped my life, taught me whatever wisdom I might have attained, and confirmed my theological vocation—not bad for ten years that, by and large, were the toughest and one or two of them the most unpleasant of my life.

In his book of meditations, *Silence and Honey Cakes*, Rowan Williams identifies the actual Church's spiritual credentials in

> the daily prayer of believers, the constant celebration of the Eucharist, meeting the same potentially difficult or dull people time after time, because they are the soil of growth. It insists that we go on reading the same book and reciting the same creeds... an inexhaustible story, a pattern of words and images given by God that we shall never come to the end of. ... In very unmagical settings indeed, inner cities and prisons, and remote hamlets and struggling mission plants, the church remains pledged; its pastors and people and buildings speaking of God who is not bored or disillusioned by what he has made—and so they speak of the personal possibilities for everyone in such a situation.[169]

Such a perspective is refreshingly free of frustrated idealism; it is not scandalised by Christian ordinariness, even by sin. God is not fazed by us, after all, and does not give up on us for all our falling short. Yet parishes can be frustrating, occasionally dispiriting and even embittering. So how might we maintain our courage and commitment?

---

[169] Rowan Williams, *Silence and Honey Cakes: The Wisdom of the Desert* (Oxford: Lion Publishing, 2003), 92-3. (Author's Note: Yes, I also used this quotation in Chapter 3. Is it not worth repeating?).

Keeping our nerve

There are some in our Church who believe that the parish system is unreformable and should be abandoned, or at least bypassed in the multiplication of new and more intentional fellowships. The so-called Emerging Church Movement, with its fresh expressions, can, of course, provide vision and resources for renewing parish life. In many places, new church plants, messy church and other family-friendly developments and outreach initiatives into the community are doing what energetic parishes, both Evangelical and Anglo-Catholic, have always done. But to give up on the parish altogether because it can be difficult, intractable and unrewarding, to my mind, means giving up on word, sacrament, and the people of God.

The good news is that a wave of spiritual energy is being made available to the Church in our generation. It began in the twentieth century with five key movements all driving the renewal of parish life. The Biblical Theology Movement and the Ecumenical Movement both helped us to recover a sense of being called as God's people—as the body of Christ. For Anglicans, this pointed us beyond the Erastian State Church model and the culturally captive, socially conservative Anglicanism that many of us are old enough to remember. The Liturgical Movement, which in the Anglican Church was called the Parish Communion Movement, or the Parish and People Movement, helped us to recover the centrality of worship for Christian identity, returning the Eucharist to its ancient and proper place at the centre of Christian life after a long absence. Those of us who grew up with Prayer Book revision might remember how exciting and liberating all this was. The Charismatic Movement helped free us from what we might call the formalistic and structural captivity of God's presence to experience more freedom and personal connection in worship, even when we did not become card-carrying Charismatics. The Movement for the Ordination of Women called our Church to greater openness, and Anglican women to a greater confidence in Christ that lead them to claim their proper place in his mission. The result of these movements has been to recover a sense of all Christians being gifted members of Christ, as St Paul taught, with a common inheritance together as saints through baptism and Eucharist.

As the apostolic gave way under Anglicanism to the Erastian, as Paul Avis explains, the Erastian has now given way to the baptismal.[170] This language is everywhere now in our worship, teaching and parish planning, even if it remains the case that many have not caught the liberating vision. So, beyond the Church as a non-distinctive branch of culture, alternatively a remote sect—my too-cold and too-hot solutions—a just-right solution is emerging as God's gift to us. A more intentional, even more mystical togetherness in Christ is being discovered in some of our parishes.

This development in the Church goes with comparable trends in wider society. What the sociologist Anthony Giddens called life politics is everywhere on the rise, as people seek local opportunities to invest themselves in rebuilding social capital and renewing a sense of identity and solidarity. Indeed, in many places, parishes provide a community focus for building wider social capital.[171]

Rather than offer a technique let alone a manifesto for rebooting parish life, I conclude instead with a word about Dietrich Bonhoeffer and what he called religionless Christianity. This term is much misunderstood. It does not mean a secular, beliefless Christianity, of the Bishop Spong or even the Don Cupitt sort. Rather, it means giving up on the idea that Christianity exists to provide us with religious services, to protect us from the uncomfortable facts of life, to preserve us from difficulty and

---

[170] Paul Avis, *The Anglican Understanding of the Church: An Introduction* (London: SPCK, 2000), 15-29. Erastianism means that the Church is significantly annexed to the State's agenda—think of Tudor England.
[171] Anthony Giddens, *Modernity and Self Identity: Self and Society in the Late Modern Age* (Stanford, CA.: Stanford University Press, 1991), 209-31.

challenge. This is how many people see Christian life, which they expect our parishes to cater for.

Wrong, says Dietrich Bonhoeffer the martyr, who believed that when God calls us, he calls us to die. Religionless Christianity means that God, worship, clergy, and parish life are not meant to serve and confirm our agenda, and our unreconstructed preferences in life. Rather, they are about the joyful liberation of our lives so that we come to serve God's needs, and others' needs, according to a big, liberating picture of the gospel. I believe that the parish's promise of a unique Christian habitus can be fulfilled once again, even in times like these, as we discover God's agenda at the heart of our life in the Church, displacing any less adequate agenda. And three cheers for that.

12

Mimesis and Ministry (2016)

> When invited to contribute to a themed edition of St Mark's Review on dangerous ideas, I realised that a frank talk I had given earlier in 2016 would fit the bill. It is about what I believe to be really necessary for the ordained ministry facing current challenges. It draws not only on my reflections as a professional theologian, now occupied for some years in explicating and applying the mimetic theory of René Girard (1923-2015), but also on how I have become a better priest through personal engagement with Girard's thought. I approach this topic not primarily as a theorist, then, but as a ministry practitioner whose outlook and approach have been transformed. Pope Paul VI said that people today want witnesses rather than teachers, and if they will listen to teachers it is because first of all they are witnesses. So, I offer these reflections as a witness. The original address was given in March 2016 to gathering of clergy and change facilitators sponsored by Fr Chris Bedding through the Anglican Parish of Darlington, Perth. It was published as 'Mimesis and Ministry', St Mark's Review 237 (2016): 19-32, and appears here by kind permission.

Christian ministry is widely perceived by many practitioners to be increasingly difficult, conflict prone and personally challenging. At a time when managerialism is being widely embraced in the Church and applied to intractable problems that are far too deeply rooted in change-resistant institutional cultures, we have a recipe for much superficial and frustrated activity. It is dangerous for clergy to be frank about these fears and burdens at a time when activist, program-centred approaches to church leadership are being imposed from above and typically dodge the really hard work of cultural transformation. Without a more profound and searching engagement than is currently on offer, many programs for growth and change in the Church end up stillborn. It is an equally dangerous idea to insist on the inescapable necessity of hard-won self-awareness and personal maturity on the part of clergy if today's Church is to find a new confidence and direction, since this is the hardest and least program-oriented of solutions.

René Girard's mimetic theory understands religion to be the primeval flipside of culture.[172] Religion is the evolutionary development whereby humanity emerged out of self-destructive violence. This threat of violence originates not in any innate aggression on our part but in the instability of our desires, which follow the desires of others. This state of affairs makes us unique and creative creatures, able to learn, share and advance beyond the scope of animal instinct. Yet, because our desires can compete, human groups are systemically prone to rivalry and violence.

The key to surviving the violent downside of our mimetic nature lies in an efficient mechanism for quietening such a crisis. This key was stumbled upon by our progenitors, involving the spontaneous discharge of pent-up violence onto a scapegoat. This apparent miracle of order springing from chaos as a result of such primal murders gave birth to our sense of the sacred, which for Girard yields various prohibitions, rituals and myths.[173] These are defining features of religion, which preserve stable co-existence and tolerable diversity within every pre-modern culture.

---

[172] For an overview see e.g., René Girard, *The Girard Reader*, ed. James G. Williams (New York: Crossroad, 1996). There is a one-page summary of mimetic theory prepared by myself and colleagues in the Australian Girard Seminar, online at http://www.australiangirardseminar.org/?page_id=2 (last accessed August 2022).

[173] See René Girard, *Violence and the Sacred* (1972), trans. Patrick Gregory (Baltimore and London: The Johns Hopkins University Press, 1977).

The truth about this state of affairs emerged slowly in history, but chiefly in the Judaeo-Christian Scriptures. We began to learn from the Psalms, from Job and from the Hebrew prophets that sacrificial victims are innocent. For Girard, it was chiefly Jesus' life and death that revealed the real sacred in the midst of this cultural by-product, the false sacred. Jesus' Kingdom was not made with hands. That is, it was not of human origin; it was not the evolved way of things. Hence, we can dispense with a violent god, and certainly a retributively violent one. For Girard this is the message of the Prologue to John's Gospel (John 1:1-18), where the word of God suffers violence and exclusion at the hands of human beings and not vice versa. Consequently, the expulsion of Adam and Eve from the Garden by God in Genesis 3 is shown not to be the truth about how God deals with human sin. Rather, this expulsion proves to be our projection, our assumption about what God is like. It is an instance of *méconnaissance*, of mis-knowing, which is corrected by the New Testament's version of the creation narrative, the prologue of John's Gospel.

So, Girard puts paid to the whole theme of divine expulsion. It is not God who expels, but we human beings are the ones who expel God, in the person of Jesus—'he came to what was his own, and his own people did not accept him' (John 1:11). And so, we come to create God in our own image—as rivalrous, disapproving, and violent, just as we humans are.

Jesus' death and resurrection, and the subsequent work of the Holy Spirit as God's advocate for the defence of victims, releases a new reality into history that eventually undermines this once-useful but fundamentally misconceived version of the sacred, since we now know how it works and can no longer uncritically rely on it. This revelation unleashes a dangerous threat of violent escalation into history, according to Girard, which is how he understands Jesus' saying, 'I came not to bring peace, but a sword' (Matthew 10:34).

Indeed, Girard is convinced that the Bible's apocalyptic literature is best understood as a prediction of this unstoppable escalation to extremes and must not be understood as if God were about to wreak an entirely human-like revenge. Rather, the Bible's apocalyptic literature points to the collapse of the false sacred and its capacity to restrain human violence.[174] Secularity, then, is the inevitable and proper fruit of the gospel, according to Girard, which he understands as providing the true meaning of Nietzsche's twilight of the gods. The incarnation heralds the collapse of religion as a functional reality in its false sacred form. The incarnation represents God's personal investment in humanity finding a new and lasting way to peace, beyond pagan religious ways of organising the world that we still see throwing up false gods: the growth economy, neoliberalism, the security state, the Islamic State Caliphate and so on. These false gods multiply victims, and, despite the false sacred collapsing, they retain more than a whiff of that archaic sacred aura.

While the carapace of the archaic sacred remains, the gospel inhabits it ecclesially in a different register. Sacrificial language and self-sacrificial dedication remain but they refer to personal consecration, not sacrificial immolation. Ritual now serves to dramatise Christ's new order rather than prop up the old pagan order. Prohibitions in the hands of Christians are best understood as prudent and practical rather than arbitrary yet unquestionable. Hence the old way of organising the world is perpetually reimagined in the Church's liturgy and ministry.

Now, if that is the mimetic theory, how might we define ministry in light of it? Ministry is a sacramental manifestation of God's breakthrough with humanity in Jesus Christ, through the Church. It taps into the heavenly promise in the midst of earth, bringing God's forgiveness and welcome to a world structured by

---

[174] See René Girard, *Battling to the End: Conversations with Benoît Chantre* (2007), trans. Mary Baker (East Lansing, MI.: Michigan State University Press, 2010).

aggressive tribalism and the legacy of sacred violence. Ministry is how things are done in the non-tribal tribe, as I am calling it, which is the Church. So, while ministry is a religious undertaking, it is subversively so. Likewise, while it is a ritual undertaking, it is transformingly rather than conservatively so. And while it enforces prohibitions, we minister discipline only insofar as discipline serves the cause of human liberation. Ministry belongs to the whole Church, but it is embodied in the diaconate, the ministerial priesthood, the episcopate and in related ways via their functional counterparts in the non-episcopal traditions. In short, ministry is what the Church does in Christ and in the Spirit for the mimetic transformation of our world, against the constant challenge of a collapsing but nonetheless stubborn false sacred.

The challenge

I regard God's transformation of a world built out of the false sacred as the primary concern of Christian ministry. In particular, I want to address the specific challenges of false sacred imagination that remain influential in our society, even though their effects are now largely disruptive and damaging because the false sacred can no longer structure let alone revive society. This is the effect of that sword brought by Jesus (Matthew 10:34), undercutting the false sacred and with it our capacity for sustaining a certain sort of peace. Here I find the most crucial imaginative and practical challenge for ministry in our churches today.

The modern Western problem, according to Girard, is what he calls metaphysical desire and its terminal condition, which he calls ontological sickness. These problems arise because we do not desire objects directly, but only secondarily and indirectly. Primarily, we desire according to the desire of an admired person or group, our model or mediator.[175] This foundational Girardian insight explains how advertising works, along with more romantic attraction than we would care to admit—do you remember that Rick Springfield song, 'I Wish that I had Jessie's Girl'?

Problems arise when the model of our desire gets in the way, in what Girard calls internal mediation. The envy and rivalry that our mimetic desiring throws up under these conditions introduces a whole new dimension of desire. We become obsessed with our model, who can become our rival, our obstacle, maybe even our mirror double, to use various of Girard's terms for this escalation through what he calls metaphysical desire towards ontological sickness. That is, our desire is no longer directed to any particular object, but fixates on the *being* of our model itself. We come to desire vaporous things rather than actual objects—things such as prestige and regard, which represent the longed-for being that our model seems to have but not we ourselves.

The spiritual writer Jim Grote describes the traditional seven deadly sins in terms of this ontological sickness.[176] In lust, gluttony, sloth and the other deadly sins, we crave the being of a model and we despise the limitations inherent in our own actual circumstances. The idea is that a lustful, greedy and lazy life may come to seem attractive in light of attractive persons who model it for us, leading responsible people to abandon their sensible habits of chastity, moderation and diligence. Hence, we pursue a phantom of someone else's desire at the expense of our own success, wellbeing and that of others who depend on us.

In one version of Girard's ontological sickness, we observe the phenomena that Sigmund Freud theorised as masochism

---

[175] See e.g., René Girard (with Jean-Michel Oughourlian and Guy Lefort), *Things Hidden since the Foundation of the World* (1978), trans. Stephen Bann and Michael Metteer (London and New York: Continuum, 2003), 294–98.

[176] Jim Grote, 'The Imitation of Christ as Double-Bind: Toward a Girardian Spirituality', *Cistercian Studies* 29, no. 4 (1994): 485–98.

and sadism. For Girard, however, these are widespread mimetic behaviours played out in public, not exotic private eccentricities confined to the sexual *demimonde*.[177] According to Girard, masochism and sadism represent two ways of responding to indifference or ill-treatment. The subject is in the grip of metaphysical desire, yearning for the greater being of their model, so they welcome indifferent, contemptuous and even violent treatment from the model because it confirms the superiority of the model's being over their own, and hence the model's worthiness. Indeed, anyone who treats this subject well cannot be a worthy model for their desire, hence their lifelong search for a more abusive partner, a more indifferent love interest to woo (or to stalk), a more impossible job to undertake, or a bigger risk to court, all because a deviated transcendence ensures that the great prize must always be just out of reach. Even the ordinarily ambitious are like this. Girard says that if we are restless and seek the fulfilment that eludes us in the realm of career, we will start to knock ourselves against obstacles, mistaking walls for doors as he memorably puts it.[178]

A parallel solution to craving the supposedly greater being of an abusive model of desire is to take on their abusive desire and become abusive ourselves. This is the sadistic option where, according to Girard, the key to the enchanted garden is perceived to be in the hands of the tormentor.[179]

I have argued that some clergy demonstrate the masochistic option in terms of chronic conflict avoidance, fawning sycophancy and even self-oblation before indifferent or else bullying laity and superiors as the price of perceived emotional wellbeing or else smoother career advancement, with a harsh and judgmental God image often thrown in for good measure. Alternatively, this abusive theology and structural violence can be internalised, issuing in a

---

[177] Girard, *Things Hidden*, 326-51.
[178] Girard, *Things Hidden*, 415.
[179] Girard, *Things Hidden*, 326-35.

pattern of bullying or abuse by clergy. In this sadistic version, the weakness and vulnerability that abusers despise in themselves is assaulted in others, with one version of this abuse in particular now coming to light in revelations about sexual abuse in the churches.

Girard makes much of the New Testament word *skandalon* and understands being scandalised as a key manifestation of metaphysical desire. We resent the success, power, and poise of others, perhaps their advantageous position—all the things that we lack—and so we begin to obsess about them. Clergy can be sycophantic, as I have said, or they can react with hostility. Though this hostility does not have to go as far as sadism and abuse. A milder version is to be the anti-hero, which Girard calls counter-imitation. The anti-hero is typically something of a nonentity, whose claim to critical lucidity represents a refusal to admit their impotent reality. So, here are two related mimetic patterns into which clergy can unhelpfully fall: the uncritically compliant and the angrily dissident.

The transformation

The transformation is a shift both in perspective and practice that involves head, heart and imagination. I am reminded of a book by Henri Nouwen that I read as a theological student, and have at last really begun to understand, called *The Wounded Healer*.[180] The idea is that only through being a transformed person can you minister God's transforming reality to others. Girardian theologian James Alison points out that Christ's desire begins to shape our desire, and we find ourselves slowly changing in ways that may only become evident to us with hindsight.

For Alison, following Girard, the sign of God's presence with us is through our desire beginning to play out differently in our

---

[180] Henri J.M. Nouwen, *The Wounded Healer: Ministry in Contemporary Society* (Garden City, NY.: Doubleday & Company [Image Books], 1972).

dealings with others, which is where the truth of who we are coming to be emerges bit by bit. Alison says that God, the 'utterly other', influences us through intruding new desires that change how we respond to the desire of 'customary' human others, also beyond any sacrificial reliance upon 'removed' others.[181] So, it is a slow, subtle and indirect process, and one not prone to easy quantification in terms of success. But, over time, we do recognise that our desires have changed. The mimetic dynamics that would once have enthralled us no longer carry the same fascination.

Girard and Alison point to biblical figures called to ministry who escaped dysfunctional mimetic entrapment. I mention three.

Alison thinks that Jonah has a lot to teach us. Jonah was scandalised by God's call to preach repentance to the unworthy citizens of Nineveh, and his resentment burned so hot that he sailed off in the opposite direction. Something about his conflicted persona obviously attracted the attention of his shipmates, however. Those pagans knew exactly what had to be done and Jonah was made the scapegoat in his own version of a pastoral crisis, ending up being thrown overboard. But God did not give up on Jonah, holding him in being in the belly of the fish until he could change his mind and resume his mission—as Alison puts it, 'spluttering up the beach to Nineveh'.[182]

Girard examines the Gerasene demoniac story.[183] There we meet a designated scapegoat—Alison's 'removed other'—who helped maintain a stable pagan sacred reality. He behaved insanely and self-harmed incessantly, which helped the rest of his community by contrast to feel sane and stable, relaxed and comfortable. Jesus' intervention caused a crisis for that community because the

---

[181] James Alison, *Knowing Jesus*, 2nd edn. (London: SPCK, 1998), 14-15.
[182] James Alison, 'Spluttering up the Beach to Nineveh', in *Faith Beyond Resentment: Fragments Catholic and Gay* (London: Darton, Longman & Todd, 2001), 86–104.
[183] Mark 5:1-20, Luke 8:26-39. See René Girard, 'The Gerasene Demoniac', in *The Scapegoat*, 165–83.

man was healed. The destructive potential of the situation was unleashed, as we see symbolised in the porcine apocalypse that followed. Thereafter, the sanity and stability of that community had to be maintained by other means, and the former demoniac was left behind as a witness to the only genuinely saving and transforming reality remaining to it, which was coming to share in Jesus' own non-rivalrous peace with God. This is a demanding apostolic role, according to Alison, this ministry of an ex-demoniac. It calls for staying put in a situation so that it might slowly undergo transformation from dysfunction towards maturity, and thus find its way to the peace of God that passes all understanding. This is why staying put in ministry can be the most important thing that a priest can do, holding our ground as a witness and agent of personal transformation in the midst of a community that may not be fixable by any other means.

Girard is also very struck by Peter, the father of the institutional Church, who was mimetic, rivalrous and violent, but who was converted. Peter was swayed mimetically by the crowd in the high priest's courtyard and on cue he betrayed Jesus. But the risen Jesus got through to him, ending Peter's rivalry so that he could become a life-giving leader in the Church.[184] I like to think that when the risen Jesus at the end of John's Gospel asks Peter if he loves him 'more than these'—more than the other disciples, that is—and Peter simply replies that, yes, he does love Jesus, without comparing himself to anyone, Peter demonstrates that he has turned a corner. Now, having abandoned envy and rivalry, Peter shows that he is ready for the high office of feeding Christ's sheep. Mind you, Peter immediately makes a small stumble in his moment of scandal concerning the beloved disciple—asking 'What about him?' Jesus tells him to get a grip, to remember that Jesus' desires and not anyone else's are to be his sole concern now (John 21:15-22). Peter's little lapse is a timely reminder about how easy it is for us to slip

---

[184] Girard, 'Peter's Denial', in *The Scapegoat*, 149–64.

back, if we are not careful, despite all the progress that we might have made.

The late Girardian New Testament scholar Robert Hamerton-Kelly describes the spiritual transformation involved: 'Since sacred power depends on the conspiracy of all to maintain it, those who withhold consent from the conspiracy are dangerous and their gracious irony threatens the foundations. They are the "nothings" that God uses to bring the "somethings" to nothing (1 Corinthians 1:28)'.[185]

The point here, for James Alison, is refusing to be run oppositionally. That way, instead of being symptoms of the system, we become 'symptoms of God's desire'. Alison sums up the task of ministry according to the mimetic theory: it is the role of professional hypocrite publicly being set free from our own hypocrisy, as a truthfulness that is not our own comes upon us.[186]

Surely Pope Francis is living proof of this. His leadership is every bit as unsettling to many around him as Robert Hamerton-Kelly would predict. But Pope Francis' humble, joyful witness as an apostle of Jesus Christ is only possible because of what he learned through the experience of conversion. The once insensitive and conflict-prone Argentinian Jesuit leader Jorge Bergoglio, like Jonah, was held in being during a period of exile away from the capital in Cordoba until the mimetic knots in his nature and approach were untied. Then, having attained to what leadership in the Church most truly requires, he was called back to Buenos Aires and made a bishop.[187]

---

[185] Robert G. Hamerton-Kelly, *Sacred Violence: Paul's Hermeneutic of the Cross* (Minneapolis, MN.: Fortress Press, 1992), 84–85.

[186] James Alison, *Jesus the Forgiving Victim: Listening for the Unheard Voice* (Glenview, IL.: Doers Publishing, 2013), 478.

[187] See Paul Vallely, *Pope Francis: Untying the Knots: The Struggle for the Soul of Catholicism*, 2nd edn. (London and New York: Bloomsbury Continuum, 2015), especially Chapters 6 and 7.

The habits

Finally, I want to share with you some worthwhile habits that seem to go with these insights into mimetic theory and ministry. The heart of it is learning how to negotiate metaphysical desire and not fall into the ontological sickness that forfeits perspective, becomes obsessive and loses touch with Christ and his desires.

In the face of mimetic rivalry, Girard offers two key pieces of advice. First, focus on the object, not on the model.[188] If we are in a conflicted and potentially rivalrous situation with someone, focus on the issue at hand, not on them or anything to do with the troubled relationship. Turning away from the object to the model would serve as a hook for mimetic rivalry to latch onto and escalate. An example. If I want to avoid the otherwise inevitable arguments with my sister, it is best simply to stick to the specifics of our aged (adoptive) mother's care needs. To help rather than hinder my mother, my sister, and myself, I have to remember that it is best to not make things about me or my sister or our relationship but only about practicalities concerning our mother. If conflict flares up anyway, Girard's next piece of advice is to abandon disputes before the mimetic doubles emerge and all hope of sticking to the matter in hand is lost—to simply not allow mimetic rivalry to take over.[189] Better to lose gracefully with few if any casualties than to lose yourself and probably the situation.

But what if we cannot walk away from a difficult pastoral situation, for instance when firm discipline is necessary and someone has to be dealt with, sacked perhaps, or at least called to account for something even though we know that there will likely be hell to pay? Then we should act as decently, cleanly and objectively as possible, not being deflected by the toxifying personal desires that surround the situation. Winston Churchill

---

[188] Girard, *Things Hidden*, 311.
[189] Girard, *The Girard Reader*, 278–79.

was criticised for the notably respectful tone of the letter he wrote to his Japanese counterpart to convey Britain's declaration of war, to which Churchill replied that if you have to kill a man, it costs you nothing to be polite.

This is a situation I once discussed with James Alison. I was in the midst of a stubborn parish conflict and I asked his advice about standing up to a situation of calculated and prolonged bullying without either capitulating or else pouring fuel on the conflict by getting too personally caught up in it. His answer began with him explaining the power of conflict to escalate and take us over which, like the fear of death, lies in our fear of losing ourselves. We stage a desperate attempt to save the being that we fear we are losing. But just as death holds no fear for an imagination caught up in the absolute vivacity and deathlessness of God, so conflict will never overwhelm an imagination grounded in the surety of God's love for us, of God's being which is non-rivalrously on our side. In other words, death is just biology, and conflict is natural, too, given the sort of systemic dynamics that we inhabit. So, to either capitulate or else overreact to the bullying would be to overstate the threat involved in a natural, explicable and eminently survivable process. Conflict demands calm resolve and self-mastery, not flailing around in the grip of being scandalised.

Here I am helped by Jesus' advice that we be as cunning as serpents yet as gentle as doves (Matthew 10:16)—to be alert to the problems of mimetic rivalry and escalation, and to take prudent steps to slither out of harm's way while being mimetically secure enough to respond firmly yet nonviolently in the face of provocation. In that way, we can avoid being caught up with our rival in an escalation that will not serve to bring the best outcome for all concerned. Three habits accompany this set of insights.

First, we learn to inhabit ourselves rightly. By this I refer to the capacity to be the calm, non-anxious presence that the family systems theorists extol. Their networked understanding of human influence, dysfunction and restorative action is explicable in terms of mimetic theory. If we are calm and sure of ourselves, we can avoid getting embroiled mimetically in group dynamics. That way, we can have a calming influence on others and help prevent the situation from being hijacked by mimetic rivalries.

Second, we learn to inhabit the institutional Church rightly. For James Alison, the right ecclesial virtues are *hilarity*, *pathos* and *irony*.[190] These attitudes come from learning to see with Easter eyes, compassionately, alert to God's future, and hence less prone to being disappointed, scandalised, fixated on whatever is wrong, and deluded that we either can or must fix everything ourselves. Instead, as we come to share Jesus' desire and that of his saints, who loved and yet transformed the Church, we find ourselves tending toward understanding and compassion rather than scandal and anger over what is amiss, irony over the fact of so much godliness and beauty woven through with so much cluelessness, and hilarity over the grace of God that puts up with us in love—along with all the other ordinary, fallible Christians, including our opponents.

Third, to rightly inhabit ourselves and the institutional Church, we must learn to inhabit God rightly. Apart from the spiritual habits of daily office, spiritual direction and regular confession that I learned at theological college and that priests do well to maintain, I have begun learning a new habit of contemplative prayer. For all the mimetic restlessness of my mind that regularly refuses to be still, nevertheless I have already confirmed in my own experience of this prayer what the Desert Father John Cassian taught long ago concerning temptation: that it is more reliable to displace temptation through contemplation than to fight it. By displacing it, we allow our desires to be led away towards God's desire, but by trying to fight it we remain mimetically entrapped in the desire we fight: scandalised, powerless and un-free. I am becoming convinced that contemplation represents a necessary means for allowing our

---

[190] See James Alison, 'The Portal and the Halfway House: Spacious Imagination and Aristocratic Belonging', in *Jesus the Forgiving Victim*, 435–79.

desires to be conformed over time to Christ's desire.[191] Indeed, I have begun to refer to contemplation as mimetic dialysis, coming to regard it as necessary if we are to avoid many pitfalls in ministry.

In closing, I want to emphasise the Christian orthodoxy of everything I have been commending here. Girard is convinced that the sort of progressive Christianity preferring psychotherapy or ideology over Scripture and tradition may be sacrificing the most radical resources of all. But that is another dangerous idea, to be pursued another time: that theological orthodoxy is edgier and more exciting than the various rationalistic, ideological or therapeutic reductions of Christian faith and practice that became popular during the last decades of the twentieth century.

Finally, here is a summing-up of the dangerous idea that I have been setting out: in the face of widespread cluelessness about how to move things along in the Church, René Girard's mimetic theory provides those of us in ministry with intellectual, spiritual and personal resources that are scriptural, experiential and, in that sense, scientific, while keeping us close to the heart of theological orthodoxy. Its insights work, too, and to that I testify as a witness.

---

[191] Helpful here is Brian Robinette, 'Deceit, Desire, and the Desert: René Girard's Mimetic Theory in Conversation with Early Christian Monastic Practice', in *Violence, Transformation, and the Sacred: 'They Shall Be Called Children of God'*, eds. Margaret R. Pfeil and Tobias L. Winright (Maryknoll, NY.: Orbis, 2012), 130–43.

13

Catholic Anglicanism for Evangelicals (2016)

> *This is a slightly expanded version of an address given to the relatively few Catholic-leaning Anglican clergy of Canberra at a 2016 consultation on 'Catholic Evangelism'. It is an apologia for the Anglo-Catholic vision at a time when the Diocese of Canberra and Goulburn has turned substantially Evangelical, as the Anglican Church of Australia is tending more generally under the widening influence of Sydney Diocese. Yet the Catholic wing of our Church, which divided over women's ordination and is everywhere in decline, seems more disposed to retreat than to advance. Anglo-Catholics might worry about the rising Evangelical tide, but this does not translate into confident dialogue with the emerging majority position based on its own vision of the gospel. Recourse to mystery is no alternative—you need theology to point to mystery. This address was published as 'Catholic Anglicanism for Evangelicals', St Mark's* Review *241 (2017): 82-89, and appears here by kind permission.*

Perhaps, like me, you have enjoyed watching *Call the Midwife* on ABC TV over recent years. It portrays a bygone world of Anglican nuns and their secular nursing colleagues who live and pray together, and who work as midwives, in the crowded and impoverished slums and docklands of Poplar, in East London. A century of such mission in the hands of so-called Anglo-Catholic slum priests and religious sisterhoods represented a vision of the world, the Eucharist and the common good held together by the incarnate love of God.

I feel an affinity with this program because the late Canon James Warner, under whom I trained at Brisbane's then quite Anglo-Catholic St Francis' Theological College in the mid-1980s, was a young curate in Poplar around my birth year, 1960, when the fourth season of *Call the Midwife* is set. Whereas the local curate is referred to as 'Mr' in the program, the clergy would of course have been called 'Father', going about their pastoral visiting in the streets and alleyways in cassocks and even birettas. They would have been known and loved by very many ordinary people, young and old, not just the churchgoers. Sunday Mass at All Saints, Poplar, would have been dignified, beautiful, musical, highly ritualistic, yet evangelistic, too, and quite enjoyable—not at all stuffy.

The sacraments were the centre of a vibrant pastoral program in such parishes: with boys clubs, girls societies, missions to seamen, Scouts and Guides, good works of all sorts, and the Church's high festivals celebrated in ways that reached out to the wider community. Anglo-Catholic parishes—like Holy Trinity, Fortitude Valley, in Brisbane's inner-city, where I served my curacy—sought to present an integral imaginative vision of the Christian life. It was centred on the Eucharist and the church year, celebrating the joy of Christ who stands at the heart of nature and its beauty, of a beloved humanity and its struggle, of human reason and aspiration, and of society at large, which cannot help but be transformed as heaven presses near to earth. This was the Catholic vision of my own Anglican formation for the priesthood.

Absent some of its characteristic liturgical trappings, aspects of the Catholic can be found in more 'central' Anglicanism. These aspects might involve emphasising the importance of traditional worship, of daily prayer discipline, of the Church mediating God's grace, of parish fellowship as a corrective to lonely individualism, and even of a little incarnate mystery in the liturgy as a corrective to today's widespread discarnate rationalism. Such a Broad-Church priest might wear the chasuble (i.e., the traditional Catholic Eucharistic vestment), though they would not regard doing so as an expression of Catholic Eucharistic beliefs.

I for one do not wish to perpetuate the old party model of Catholic Anglicanism in opposition to Evangelical Anglicanism. The former, when truest to itself, has always been missional and evangelistic. However, there are differences in theological emphasis, and in how both Church and mission are conceived. In what follows, I want to highlight distinctively Catholic emphases under the headings of Vision, Eucharist and Church.

Vision

Our word 'Catholic' comes from the Greek words *kata holos*: according to the whole. It is a holistic vision of God's unstinting embrace of a much-loved world, and of a deeply beloved though admittedly wayward human species. There is generosity in the Catholic vision of humanity, though it is not naive: we humans are restless for God, and yet easily diverted, even perverted. So sin, yes, but total depravity, no. And grace, too, of course—though not grace conceived narrowly. Catholic grace is more free range. It surfaces in our natural inclinations toward loving relationships, just as it connects us to God whenever we find ourselves extended beyond ourselves in every impulse of creativity and wisdom, along with every worthy self-sacrifice. If the Catholic imagination is right, then creation, incarnation and redemption are making their presence felt.

There has always been a Catholic movement in Anglicanism, long before the early nineteenth-century Tractarians and their Anglo-Catholic descendants. The marks of it have included an openness to human reason in the light of God's word, a delight in creation with eyes sharpened by the promise of God's new creation, and in particular a sense of continuity with the early undivided Church. The ancient Fathers and Creeds were claimed as a crucial part of Anglican patrimony by the Tractarians (i.e., locating Anglican origins well before the Protestant Reformation), just as the later Anglo-Catholics looked to medieval and Baroque-era Catholic expressions for liturgical resources to express their burgeoning Catholic sensibility. This is where the Eucharistic vestments and the Catholic ritual came in, to transform worship in depressed places like Poplar with colour, beauty and vibrancy.

It was Catholic-minded Anglicans who took up modern currents of thought such as historical criticism and evolutionary biology. These so-called Liberal Catholics came to see that the truths of revelation needed to be interpreted in dialogue with new discoveries, perspectives and aspirations of the modern world. Theology is understood in Catholic Anglicanism as the handmaid of faith and the companion of practice—as faith seeking understanding, and practice coming to articulate its underlying logic. So, behind the wide sympathies and extensive gathering of liturgical and musical resources by Anglo-Catholics, a guiding passion was at work. Theirs was not simply an odd mix of intellectual novelty and antiquarian bricolage. Rather, it was a vision as wide as creation, as sympathetic as incarnation, as no holds barred as crucifixion, as path breaking as resurrection, as joyful as Pentecost, and as hopeful as the seer's vision of a new Jerusalem (Revelation 21-22).

This breadth of vision included a comprehensive celebration of the saints. This accompanied prayer for the dead, especially in the traumatic aftermath of World War I, including the erection of shrines and Calvaries outside churches such as had not been seen in England since the Reformation. These developments gave Anglo-Catholicism significant pastoral traction and fuelled its increasing prominence, up to a peak in the 1930s. Prayers and Masses for the dead, while a departure from established

Anglican principle, proved to be a blessing for the community and powerfully evangelistic.

So, here is a Catholic vision sharing the zeal of Evangelicalism but differently expressed. It acknowledges sin, yes, though without the potentially vertigo-inducing demands of Calvinist theological anthropology. It insists on humanity coming to dwell at peace with God through Jesus Christ, but it is our human hearts that change, not God's. It regards the incarnate life and bodily resurrection of Jesus as framing and situating the message of his cross, making salvation a warm-blooded process of inclusion rather than a forensic transaction or imputation. It acknowledges the active, conscious participation of Christian disciples in God's grace, though it regards grace as ecclesial and prophetic before it is individual and moral. And it is so firmly anchored in the word that it eagerly welcomes the lavish overflow of that word into the concrete grace of the sacraments.

Eucharist

The Catholic imagination is essentially sacramental, in the sense that Christ is triumphantly gathering-up all creation and human life in the sweep of his resurrection. This is made most concrete in the sacrament that is Christ's body. But which body is that? Up to the early-medieval period, a threefold body of Christ was perceived by Christians. There was the Lord himself, with his body on earth now risen to heaven; there was his body the Church, and there was his body really present in the sacrament of the altar. Later developments, from the ninth to the eleventh centuries, emphasised Christ's real presence on the altar at the expense of Jesus himself and his teachings in the Gospels, and at the expense of his gathered people comprising Christ's body the Church. A subsequent loss of gospel focus and of lay discipleship helped drive the Protestant Reformation as a corrective. In response, a triumphalist Roman Catholicism arose for which the Church's sacramental monopoly enforced its institutional power. Since Vatican II, however, the Mass is back in tune with the word and understood fully in the context of Christ's body gathered, which is where it belongs.

An Evangelical student asked me recently why it is not enough for Catholic Anglicans to rejoice in God's promises through the word, rather than insisting on so prominent a place for the Lord's Supper beyond simple obedience and devout remembrance. This is a good question. My answer will not appeal to those who favour a non-sensual rationalistic minimalism in religion, and who expect fully articulate and zealous engagement from all worshippers. My answer was that *the Word becomes flesh, and we dishonour the incarnation by turning that flesh back into word*. Instead, we see that flesh as inseparable from God's saving word in Scripture, and so we recognise Christ's body and blood in the Eucharist as the pledge and overflow of God's word.

Ultimately, Catholic Anglicanism approaches Christ's presence in the Eucharist with a confident realism because of God's promises that we receive at Christmas, Easter and Pentecost. Whether it be Richard Hooker's confidence that Christ is truly received in the Eucharist, tempering both Tridentine and Puritan emphases, or a fully-fledged Anglo-Catholic belief in the real presence with genuflection, tabernacles and even Benediction of the Blessed Sacrament, what we see is a confidence based on God's promises. Christ is not confined in heaven, or in the past, but is vibrantly alive among his people in the midst of his world.

Hence the priest's language at the altar does not just declare facts about God's intentions or about Jesus' past, nor are his or her words simply for the evoking of memories and devotional feelings. Rather, the Eucharistic words create a state of affairs. Using the linguistic philosopher J.L. Austin's terms, they are not just *locutionary*, or fact-stating, and they are not just *illocutionary*, or evocative of new connections. They are also *perlocutionary*, which means that they bring into effect what they state. If such confidence in the real presence seems too Catholic, its groundedness in the word and in the confidence of faith reveals what I like to think is an Evangelical impulse.

Church

It is not for nothing that Catholic Anglicanism has also been referred to as High-Church. That term has old-fashioned, Tory Royalist echoes which are out of tune with some Anglo-Catholic developments, not least its affinity with Christian Socialism. But, in general, being Catholic does entail an elevated assessment of the Church as a vehicle of grace. Hence, our Church is the mother of Christians, and not an organisation formed by them. It is hardware, not software. Church is not an app that we use, to assist us as we make our essentially private arrangements with God. Nor does being Catholic entail a static ontology, with divine mercy dispensed in measured doses via an ecclesiastical bureaucracy. Rather, it is about God's new creation discretely but dynamically extending itself through history. High-Church means high confidence that Jesus' high priestly prayer (John 17) has actually been answered.

The Church as *mater et magistra*, mother and teacher, is also a prophetic sign among the other institutions and powers of this world. This is seen in the Church's being, its saints, its actions, and not just in its words. The world needs to see a community so liberated by God's love that it does not need to play by the usual self-justifying rules. As American Catholic theologian John Cavadini put it, 'it is only a community that is not formed on the basis of claims of human purity, achievement, or excellence, however unique, that can mediate perspective simply by its very presence in the world, on those that are'.[192]

---

[192] John Cavadini, 'Review of *Evangelical Catholicism: Deep Reform in the 21st-Century Church*, by George Weigel'. Online at: https://www.firstthings.com/article/2013/08/church-as-sacrament (last accessed August 2022).

An imperfect Church, not obsessed with its own ideological and moral purity, but confident instead in Christ's mercy and forgiveness, gives rise to an attractive Catholic humanism—one that is convinced but not closed-minded, open-hearted and curious rather than peevish and narrow, and merciful rather than either lax or harsh. That is, a Christian humanism that avoids certain besetting tendencies of both Christian liberals and conservatives.

An important aspect of the Church according to the Catholic imagination is its pastoral structure. The Church is integrated into every community, while embedded also in wider geographical, social and cultural commonalities through its basic unit the diocese (not the congregation). The pastoral structure of parishes centred on the church building and the Eucharist points to heaven's embrace of earth, through the everyday pastoral ministry of service, nurture, teaching, community building and making disciples.

However, the parish in theory is not always the parish in reality, as all clergy discover. This has implications for our witness and mission. In mid-twentieth century France, the Catholic Church recovered a remarkable zeal for mission. In the so-called Mission to France, they favoured young Christian worker groups, which were led by lay people trained and supported by worker priests who lived among the urban proletariat and came to share their struggles. In these circles, parishes were sometimes seen as a problem that had to be circumvented. Typical congregations proved themselves unwilling and unable to receive and nurture new converts—they were too bourgeois, tame and respectable to accommodate the lively, worldly, sometimes rough and uncouth young workers who started to show up.

Other French Catholics of the day, such as l'Abbé Michonneau, in his post-war book *Revolution in a City Parish*, recognised that the parish is in fact the one concrete element in the evangelising task. Still, he acknowledged that there was quite a mission of parish renewal required. Regarding many typical parishioners of his day, Michonneau's conclusions reach across oceans and decades to strike us with undiminished relevance: 'They have not had to find the pearl of great price for themselves, and so, they do not feel impelled to call others to rejoice with them. They cannot quite imagine themselves as apostles'.[193]

We must acknowledge, without being scandalised or unduly frustrated, this disjunction between theory and practice, and that many parishes offering elements of Catholic Anglicanism need help to appreciate and unlock all the good gifts that I am describing. Religious education, catechumenal programs, better liturgy and music, enhanced ministries of welcome to children and families, and the never-ending task of preaching and teaching and pastoring so that all these elements begin to gel, are all indispensable. Yet without an intentional commitment to more Anglicans growing in the seriousness of their discipleship, the Catholic vision that we put out there on Sundays, despite its considerable attractiveness, will only be folded up and put away again, with little ongoing impact.

We cannot wait for everything to be right in the Church and the congregation before we undertake mission and evangelism, nor need we. The actual doing of mission can also unlock faith's riches, even if those who do it are not thoroughly formed as disciples or fully equipped for specific lay ministries. Indeed, the Catholic whole-of-life approach provides many opportunities for more nominal believers to get a taste of God at work through being involved in mission, without having to be too explicitly evangelistic, so that they are surprised and even converted by that experience.

The big challenge for many of our parishioners is to be able to talk about Jesus, which if it is authentic does not of course need to be polished and word perfect—as clergy unfailingly discover when they try to do it with the curious and open minded, along with

---

[193] Georges Michonneau, *Revolution in a City Parish* (Westminster: Newman Press; Oxford: Blackfriars, 1950), 65.

the sceptical and indifferent. But the good news on which Catholic faith is based is that God is at work, creating and redeeming through Jesus Christ and enlisting us in this enterprise through the Holy Spirit out of love for the World. The good news is that we do not have to do it ourselves, as if God just sits back watching us scramble about. In this sense, our Church's mission is rather like that of the midwife, playing a significant but nevertheless subordinate role in birthing God's future.

14

How Can We Sing the Lord's Song in a Strange Land? (2017)

> *This chapter is about secularisation and what it means for the Church. I develop Peter Berger's options of reduction, deduction and induction, favouring the latter—a confident return to the roots of faith and ecclesial belonging as an alternative to current anxiety-driven responses. This was a public lecture given at the Port Macquarie campus of Charles Sturt University in April 2017. I was meant to share the platform with Roy Williams, author of* Post-God Nation *(2015), against whose assessments I offer a more positive theological reading of the secular, though he cancelled at short notice. This piece was published as 'How Can We Sing the Lord's Song in a Strange Land'* St Mark's Review *248 (2019), 45-53, and appears here by kind permission.*

On behalf of God's ancient people, exiled far from home in Babylon, the psalmist asks, 'How can we sing the Lord's song in a strange land?' (Psalm 137:4). The question rings true for many Western Christians today, who experience life under secular modern conditions as an exile from the wellsprings of faith. In consequence, some Christians seek withdrawal from the secular modern world in order to protect their faith.

Deductive, reductive and inductive options

In the United States, we find an Evangelical religious subculture seeking to preserve a form of life harking back to the old South and to supposedly simpler times. In fundamentalist Christian schools and universities, family values, home-schooling, Christian TV and even Christian theme parks, a coherent if cognitively deviant world is preserved in defiance of wider culture. In conservative American Catholicism, too, there are attempts to revive the sort of Catholic ghetto familiar before World War II—though such Catholic subcultures typically took an ethnic form, whether Irish, Polish or Italian. Today, however, conservative American Catholicism has discovered a new slogan, the so-called Benedict Option—the idea being that Christian retreat from a collapsing Empire, which is how they interpret the witness of Benedictine monasticism from late-Roman times, is now required of mainstream Catholics in all walks of life. These are *deductive* options, as the sociologist Peter Berger would identify them.[194] The pattern of faithful Christian life is *deduced* from Scripture or from Church tradition, resisting the accustomed mindset of our modern world.

Alternatively, there are what Berger calls *reductive* options, which uncritically embrace the secular modern. The idea is that an older, closed world of faith has to be let go of so that the Church can catch up. According to this approach, Christianity must adapt to modern conditions of knowledge, and to today's mood of aspirational, therapeutic individualism. Hence the distinctive traditional content of Christianity is *reduced* to what makes sense and fits in today. Liberal Christianity of this sort has been accused of subordinating Christ to culture. The pursuit of social justice and human rights is central to this agenda, as is the removal of past constraints on gender expression and sexual freedom.

---

[194] Peter Berger, *The Heretical Imperative: Contemporary Possibilities of Religious Affirmation* (New York: Doubleday, 1979).

Yet neither of these options necessarily strengthens Christian life. The *deductive* approach locks up truth in a literal reading of the Bible or else an inflexible adherence to Church traditions. As a result, many well-established insights into the world have to be rejected, from evolutionary biology to climate change to the statistical normality of exclusive same-sex attraction in around 3% of the population. Such denial is supposed to represent Christian faithfulness and purity of heart, but it risks falling into mendacity and self-righteousness. This is an approach well represented among the conservative Evangelicals who helped elect Donald Trump, who were prepared to excuse Trump's glaring moral failings for the sake of his opposition to a liberal agenda embodied by the likes of Hillary Clinton.

On the liberal side, the cause of justice, equality and human rights loses ground in America for want of a unified and credible Christian community to embody it, and hence reliably to commend it. Liberal theology, by underplaying Christian doctrine and many long-nurtured church disciplines, seeks to enhance Christianity's appeal. But it is as a confessing Church rather than a group of right-thinking spiritual individualists that God calls Christians. And it was like that from the beginning. Without the rule of faith and the Church structures that early Christianity quickly adopted, the new religion would have lacked the coherence and the discipline to engage and eventually to shape Western culture. My concern about the *reductive* approach is that it cannot galvanise and unify Christians in a common cause, leaving them instead to lives of isolated spiritual bricolage.

Beyond the *deductive* and *reductive* options, Peter Berger commended the *inductive* option. Here the Church returns to first principles and the wellsprings of its faith and mission. This is an approach grounded in hermeneutics: the discipline of attending to Scripture and tradition in dialogue with prevailing culture. Such dialogue is how Christian tradition has always tended to develop, engaging with forms of thought and life wherever Christianity has taken root. Culture puts its questions to the Church, encouraging Christians to interpret Scripture and develop tradition in fresh ways. Likewise, wider culture is shaped by the Church that abides within it. Scripture and tradition are like a tea bag steeped in the boiling water of culture. The water enters the tea bag and stimulates it to release its essence, while in turn that essence infuses the water and changes it into tea.

The Church was never meant to be a ghetto, then. Benedictine monasticism, despite its withdrawal in walled communities, did much to shape modern Europe—through the monks' development of farming technology, refinement of the calendar, and preservation of classical learning through the Dark Ages. None of this robust engagement with the world remains in today's Benedict option, however, which retreats from the world rather than boldly inhabiting that world with confidence in the gospel.

So, Roy Williams, whose Australian book, *Post-God Nation*,[195] addresses such questions, is right to remind us of Christianity's major role in forming strong cultures in Europe, England and Australia. Yet he is concerned about its waning influence. Williams laments the Church's loss of moral authority, and of its foothold in public consciousness through the general decline of religious literacy—that, and Christians' widespread obsession with sexual boundary violations, which no longer plays well to a younger demographic. Williams' helpful insights into the Australian churches' declining fortunes and his proposals for reversing them provide much food for thought. I will try to address this issue of secularisation positively, however. It is not all bad news for Christians. Having set out the meaning and ramifications of secularisation, I will suggest that God actually drives the secularising trend that shapes modern culture. I will then close with some brief proposals about the way forward for Australian Christians.

---

[195] Roy Williams, *Post-God Nation: How Religion Fell off the Radar in Australia—and What Might Be Done to Get It Back On* (Sydney: ABC Books, 2015).

The secular: what it is and what it is not

Secularisation is a way of talking about the transformation of Western societies that has given rise to our modern world and that now advances in tandem with other modern developments. In an older, tribal society—a unified traditional society—there is a powerful sense of life as all of a piece, typically experienced in terms of ordered belonging. It is a form of life structured by the sacred that penetrates and knits together every aspect of existence, from language, customs, agriculture and technology to the social scaffolding provided by defining myths, moral norms and public rituals. It is not appropriate to refer to religion as a separate category in such a practically and imaginatively integrated society.

The secular impulse disrupts this unified world, and social functions begin to differentiate. Spheres of knowledge and action separate out from a formerly cohesive whole. So, for instance, science and religion emerge as distinct realms, while new versions of the Christian Church arise. Some of these, such as the Church of England, accompany our modern world's characteristic creation, the Nation State. Long embedded practices yield to discrete modern specialisations, from education to economy to entertainment, as an institutional whole once knit together by the sacred becomes a diversity of managed activities and organisations. Such secularisation is inseparable from the emergence of modernity, in which the tribal gives way to the individual, the given yields to the chosen, and belonging becomes aggregating. Thus, a sacred cosmos is replaced by a social contract, with optional spirituality.

It is important to note that secularisation does not mean the end of traditional religious practice, though it does mean that such practice becomes a matter of choice—an optional extra in a world that is no longer *integrally* religious. Note, too, that secularisation is not an ideology—it is not an 'ism'. That would be *secularism*, which weaponises secularisation in programmatic opposition to religion. Secularism seeks to reduce the Church's influence in wider society, to keep it out of public education and to repress the invocation of God in favour of modern scientific rationality. Secularism is the ideology of Richard Dawkins and others among the so-called new atheists, but secularism is not necessarily entailed by secularisation.

Indeed, *deductive* forms of religion can be seen as a push-back against secularism—especially among ethnic minorities that remain significantly reliant on their religious identity. Hence, we see militant Islam on the rise in reaction against perceived threats to Muslim identity from secular Western states and an increasingly globalised economy. Then, tit for tat, heightened expressions of conservative Christianity rise up against militant Islam, with their crusader rhetoric further inflaming jihadist reaction. So, it is plainly naive of secularists to believe that religion is finished, even if the social functions of religion have changed and shifted as a result of secularisation.

Let me make one further point here. There is a new term afoot, 'post-secular', which refers to a positive reappraisal of religion for what it can contribute to social harmony and personal well-being. Even a non-religious philosopher like Jürgen Habermas believes that secularism is a step too far in today's secular world. Religion can thus resume a place of honour in the public square, whether its claims are believed or not, according to the post-secular twist on secularisation.

But it is not only traditional religions that persevere in secular modern cultures, albeit in more freely chosen ways. The one-time social glue provided by religion returns in new forms, which we may not immediately identify as religious. Secularisation not only separates out the religious function, then, but it can also redirect it. The unifying function of religion as an integral dimension of tribal societies reappears in secular societies—albeit in less integral ways, and via new social realities.

The sociologist Max Weber famously spoke of this in terms of disenchantment, by which he meant a shift of religious discipline from the medieval monastery to the disciplined, frugal, modern Protestant workforce.[196] The Nation State, the modern economy, and the defining enmities to which many nations cling all fulfil some of the former religious function, even retaining a whiff of the old sacred awe. Think of the feeling that attaches to national flags, and the new priestly authority of those largely incomprehensible economic talking heads on television. A religious aura clings to sport, too, to film and theatre, to some of the popular music that unifies a culture, certainly to romantic love and sexuality, and of course to wild nature, which has fascinated urban moderns since the Romantic period. Secular imagination, for which traditional religion is no longer integral, can still crave a holistic vision, with some transcendence sought at the heart of community life, though this is now pursued in newly differentiated zones of experience. Once again, the secular does not spell the end of finding the sacred via the social, though it does spell deregulation of that sacred.

This shift of the religious function helps explain why spirituality has come adrift from Christian churches in the modern West. Enchantment has skipped the traces of traditional church practice so that, having lost its integral role in an imaginative whole, the Christian way of life as a newly optional choice loses much of its appeal. It is not that everyone was a convinced Christian believer and regular churchgoer in pre-secular times, but religion was a dimension of social belonging and of expected social behaviour that no longer apply. Today, the active Western Christian is likely to have made choices about their religious belief and practice that their pre-secular forebears could not have conceived. This is what Peter Berger refers to as today's 'heretical imperative', meaning that religious involvement is now typically a matter of personal choice.

---

[196] Max Weber, *The Protestant Ethic and the Spirit of Capitalism* (1904-05), trans. Talcott Parsons (New York: Scribner's, 1958).

This is just as true for genteel Anglicans in Woollahra as it is for radicalised Islamic youth in Lakemba.

God, the secular, and the Church of tomorrow

Now, where is God in all this? I for one believe that the secularising impulse is a biblical one, a prophetic one, as the tribal deities and their closed pagan world yield to the one true God on the way to our world becoming more open and global. And the only way that such an open, global world can sustain itself is if it becomes a world of peace and mutuality. This is the gift and task of secularisation, which I interpret as a divine impulse. The gift is a culturally rich, open, diversified world, with a strong global economy, featuring what in many places is a high level of religious tolerance, with the static and fearful world of archaic spirits yielding to the dynamic and confident world of modern science. Yet if this is the best of times, it is also the worst of times. We must face the risk of nuclear and environmental disasters *globally* while a new awareness of inequality and injustice, along with new tribalisms and their accompanying sacred enthusiasms, combine to unsettle people *locally*.

As a theological interpreter of the late French American theorist René Girard, I am alert to the role of scapegoating violence in stabilising all those closed pre-modern social worlds. Girard explored the functional role of religion that sociologists had long recognised. This functional sacred is a felt experience of togetherness, a form of group transcendence, which is expressed and preserved in taboo, myth and ritual. And it is this totalising reality that gives way with secularisation. What Girard offers is an account of secularisation that is not only sociological and anthropological but also theological.

At the origin of human togetherness, for Girard, a functional sacred emerges naturally following the collective turn of group hostility upon a victim. Their lynching or stoning or drowning releases a seemingly miraculous peace where, previously, escalating rivalries in the group had threatened to tear it apart. This peace is preserved as a sacred aura attaching to rules, rituals and mythical stories that shape and stabilise such societies, with language, legal systems, law enforcement and other cultural institutions eventually developing on this functional sacred foundation.

Girard understands the closed pagan world of the functional sacred to be challenged by the Bible: in Psalms where victims declare their innocence, in the condemnation of human sacrifice, in the prophets' challenge to Israel whenever official religion lost its way and, chiefly, in the life, death and resurrection of Jesus. Beyond a world of sacrifice, mythology, and demonised enemies, a new version of the sacred emerges. A sacrificial social order that had been sanctified and mythologised is subjected to a secularising, deconstructive undoing. And this is God's work.

The impact of secularising impulses thus understood, which received their charter in the Judeo-Christian Scriptures, began to shape a new Christian culture. Girard draws particular attention to early modern developments such as the decline of European anti-Semitism along with the prosecution of witches.[197] It is not that science liberated modern minds from religious superstition. Instead, revealed religion—non-functional religion, the gospel of Jesus Christ—liberated Europe from superstition and its sacrificial underpinnings. Consequently, natural causes could be discovered through scientific investigation once we no longer blamed Jews or witches for plagues, crop failures or monstrous births.

Functional religion represents a bygone phase of human history, then, much as St Paul in Galatians viewed the Old

---

[197] René Girard, *The Scapegoat* (1982), trans. Yvonne Freccero (Baltimore and London: The Johns Hopkins University Press, 1986). See also my *René Girard and Secular Modernity: Christ, Culture, and Crisis* (Notre Dame, IN.: The University of Notre Dame Press, 2013).

Testament law as a necessary guide for God's people until Christ could be revealed (Galatians 3:24-26). The secular impulse emerges as a gospel impulse, and Christians should not attempt to put the genie back in the bottle. Hence, I am concerned by both deductive and reductive attempts to reclaim social prominence for religion—to re-knit a weave that God has been unpicking. And here is my one concern with Roy Williams' *Post-God Nation*: it is not clear to me that the recovery of so-called Christian society—a society that Williams admits was forged by Christians of very mixed commitment, church involvement and theological orthodoxy—is in fact what God has in mind.

Roy Williams rightly emphasises educational reforms to enhance public knowledge about religion, which is a very prudent proposal in keeping with newer post-secular insights. He believes, however, that this will also strengthen Christianity's fortunes. Yet religious knowledge is insufficient to make converts, just as kindling is insufficient to make fire without a spark to ignite it. I believe that Roy Williams is on surer ground when he calls the churches to be more intentional, more evangelistic, more committed to living and advocating a generous and humane vision. And with some brief thoughts about the recovery of that converting spark I draw to my conclusion.

I fear any attempted retrieval of the old functional sacred, toward which the deductive approach of Christian conservatism can tend. A return is sought to more integral religion, a more influential Church, a more religiously defined and disciplined society. While we may lament today's widespread decline of civility, and wish to see some more of the old virtues, we do not want what the Taliban want in their hatred of modern freedoms. The historian Charles Taylor is right, in his classic *A Secular Age*,[198] that secular modern individuals are less *porous*, more *buffered*, as he puts it, which means unassimilable to an older socio-religious

---

[198] Charles Taylor, *A Secular Age* (Cambridge, MA.: The Belknap Press, 2007).

amalgam. We cannot imagine returning to a more integral world lacking the openness, the freedom of choice and the requirement of mature, self-aware commitment that Christianity in a secular age represents.

Yet I also fear that reductive, liberal alternatives are missing the boat. In light of today's post-secular recovery of a place for traditional religion in modern societies, Christianity ought not to shed its distinctive features in pursuit of cultural relevance right when this new post-secular mood grants it a potentially warmer welcome.

My favoured option is quite simple: that the Church concentrates on building faith and discipleship among its members in open-minded (though not uncritical) dialogue with modern culture. This is Berger's inductive option, whereby Christians return to the faith and practice of Scripture and tradition without either retreating from or capitulating entirely to secular modernity. Indeed, if the secular modern is interpreted not as a threat but actually as an outgrowth of the gospel, as René Girard argues, Christians will best ensure that they engage it neither negatively nor uncritically.

This will require the Church to be more committed, more converted, more prayerful, more worshipful, more theological, more pastoral, more humane, certainly more joyful, and altogether more formed in the gospel's defining narrative—neither sectarian, nor laissez faire, but certainly *intentional*. We do not want to roll back the secular, nor to uncritically embrace its every feature. What we do want is to inhabit secular modern culture in a distinctive way, having freely chosen to live as Christians and to be the Church *in* this world though not *of it*. I may read the secular in a more positive theological light than Roy Williams. And I may not share all his concerns about an older religious world that is passing away—a world that to my mind was at best nominally Christian. Yet I fully endorse his call for a more intentional, evangelistic Church today.

15

Theology in the School of Humility (2021)

> *This most recent item was commissioned for a themed edition of* St Mark's Review *marking the retirement of Revd Dr Jane Foulcher from the Charles Sturt University theology faculty and St Mark's National Theological Centre, Canberra. Jane's fine book on humility and monasticism inspired me, and so I wrote about how to be a humble theologian as part of the Church's ministry and mission—a humility far easier to maintain thanks to the near-invisibility of theology and theologians in Australian Anglicanism! I had been doing research for a book about René Girard and John Milbank and was thinking about Milbank's uniquely pugilistic approach to theology. From a Girardian perspective, I was alert to how self-defining rivalries are antithetical to the primary Christian vocation of ecclesial abiding in peace. Likewise, I was concerned about staying open to the real world while being continually formed in the Christian narrative. This joint calling of theology has been central to my own modest contribution to the field over nearly 35 years, and here I try to articulate it. This essay was published as 'Theology in the School of Humility', * St Mark's Review *256 (2021): 29-38, and appears here by kind permission.*

The Christian monastery is meant to be a school of humility thanks to its immersive scriptural and liturgical culture, which aims at nurturing gracious mutuality through life together under the rule. This is an evolving and diversifying story, of course, as Jane Foulcher capably shows.[199] But one constant has been the intentional avoidance and de-escalation of rivalry between monastics, as key to fostering a community's collective ascent towards holiness. To this end, the example of Christ is not only privately contemplated but also programmatically followed via habits of openness, accountability and service. The spiritual currency of Benedictine monasticism's school of humility is amply demonstrated by Abbot Andrew Marr in his *Tools for Peace: The Spiritual Craft of St Benedict and René Girard*.[200]

But this is an essay on theology not monasticism. I only mention the latter because the former grew up as a monastic undertaking, sharing in the monastery's cultivation of humility and holiness. So I hope that theology can persist in the humility integral to its formative scriptural, liturgical and ecclesial origins despite its shift from monastery to university and from sanctified contemplation to scholastic disputation from the fourteenth century.[201] In what follows, I will show what modern theology might look like if it chooses to persevere in the school of humility.

From rivalry to ecclesiality

Constructive theology is a creative undertaking with obvious parallels in art and philosophy. Modern artists seek to represent and reconfigure reality and its perception in ever new ways, with differing schools and methods vying for attention. Rivalries have proved central to this enterprise, ever since originality in modernity displaced earlier fidelity to tradition—consider the

---

[199] Jane Foulcher, *Reclaiming Humility: Four Studies in the Monastic Tradition* (Collegeville, MN.: Cistercian Publications [Liturgical Press], 2015).

[200] Andrew Marr, *Tools for Peace: The Spiritual Craft of St Benedict and René Girard* (Lincoln, NE.: iUniverse, 2007).

[201] See Hans Urs von Balthasar, 'Theology and Sanctity,' in *Explorations in Theology*, Vol. 1, *The Word Made Flesh* (1964), trans. A.V. Littledale and Alexander Dru (San Francisco: Ignatius, 1989), 181-209.

relationships of Matisse and Picasso, Manet and Degas, Pollock and de Kooning, also Lucien Freud and Francis Bacon.[202] Likewise modern philosophy advances as each generation and leading contributor seeks to outperform and defeat predecessors and contemporaries, with the achievement of greater comprehensiveness and radical new perspectives making the reputation of practitioners.[203] In today's post-truth world, with will to power regularly trumping basic logic and solid evidence, the scope for rivalry to dominate thought and to sideline contrary testimony seems irresistible. Hence the necessary emergence of epistemological ethics.[204]

Theology is no stranger to any of this. As with competing schools and individuals in art and philosophy, along with public debates where antagonists talk past each other in pursuit of ideological advantage, theology is widely implicated in rivalry. A version of the culture wars is manifest in theology's liberal/conservative divide, apart from the older confessional differences. These latter traded on self-defining rivalries that extended to mutual anathematisation. Thankfully Vatican II and the Ecumenical Movement have moderated this state of affairs. Though a version of such anathematisation continues even in mainstream theology.

Progressives typically embrace a range of issues that are treated with suspicion by theological conservatives. They draw on secular sources such as Marxism, feminism, deconstruction and, more recently, genderqueer perspectives. Liberation Theology, Feminist Theology and what we might loosely call postmodern theologies often take aim at theologies deemed to be conservative—those

---

[202] See Sebastian Smee, *The Art of Rivalry: Four Friendships, Betrayals, and Breakthroughs in Modern Art* (New York: Random House, 2015).

[203] See Allan Megill, *Prophets of Extremity: Nietzsche, Heidegger, Foucault, Derrida* (Berkeley: University of California Press, 1985); Stephen L. Gardner, *Myths of Freedom: Equality, Modern Thought, and Philosophical Radicalism* (Contributions in Philosophy, 62. Westport, CT.: Greenwood Press, 1998).

[204] Miranda Fricker, *Epistemic Injustice: Power and the Ethics of Knowing* (Oxford: Oxford University Press, 2007).

typically making claims for fixed reality and authoritative canons of meaning. Such perspectives are regarded variously as privileged, self-serving, abusive, racist and corrupted by patriarchalism. Conservative voices regularly reply that their progressive critics have abandoned Scripture and tradition, substituting a hostile and destructive modern or postmodern agenda for abiding in a more recognisable and reliable Christian narrative.

There is truth on both sides, and indeed much creative overlap. Progressives make a strong case when they are seriously scriptural, as Latin American Liberation Theology has long sought to be. Feminist and LGBTQI readings of Scripture have also revealed significant and never-before-appreciated perspectives.[205] On the more conservative side, as in the pugilistic Radical Orthodoxy push led by John Milbank, there is nevertheless serious engagement with deconstruction in an epistemology indebted to latest French philosophy—both to phenomenology and the revival of Neoplatonism.[206] Here, a radical reappropriation of theological tradition is used not only to critique but to out-narrate the claims of secular ideology.

The mistake for conservatives is to think that Christian tradition has ever developed apart from wider cultural cross-fertilisation,[207] while progressives can underestimate the radicality of abiding Christian orthodoxy. Both oversights represent a failure of ecclesiology, and hence of humility. Instead, remembering the inclusive gift of grace through baptism and the reality of

---

[205] See Carol A. Newsom and Sharon H. Ring, eds., *The Women's Bible Commentary* (London: SPCK; Louisville, KY.: Westminster/John Knox Press, 1992); Deryn Guest, Robert E. Goss, Mona West and Thomas Bohache, eds., *The Queer Bible Commentary* (London: SCM Press, 2006).

[206] See John Milbank, *The Word Made Strange: Theology, Language, Culture* (Oxford: Blackwell, 1997).

[207] See Kathryn Tanner, *Theories of Culture: A New Agenda for Theology* (Guides to Theological Inquiry. Minneapolis, MN.: Fortress Press, 1997); Terrence W. Tilley, *Inventing Catholic Tradition* (Maryknoll, NY.: Orbis, 2000).

Eucharistic fellowship puts such differences in perspective, ensuring that the ecclesial reality (and the reign of God to which it points) is not supplanted by any lesser allegiance. Christian humility entails something like a family mentality in which inevitable differences of opinion and practice are relativised in light of a greater solidarity.

Conservatives and progressives are invited in humility to be friends and collaborators, willing to meet halfway and to work through their inevitable and proper disagreements within the bond of unity. The alternative, which is to become scandalised and to break fellowship over presumed non-negotiable differences, or else retreat into a posture of stubborn contrariness, represents a serious spiritual lapse. This is the logic of today's wider culture wars, which Christians might be expected to reject. We do well to remember St Paul's reminder, regarding just such a divided situation, that 'Knowledge puffs up, but love builds up' (1 Corinthians 8:1).

This is not a pious injunction. It goes to the heart of what Christian orthodoxy entailed from the beginning. James D.G. Dunn traces how the range of acceptable canonical diversity emerges in the New Testament period—a state of affairs that has never gone away—though it is constrained by two abiding principles: 'diversity which abandons the unity of the faith in Jesus the man now exalted is unacceptable; diversity which abandons the unity of love for fellow believers is unacceptable'.[208] The holding together of opposed positions in emerging credal orthodoxy represents an outworking of this early orthodox principle. God's truth is not exhausted by rivalry nor necessarily implicated in it but is best sought in the patient dialogue of ecclesial solidarity.

That is not to say that theology should be narrowly, ecclesially confined and critically quiescent. There is a properly prophetic dimension to theology's role in the Church's service. In this it is in step with holiness and sanctity, which are likewise inseparable both from loving the Church and from influencing its reform.

---

[208] James D.G. Dunn, *Unity and Diversity in the New Testament: An Inquiry into the Character of Earliest Christianity* (London: SCM Press, 1981), 378.

I now wish to shift focus from theology in an ecclesial culture of humility to the present ecclesial conditions for theological work, chiefly in the Australian context. Here we will also find ample opportunity for cultivating theological humility.

Australia, true to certain early historical decisions, did not develop a university theology sector until recent decades (and even now it is a shadow of what is taken for granted in Europe and North America). The resulting confinement of theology in Australia to the churches' seminaries and theological colleges forced a humbler role on theology than is found in Europe and America. Australian theology has thus been less of a public intellectual presence and more of an adjunct to the socialisation of prospective clergy, confined to understaffed and under-resourced church training institutions. Experience in this sector might lead one to conclude that theology is more tolerated than loved, being widely seen as having little to offer in one's preparation for pastoral work. So, the relatively few constructive theologians that Australia produces fulfil a humble role indeed if they are to keep at it, either heavily burdened while typically marginal within the system, or else institutionally adrift outside it.

This state of affairs both reflects and contributes to an abiding anti-intellectualism in Australian Christianity, which in turn reflects our wider culture. The situation is worsened under today's ecclesial conditions of institutional survivalism, with a turn to managerial approaches in the hope of reviving the Church's fortunes. This local refraction of an English and wider trend is rightly subject to theological critique, in the service of a deeper ecclesial loyalty.[209]

---

[209] See e.g., Richard H. Roberts, 'Ruling the Body: The Care of Souls in a Managerial Church,' in *Religion, Theology and the Human Sciences* (Cambridge: Cambridge University Press, 2002), 161-89; John Milbank, 'Stale Expressions: The Management-Shaped Church,' in *The Future of Love: Essays in Political Theology* (London: SCM Press, 2009), 264-76. I once wrote a theological book about the Emerging

The theological vocation must maintain a corrective emphasis on faith and gospel, and on God's purpose and agency, wherever the Church is seen as a struggling organisation in need of reinvigoration by largely human means. Here the theologian must step up as teacher, writer, preacher and prophetic voice in councils of the Church. A better perspective on how to approach such difficult motivational challenges is attributed to the French aviator and writer Antoine de Saint-Exupéry, whose sentiments I entirely endorse: 'If you want to build a ship, don't drum up people to collect wood and don't assign them tasks and work, but rather teach them to long for the endless immensity of the sea.'[210]

But this cannot be a matter of reactionary retreat into biblicism, or else commending some sort of nostalgic metaphysical closure as an alternative to today's secular identity markers. Instead, theology demonstrates an appropriate humility by attending to the developing phenomenality of faith, which it serves and articulates in critical dialogue with pressing questions of the day. Here theology proves truer to authoritative pointers at the heart of faith.[211] How might this play out?

From closedness to openness

This end is best served by a supple and flexible theology that travels light in the wider world of meaning. Not light in terms of faith and belief but, rather, light in terms of structural scaffolding and defensive armour. The work of two UK Anglicans, Rowan Williams and Ben Quash, has helped me to conceive the theological task in these terms.

Church featuring some unsparing critique of this cult of managerialism but, this being Australia, it sank like a stone: see my *God's Next Big Thing: Discovering the Future Church* (Melbourne: John Garratt Publishing, 2004).

[210] (Author's Note: this well-known quotation appears in various places, but I could not readily find an original source).

[211] See Joseph S. O'Leary, *Questioning Back: The Overcoming of Metaphysics in Christian Tradition* (Minneapolis, MN.: Winston Press, 1985).

Theology's need to stay close to the practice of faith, and hence to show some humility in its systematic aspirations, is a characteristically Anglican position. It is the Catholic faith, though not in the more crystalline form that we recognise in *The Catechism of the Catholic Church*, likewise in the various Reformation confessions (despite the tendency of some Evangelical Anglicans to regard the *Articles of Religion* as one more sixteenth-century confession, alongside Lutheran and Reformed ones). Accordingly, Williams insists that 'Theology can be no more and no less (and not otherwise) "systematic" than the processes of faith to which it is answerable, and if it is confident of itself in ways divorced from this, it loses its integrity'.[212] Behind this claim lies a distinctive sense of how God is revealed, attentive to context and inseparable from participatory involvement.

Quash favours theological dramatic theory in addressing these concerns. Drama provides a framework for conceiving of revelation and divine action in the context of human knowing and acting. It brings a 'vital unframeability' to theological investigation so that, for Quash, 'drama as an art form is uniquely positioned to manifest complex, pluriform, multiply interpreted truth in changing circumstances. It is *involving, particular, social and anticipatory*'.[213] The point is that humans can only know God humanly—that is, not apart from how all human understanding emerges in history through finite actions and interactions and hence by cleaving naturally to narrative form.[214] This is who we are as God's creatures, and so this is where theology finds its parameters. Anglican sensibility presses the Catholic faith to be more local and reserved, and less ambitious for achieving closure.

---

[212] Rowan Williams, 'Theological Integrity,' in *On Christian Theology* (Challenges in Contemporary Theology. Oxford: Blackwell, 2000), 3-15, at 14.
[213] Ben Quash, *Theology and the Drama of History* (Cambridge Studies in Christian Doctrine. Cambridge: Cambridge University Press, 2005), 36 and 37 respectively.
[214] Quash, *Theology and the Drama of History*, 3.

Quash helpfully compares Roman and Anglican theological approaches to the Catholic faith with how Roman law and its universal natural law principles differs from the case-based alternative of English common law.[215] In English common law, there are rules, but they tend to operate and develop in an additive way through the cases.[216] Accordingly, for Quash, 'no doctrine of the Holy Spirit, and no Christian theological account of history, that cannot survive exposure to actual cases is worthy of the name'.[217]

Rowan Williams describes this as honest theology, but it could equally be seen in terms of proper theological humility. For Williams, 'A religious discourse with some chance of being honest will not move too far from the particular, with all its irresolution and resistance to systematising: it will be trying to give shape to that response to the particular that is least evasive of its solid historical otherness *and* is also rooted in the conviction that God is to be sought and listened for in all occasions.'[218]

The category of drama applied to theology sets God's work in, with and under the work of time bound, context dependent, cognitively limited and morally vulnerable human beings. Scripture is perennially interpreted and reinterpreted, and doctrine develops. It is a participatory process, and human identity emerges as the drama plays out. This is how Christians come to know Jesus, as in the road to Emmaus story (Luke 24:13-35)—a journey that was relational, hermeneutical, confounding, mind-expanding and only thus revelatory. So, we seek divine revelation at the dramatic intersection between lived life and Christian narrative. For Quash, this is better than the alternative: 'Seeking the truth by striving for a God's eye view ... leads to *spectatorship*; seeking the truth in intensive encounter leads to *discipleship*. The God

---
[215] Ben Quash, *Found Theology: History, Imagination and the Holy Spirit* (London and New York: Bloomsbury, 2013), 20.
[216] Quash, *Found Theology*, 231.
[217] Quash, *Found Theology*, 288.
[218] Williams, 'Theological Integrity', 6-7.

who accompanies history asks us to follow him—in reliability, in abiding. It is as a "way" that God in Christ is a "truth"'.[219]

By God I ask you mariner, now tell me that song ...

I conclude with two images from Jesuit spirituality, which have provided a constant reference point for me throughout my theological career. The first is an icon of St Ignatius Loyola by the American Franciscan iconographer Robert Lentz, which has sat on my desk since I began graduate studies. The second is from a Spanish poem in the hands of a Jesuit theologian, which helped me tie together the conclusion of my doctoral dissertation on the nature of modern faith in Jesus Christ.[220] First, consider the icon and especially St Ignatius' two hands.

---

[219] Quash, *Found Theology*, 291.
[220] Scott Cowdell, *Is Jesus Unique? A Study of Recent Christology* (Theological Inquiries. Mahwah, NJ.: Paulist Press, 1996).

They represent two dimensions of the theological task as I have outlined it, as part of the Church's life and mission and undetachable from its moorings in liturgy and discipleship.

St Ignatius' left hand, with the index finger raised to his lips, calls for silence and attentiveness. We are bid to listen for God's voice in the voices of the world around us in all their particularity. This is not an easy task. It requires humble listening. We might see this as the particular contribution of progressive theologies, but also of the more Anglican approach to which I have pointed. This allows no retreat into biblicism or dogma for the attainment of closure and the banishment of doubt, let alone for any such recourse to be weaponised in theological rivalry. Instead, it calls for humble recognition of our limitations as creatures making our way as best we can under God.

St Ignatius' right hand is extended to the viewer in a gesture of invitation. We are bid to join his adventure of discipleship with Christ and his saints in the Church. Such participation is the other indispensable condition of theological understanding, apart from which even the most orthodox belief becomes diminished. This call to abide in the faith of Christ and his Church is more typically associated with theological conservatism, though it is surely incompatible with any hubristic contempt for less conservative Christian theologians. The left hand, extending an invitation to listen attentively outward towards the world, when combined with the right hand inviting us deeper into ecclesiality and discipleship, suggests that revelation is experienced in stereo not mono—which, of course, creates a rich and blended soundscape rather than the opposition of unintegrated voices.

This dual invitation is also present in the sixteenth-century Spanish romance 'El Conde Arnaldos', which is contemporary with St Ignatius and his movement. In this poem, Count Arnaldos looks out to sea on the feast of St John and sees the most perfect and mesmerising image of a ship sailing landward, with a helmsman whose song is so entrancing that the wind and sea are stilled while both fish and birds are drawn to the ship from their separate elements. The Dutch American Jesuit theologian Frans Jozef van Beeck concludes his massive study on the nature of Christian proclamation by using this poem as an illustration. His conviction is that there is only one reliable way for theological truth to emerge in our time: 'Words will come to those Churches and those Christians that are united with Jesus Christ, and united with him in his love for the world. No new knowledge without participation in the experience'.[221]

The poem imagines God's love for the world in the enchanting of creation around the figure of Jesus Christ abiding in his Church, which is associated traditionally with the image of a ship. Here I am reminded of St Ignatius' attentiveness to the world in the Lentz icon, seen as a call to humble listening. Count Arnaldos is compelled to seek the truth of this song. His is the perennial theological quest, and in terse and unromantic Spanish this is what he calls out to the helmsman:

> *Por Dios te ruego, marinero,*
> *digasme ora ese cantar.*
> (By God I ask you, mariner, now tell me that song.)

For van Beeck, what the helmsman replies to Count Arnaldos 'is that only those will know who join in the venture—in its risks and in its rewards'.[222]

> *Yo no digo esta canción,*
> *sino a quien conmigo va.*
> (I tell that song only to him who comes with me.)[223]

And there in sum is what theology looks like if it has learned its craft in the school of humility.

---

[221] Frans Jozef van Beeck, *Christ Proclaimed: Christology as Rhetoric* (Theological Inquiries. Mahwah, NJ.: Paulist Press, 1979), 574.
[222] van Beeck, *Christ Proclaimed*, 574.
[223] van Beeck, *Christ Proclaimed*, 574n144. The original is in *Canconiero de Romances* (Anvers, 1550), ed. Antonio Rodriguez (Madrid: Editorial Castalia, 1967), 255 (spelling modernised; trans. van Beeck).

www.ingramcontent.com/pod-product-compliance
Lightning Source LLC
Chambersburg PA
CBHW012004090526
44590CB00026B/3862